ARCHAEOLOGICAL ETHICS, SECOND EDITION

ARCHAEOLOGICAL ETHICS, SECOND EDITION

EDITED BY
KAREN D. VITELLI AND
CHIP COLWELL-CHANTHAPHONH

A Division of

ALTAMIRA
PRESS

ROWMAN & LITTLEFIELD PUBLISHERS, INC.
Lanham • *New York* • *Toronto* • *Oxford*

ALTAMIRA PRESS
A division of Rowman & Littlefield Publishers, Inc.
A wholly owned subsidary of The Rowman & Littlefield Publishing Group, Inc.
4501 Forbes Boulevard, Suite 200
Lanham, MD 20706
www.altamirapress.com

PO Box 317, Oxford, OX2 9RU, UK

British Library Cataloguing in Publication Information Available

Library of Congress Cataloging-in-Publication Data

Archaeological ethics / edited by Karen D. Vitelli and Chip Colwell-Chanthaphonh.—2nd ed.
     p. cm.
     ISBN-13: 978-0-7591-0962-9 (cloth : alk. paper)
     ISBN-10: 0-7591-0962-1 (cloth : alk. paper)
     ISBN-13: 978-0-7591-0963-6 (pbk : alk. paper)
     ISBN-10: 0-7591-0963-X (pbk : alk. paper)
     1. Archaeology—Moral and ethical aspects. 2. Antiquities—Collection and preservation—Moral and ethical aspects. 3. Cultural property—Protection—Moral and ethical aspects. I. Vitelli, Karen D. II. Colwell-Chanthaphonh, Chip, 1975– .
  CC175 .A715 2006
  930.1—dc22

                                                                                    2005024136

Printed in the United States of America

∞™ The paper used in this publication meets the minimum requirements of American National Standard for Information Sciences—Permanence of Paper for Printed Library Materials, ANSI/NISO Z39.48-1992.

CONTENTS

Part II: Archaeology and (Inter)National Politics

Part III: Affected Peoples

Part IV: Reburial, Repatriation, and Representation

Part V: The Professional Archaeologist

Introduction

WHAT A DIFFERENCE A DECADE MAKES. Since the first edition of this collection appeared, the Internet has taken over our lives, and looting of archaeological sites and museums makes national news, as did, for a while, the battles over Kennewick Man—the "Ancient One"—and the destruction of the Bamiyan Buddhas. The wars in Afghanistan and Iraq have resulted in massive looting of museums and sites in those unfortunate countries, and endless reports in the media explain what has been stolen and destroyed, by whom, and why. The Society for American Archaeology (SAA) has begun holding an Ethics Bowl at its annual meetings, and in its second year that event already drew teams of students from universities around the country. Members of the Archaeological Institute of America worked tirelessly and proactively—if in the end, unsuccessfully—to prevent the worst of the looting in Iraq. In 1985, the World Archaeological Congress (WAC) formed to protest apartheid in South Africa and bring attention to the social, political, and economic role archaeology plays in our modern world. Today it is an influential organization with a broad international base representing more than 90 countries.

In the first edition of this collection, the editor used the introduction to encourage colleagues to teach a course on archaeological ethics, to emphasize that it was important for students and faculty to talk about these issues, and to reassure everyone that, in fact, it was a very rewarding, fun, and lively class. A decade later, dozens of colleagues have discovered that for themselves, and some discussion of ethics is now routinely included in many, if perhaps not yet most courses on archaeology. For any colleagues still unsure of how to approach such a course or how to work the topic in to general discussions about archaeology, the SAA's Making Archaeology Teaching Relevant in the XXI Century (MATRIX) project has plentiful examples and suggestions.

For the first edition of this volume, the editor worked from piles of Xerox copies, which the publisher then had to retype. This edition is compiled entirely electronically, exchanged between editors at opposite ends of the country and a publisher in the middle. Most readers of this edition are already expert users of the Web and can easily find up-to-date information and plentiful bibliographies on any topic, including archaeological ethics. We have, therefore, omitted the Resource Guide of the last edition, using the saved space for additional articles, to each of which we have added some suggestions for further reading, along with questions to help begin discussion and develop research into particular topics. Most of the articles in this edition are new, fresh looks at familiar, and, we suspect, not-so-familiar issues, although we have carried over a few chapters from the first edition because they still present good introductions to particular subjects. Most of the articles appeared originally in *Archaeology*, which continues to do a terrific job of addressing important issues in the field in a very accessible way. For a few chapters, we have gone further afield, a move that reflects the expanding interest in and coverage of ethical issues in both scholarly and popular publications.

If a decade ago colleagues were grateful for a collection of articles and information that was difficult to assemble on one's own, now it is perhaps more useful that we have made a selection from among the sometimes overwhelming abundance that is available. But, while we have aimed for diversity of topics and issues, along with recurring themes that we invite you to identify, we have certainly not covered everything, and even the topics addressed here provide only beginnings for discussion, never the final word. Everyone we know who has taught a course on ethics has found that current events always add something relevant, and that it is often these events that most engage everyone in the room precisely because of their immediacy. Former students tell us that their copies of the first edition are dog-eared from repeated consultation, often in reference to newly presented circumstances. We offer, therefore, this new collection to challenge and guide archaeologists and visitors to archaeology in this ongoing and fascinating discussion.

Approaches to Ethics

Although discussions of ethics are relatively new for professional archaeologists, philosophers have pondered human behavior for millennia. In the Western tradition, thinkers such as Aristotle and Plato focused on ethics, while in the East, Confucius and the Buddha were early influences. Today, the field of moral philosophy is extremely complex as scholars seek to understand an array of ancient and modern ethical systems to answer provocative questions about abortion, world hunger, and animal rights. Moral philosophers, in short, study how humans ought to live. Typically using "morality" and "ethics" interchangeably, philosophers fo-

cus on norms—questions of "ought" and "should." In this way, the philosophical study of ethics is not really descriptive, as is the work of an ethnographer
studying a tribe, or a psychologist analyzing a patient. Instead, philosophers try to
understand which human actions are justified and why.

Many people think that ethics is the same thing as the law. While the two are
connected, the law is different because it is codified, enforceable, and usually sets
the bar for good behavior at the lowest threshold. Ethics need not be codified, are
often obligatory but unenforceable, and imagine ideal and perfect models. What
is legal may not be ethical and vice versa. Slavery, for example, was long legal in
the United States, but that did not make it ethical. We are not legally obligated to
feed the poor, tell the truth to strangers asking for directions, or lend money to
friends in need, yet these are all morally sound deeds.

Many people think that ethics are relative—that there are no universal or objective truths in ethics. Most philosophers, however, are skeptical about this position. They contend that while different cultures have different beliefs about
morality, this does not mean that there are no universal principles. As philosopher
James Rachels argues by analogy, "In some societies, people believe the earth is flat.
In other societies, such as our own, people believe the earth is (roughly) spherical.
Does it follow, *from the mere fact that they disagree*, that there is no 'objective truth' in ge-
ography?"[1] Rachels goes on to write that relativism is also problematic because if
all moral systems are truly equal then we could not legitimately disapprove of ab-
horrent cultural phenomena such as Nazism in Germany or apartheid in South
Africa. Furthermore, every society, by virtue of its existence, must share certain values. Societies would not last very long without trust, reasonableness, or honesty.

Three ethical frameworks dominate contemporary moral philosophy. Utilitarianism, as a formal theory, began in the eighteenth century with the work of David
Hume, and gained prominence with Jeremy Bentham and John Stuart Mill. In this
view ethics is a kind of cost benefit analysis, where we can know if an action is
right or wrong entirely based on its consequences. Classical utilitarian theory dic-
tates that if we are faced with a moral decision we must decide on the course of
action that will bring the greatest amount of happiness to the greatest number of
people. So, for example, utilitarianism would say that it is morally permissible to
torture an innocent man who happens to know where an atom bomb is planted in
London; the happiness of the millions of potential victims outweighs the well-
being of one individual.

The second theory is called deontology or duty-based ethics, and is closely associated with the eighteenth-century German scholar, Immanuel Kant. Kant, rather than
evaluating action based on consequences, thought that actions are intrinsically right
or wrong—that ethical rules are absolute. He recognized that the future is hard to
predict and therefore people should be applauded or reproached only for actions they

can control. This means an emphasis on what we can will or desire, not on what we can achieve. Developing what he called the Categorical Imperative, Kant famously argued that you should "act only according to the maxim by which you can at the same time will that it should become a universal law." In other words, moral action involves creating rules that any individual would want everyone to follow in all situations. To use the example of lying, people often think it is okay to lie if the outcome is good, as in lying to a murderer about the hiding spot of his prey: Rachels responds, in *The Elements of Moral Philosophy*, that "we can never be certain about what the consequences of our actions will be; we cannot *know* that good results will follow. The results of lying *might* be unexpectedly bad. Therefore, the best policy is always to avoid the known evil—lying—and let the bad consequences come as they will. Even if the consequences are bad, they will not be our fault, for we will have done our duty." Kant's theory has been likened to the Golden Rule—do unto others as you would have them do unto you—because a moral rule is the only one by which everyone will abide.

The third theory is Virtue Ethics, which is derived from ancient Greek philosophers such as Aristotle, but is also connected to non-Western philosophies in India, China, and native North America. Virtue Ethics does not start with questions of consequences or duties, but rather, with questions of character, asking what traits of character make a person good. While different virtues serve as a means of discussing ethical behavior—justice, honesty, generosity, mindfulness, trust—this ethical framework is more deeply concerned with moral agents than with moral actions. Ethics in this way is not about isolated acts, but how individuals cultivate integrity over time.

Whatever one's explicit or implicit theoretical perspective, moral philosophy involves certain ground rules that bolster any discussion about ethics. When talking about what actions are right and wrong, it is important to know the facts as well as possible. This is important because we must justify our claims based on the reality of the world as we know it. Philosophy also demands that we try to base our arguments in reason—that we aim to be logical and consistent. If we argue, for example, that a person should lie to achieve a moral outcome in one case, we should not then say in another case that people must always tell the truth. Finally, it is important in discussions about ethics to try to be as impartial as possible. When talking about ethics, we should not privilege our own personal interests or be arbitrary in evaluating the interests of others. Ethics is not about validating our own beliefs and behaviors, but rather understanding what is good for everyone.

Archaeological Ethics

In the early 1990s, most professional organizations of archaeologists formulated or re-formulated professional codes of ethics that set out guidelines for their members for appropriate professional behavior that would bring the greatest good to the archaeological record and those connected with it. In each organization, the procedures for creating the code were somewhat different, but in all cases, the elements of the code came, necessarily, from the recent experience of archaeologists. The codes address issues and behavior that were perceived as problematic at the time the codes were being developed.

The codes of the different organizations have much in common, but also a number of differences that reflect the specific experiences, circumstances, and concerns of the groups served by the organization. In fact, it is useful and instructive to compare the various codes, which can be found readily on each organization's webpage. Individuals who are members of more than one such organization may even find themselves facing conflicting guidelines for occasional issues: a member of WAC and the SAA, for example, might feel torn at times between WAC's emphasis on archaeology's obligations to indigenous peoples and the SAA's assertion of primary obligation to the archaeological record. We encourage readers to download, read, and discuss the ethical codes and statements of WAC and the SAA, as well as other organizations such as the Register of Professional Archaeologists, Archaeological Institute of America, and Australian Archaeological Association. We elected not to include the codes in this volume, as was done in the first edition, because they are now so readily available, and more importantly because it is likely that some, perhaps all, will see revisions in the coming decade, as the profession adjusts to new and rapidly evolving issues—some perhaps unintentionally created or highlighted by the current codes. Already committees are discussing whether we might need to rethink what are the most appropriate and beneficial relations between archaeologists and (at least some) collectors, and whether some codes overstate archaeologists' claims as primary stewards of the archaeological record. Several organizations have already amended their original codes to address aspects of the electronic age. These professional codes are not final statements intended to settle all potential conflicts, but are works in progress that require continuous debate and reassessment in light of ongoing experience. The codes are not regulations or laws. They are guidelines that are meant to invoke thoughtful action, not to prescribe ethical behavior. Certainly a primary goal of all the organizations' codes, and indeed, of this volume, is to encourage archaeologists to think of their profession, and of all their behavior as professionals, as having an ethical dimension, with the potential to affect many people and the archaeological record in a wide variety of ways, good and bad.

For the older archaeologists among us, an awareness of this fact began with the ratification in 1970 of the UNESCO Convention on the Means of Prohibiting and Preventing the Illicit Import, Export, and Transfer of Ownership of Cultural Property (known in shorthand as the UNESCO Convention on Cultural

Property). That date is also generally used to mark the international change in attitudes toward the antiquities market and the collecting of antiquities. For example, when museums and others are considering whether to buy an artifact or accept it as a donation, most will accept an object that can clearly be demonstrated (as opposed to simply "claimed") to have left its country of origin before 1970, before the world community acknowledged the destruction and damage caused by such activity. Objects that have surfaced since 1970 and appear on the market violate the principles of that Convention, and are today rarely acquired by major museums.

The Convention itself has no legal force. Individual nations have to develop their own means of implementing the Convention and deposit instruments of ratification to become States Parties to it. (UNESCO's website currently lists 102 States Parties, including the addition, in the last decade, of several major importing nations.) In the United States such implementing legislation did not pass until 1983. The years spent in developing support for that legislation introduced many archaeologists to the antiquities market and made them begin thinking seriously about both national and international sales of antiquities as presenting pressing ethical issues for the discipline. Certainly since then archaeologists have paid much more attention to the whole set of questions encompassed by the one we have used as title for our first section, "Who owns the past?" It is not clear, however, that those attentions have done anything to diminish market activity. The website of an important dealer in antiquities (who also sells scholarly books that are considered helpful to the collector) highlights on its home page a recent headline from *The Art Newspaper*: "The Market for Ancient Art Continues to Accelerate." All other signs point in the same direction. Clearly the matter still needs attention and probably some brave new approaches—a challenge for the next decade.

Part I of this collection, therefore, looks again at some of those who buy and sell and otherwise claim ownership of a part of the past, in both old and new ways. The first chapter reappears from the first edition; it is still a good introduction to the general subject, especially for those who may not have given it much thought before. The other chapters in this section, which combines the first two sections of the last edition, are all new. The articles included in the earlier edition are not as out of date as some archaeologists might have hoped, but many new, fresh articles have appeared that raise similar questions and add new dimensions that we think are important to bring under discussion. Others, like Ricardo J. Elia's eloquently damning review of Colin Renfrew's 1991 book, *The Cycladic Spirit*,[2] we have omitted for other reasons. That chapter was, in fact, a favorite in classes: most students were aware of the towering reputation of Professor Renfrew and were stunned by his bad judgment—and that a junior colleague had dared to criticize him in print. The article raises many provocative and useful questions that are still relevant, but Renfrew's subsequent actions were very much in keeping with the scholar who, in fact, loves to debate and who takes valid criticisms to heart: he has since founded the Illicit Antiquities Research Centre, with its excellent newsletter, *Culture without Context,* available in paper and online, and has become an outspoken and leading critic of the antiquities market. Thus it seemed hardly fair to again focus discussions on that controversial book.

Looting in the United States has its own special complexities. Unlike most other nations where the national government claims ownership of all antiquities, in the United States, antiquities on private property belong, with a few exceptions, to the landowner. Thus, the landowner, or others with his or her permission, may dig, buy, and sell artifacts from private property. Local laws can put restrictions on this activity, and in a few places they have, but powerful individuals and the strongly embedded values of ownership rights work against it. Once objects from private property are out of the ground, it is all but impossible to prove, short of catching the diggers in the act, whether they have come from public or private lands. Chapter 2, "Trafficking in Treasures," explores some of the ramifications of U.S. antiquities laws and the local looting scenes. Chapters 6 and 7 describe two other manifestations of archaeological preservation that are unique to the United States—a subdivision where homeowners must agree to certain practices covering the extensive archaeological remains on their property, and The Archaeological Conservancy, which proactively acquires private property to preserve archaeological sites.

While U.S. law gives looting its own peculiar twist in this country, looting here still has much in common with the practice elsewhere. The other chapters in Part I address the international scene. In "Guardians of the Dead," journalist Roger Atwood, in a story that is further elaborated in his book, *Stealing History,* shows how archaeological discoveries of dazzling Moche remains in Peru spurred looting to supply a hungry, wealthy market by people with little access to other gainful employment, in a country with strong antiquities laws—that are rarely enforced, especially when powerful individuals are among the guilty. Although this study is set in Peru, the same story could be documented in any number of other places. Influential individuals also play prominent roles in "Faking Biblical History," which further adds religious zeal to the mix, and major attention from, and manipulation of the media. The result brought archaeology to the public in a most unflattering light. Perhaps the greatest leveler of variations in antiquities laws and in offering near universal access to the antiquities market is the World Wide Web, which has emerged in the last decade as an important means of buying and selling everything, including artifacts, apparently as often fake as genuine. As told in "The World Wide Web of Antiquities," Internet-based sales seem to be replacing, or at least vastly extending, local flea markets as an outlet for, small-scale (or lower end) collectors especially. As in Peru, such sales provide badly needed cash for many, especially rural people. The Web has made the market in artifacts more widely accessible and more visible—and easier for archaeologists to explore and analyze. We can hope that the next decade will see some brilliant new ways to turn the Web to the advantage of scholars, descendent communities, and the archaeological record.

The chapters in Part II raise some of the questions that arise in the context of archaeology and archaeologists' involvement in national and international politics. The recent wars in Afghanistan and Iraq have certainly brought some of these to international attention. Included here are but two of the many articles about the destruction there. For Afghanistan (Chapter 8), we intentionally chose a story about a controversial individual and his project—some think his museum is nothing more than a ploy that supports collectors (you should consider why)—because it raises some tough questions. Selecting a story on Iraq from the vast number available was harder (Chapter 9). A new Web-based organization called Saving Antiquities for Everyone (SAFE) has useful bibliographies and debate forums, as does *Archaeology's* webpage. An Iraqi colleague at Baghdad University recently wrote in an email that, "advanced cultures have proved practically that they are not advanced enough and should not be trusted further to protect the cultural heritage of human civilization." Is it too late to prove him wrong? With that question in mind, we thought it worthwhile to look at reconstruction in another place that had long suffered the ravages of war, Beirut (Chapter 10). The rich archaeological heritage in that city was, initially, very much included in the reconstruction plans. Perhaps there are lessons there for the eventual reconstruction further east.

Another difficult situation where archaeologists were at center stage is presented in "Flashpoint Ayodhya," which takes us to India. While the specifics of the case are unique to India, it is not too difficult to imagine comparable situations elsewhere, and to consider how archaeologists might do a better job next time. The last entry in this section, "Cloak and Trowel," asks us to consider how to behave when patriotism and professional skills collide. For some, stories of archaeologists serving as spies may sound like the stuff of pulp fiction, but it has happened and could happen again. Does it matter?

In a sense, all of the chapters in this collection are about people affected by archaeology, but Part III asks readers to focus on the people most deeply affected and moves to parts of the world less well-known today, but with histories as rich as any. Chapter 13 explores this issue and some of the ramifications, for the people themselves and for the discipline of archaeology. "When Artifacts Are Commodities" reports on Hollowell's recent study of the exceptional legal market in antiquities on St. Lawrence Island, Alaska: how it came to be, why the Islanders continue to exploit their ancestral heritage, what we can learn from them, and what archaeologists can (or cannot) do about the disappearing archaeological record in the Bering Sea area. Brent's account of looting and its effects in Mali is one of the chapters carried over from the earlier edition (Chapter 15). It is a vivid and disturbing account, and worth considering now, even though the situation has changed somewhat since it was written. "Terracottas and archeological objects traffic has decreased a bit," Brent recently wrote to us in an email, " since this form of art is not anymore the highlight of the international tribal art market. But still looting goes on and the illicit trade of ethnographical objects is more prosperous than ever." For a happier account of some recent developments in Mali see McIntosh et al. (in the recommended readings) which describes developments under a new government—with an archaeologist as president—and with Cultural Missions working effectively on public outreach.

The phenomenon of the last decade of public outreach by archaeologists is not directly addressed in this collection. Codes of ethics have made it a professional obligation to do a better job of explaining the goals and methods of archaeology to the non-professional public, and to involve them more in the process of our work. More and more archaeologists over the last decade have taken this commitment seriously and many wonderful projects are in progress. Archaeologists are learning slowly that giving up some power and authority can bring tremendous rewards; it can also be very difficult to move outside our professional mindset and truly listen to and value the questions and desires of non-professionals, be they descendant communities or local people with an interest in their cultural heritage—or, in many cases, with no interest. Sometimes it is hard for an archaeologist to accept that people have valid interests and needs that take precedence over their archaeological heritage. But, as the readings on looting should make clear, poverty and lack of opportunity are the taproot of that unruly vine, and archaeologists have begun to think of ways our discipline can make an economic contribution to the communities where we work and whose people and heritage we care so deeply about. One response to addressing local economic needs while also benefiting the archaeological record seems obvious: the development of archaeological sites for tourism. Chapter 16 looks at one example of this kind of development; we hope it stimulates lively discussion on the pros and cons, pitfalls and opportunities, the costs involved, and the actual beneficiaries of such endeavors.

If the UNESCO Convention galvanized an older generation of archaeologists around ethical issues, it was the Native American Graves Protection and Repatriation Act, NAGPRA (1990) that struck the soul of the next generation, and not only in the United States. Part IV takes up NAGPRA and related concerns about reburial, repatriation, and representation. A decade ago, NAGPRA was still new, and dire predictions of its negative impact on the discipline of archaeology were common, if not all recorded in print. We think the papers from the first edition, with the opposing early views of Clement Meighan and Larry Zimmerman, still make a

good introduction to the subject, and set the scene as it was in the early years after passage of the legislation. The short piece "Banned Books" should provoke
additional thought and discussion on the evolving relationship between archaeologists and Native Americans. "Out of Heaviness, Enlightenment" is but one of
many reports available on how NAGPRA is playing out 15 years later—how it is
changing many aspects of archaeology, not in the dire ways predicted (though
some still disagree), but certainly in revolutionary ones. Of course, these chapters
are only a beginning point for discussion, as these issues now pervade archaeological practice in Canada, New Zealand, Australia, and elsewhere. "Remembering
Chełmno," reports on archaeological work at a Nazi death camp, and raises many
of the same issues archaeologists face when excavating Native American and Aboriginal graves. It is also instructive to compare one's response to the Chełmno project with that to excavation of Native American graves or Christian cemeteries.
Finally, in this section, the construction of the new Acropolis Museum in Athens
reminds us that repatriation is an issue that was around long before NAGPRA
(Chapter 21). Other controversies surrounding this new museum lead to consideration of another growing trend, that of developing museums on archaeological
sites, indeed, of the whole concept of archaeological museums and what they
should exhibit and "be about" and why, or why not.[3]

The last section invites archaeologists to look inward, at the professional archaeologist, and what he or she brings and contributes to the discipline and the
perception of the discipline by outsiders. That archaeologists record and make
public the primary information about the artifacts and their excavation contexts is
a critical distinction between looters and treasure salvors, and archaeologists. Fagan's article from the earlier edition reminds us of this in a compelling way; it is
still an issue not taken seriously enough by all colleagues. Questions about intellectual property rights, on the other hand, are an emerging issue within archaeological ethics. No one is yet sure how these issues will play out, as archaeologists
begin to acknowledge colonialist practices, and wronged individuals and groups
are more inclined to protest abuses of their rights. The potential has always existed
for the misuse of ideas, images, and information that rightfully belong to others,
and for the intellectual property of archaeologists themselves to be misappropri-
ated. Hollowell and Nicholas draw attention to some examples, along with the
problems the abuse causes, inviting us to think about other contexts in which intellectual property rights might be involved (Chapter 23). Their suggestions for
avoiding the problems bring us back to the need for respect for, and consultation
with, other stakeholders in the archaeological record.

"Lure of the Deep" is, on the surface, a brief historical review of (a part of)
the specialized field of shipwreck archaeology. It serves also to remind us of archaeology's indebtedness to other fields, indeed, to world events, but we include it

here primarily to generate discussion about perceptions of the archaeological record that happens to be preserved under water. Scuba enthusiasts are many, worldwide, and most pride themselves on a careful respect for the natural resources—the wonders of the fish, shellfish, and coral reefs that pull them to their sport. Cultural resources preserved under water, however, are too often still thought of as being there for the taking. The old Law of the Sea exerts a powerful influence.

The last two chapters differ from all the rest by putting real people in the foreground. Both are biographical accounts, the first, of a non-archaeologist who has, nevertheless, brought the rapt attention of millions of people to the rather arcane field of early Stone Age archaeology (Chapter 26). The success of Auel's series, *Earth's Children*, raises questions about the ways that archaeologists present their findings to the public, surely a reflection of how we think about our work. Are archaeologists caught in a vicious circle, i.e., that because we are trained that proper scientific writing is formal and objective, we have come to think about our discipline in the way we have been taught to write about it? Do we produce "sleep aids," that send our readers off to dream of beautiful objects, rather than of the lives of those who made, used, and valued those objects? Have we forgotten the people behind our work?

The last chapter is a lively and sobering autobiographical sketch of Joe Watkins, an archaeologist who also happens to be among the rare Native Americans in the discipline, and who has come of age at a time when that lineage draws suspicion from both sides. His story is full of challenges. He writes, for example, that he initially thought he could avoid the controversy of reburial by moving his interests to French archaeology. We all know students and colleagues who have contemplated, or made, similar changes in focus hoping to avoid controversies, only to discover similar or equally difficult problems in the new field. One can't escape ethical obligations. Watkins's story has many other lessons, but perhaps the most intriguing comes at the end of the chapter, with his quote from Thoreau's *Journal:* "Wherever men have lived there is a story to be told, and it depends chiefly on the story-teller or historian whether [it] is interesting or not." He might equally have cited the long and sparkling tradition among Native Americans of meaningful storytelling. Surely that is a skill about which Native Americans could teach archaeologists a great deal. Perhaps, if archaeologists more easily allowed real people to inhabit their "data," they would have a much easier time of letting other real people into planning and carrying out archaeological projects as well—not to mention what it might do for the quality of archaeological prose and the increase that, in turn, would bring to the audience for archaeology.

Having said that, it is with some trepidation that we close with an archaeological story that Vitelli wrote for the first edition. It is about the significance of context for archaeological knowledge, indeed, for all of archaeological practice, as well as a thrilling moment in one archaeologist's career. Even with—or perhaps because of—all its challenges, the discipline of archaeology is still a very satisfying and rewarding one with which to fill one's life.

Paleolithic Obsidian from Franchthi Cave: A Case Study in Archaeological Context

Franchthi is a large prehistoric cave on the southern tip of the Argolid on mainland Greece, with occupation extending from the Upper Paleolithic through the Neolithic. It was excavated in the late 1960s and early 1970s, using many techniques that were quite innovative at the time. All the excavated soil was passed through a sieve, much of it through a water sieve, the first in Greece. The 5mm mesh sieve produced small mountains of what looked like pea gravel, all carefully labeled as to stratigraphic origin, and in need of laborious sorting into its components. Everyone on the project took a turn, sitting with a pile of "residue" and a paintbrush, moving the pile, piece by piece, into smaller piles of marine or land shell, carbon, flaked stone, ceramics, bone, etc. Some years we hired local teenagers to work steadily on the sorting. We devised elaborate systems of sampling, so that we might have useful information available before we all reached retirement. Meanwhile, we went ahead with our analyses of the larger materials recovered from the trenches.

In 1978, years after we had stopped excavating, we had the first of several symposia in Bloomington, Indiana, for all members of the publication staff to get together, exchange, and compare information from our analyses to date. Fifteen or twenty of us sat around the large seminar table, already exhausted from the intensity of several days of discussion. We were considering the sequence of excavated units that removed the Upper Palaeolithic and earliest Mesolithic deposits in the cave. We had heard Bill Farrand, our geoarchaeologist, present his analysis of the rate of sedimentation for the deposits. Nancy Whitney had reviewed their land snail content. Judith Shackleton had graphed the changing patterns of marine shell remains. Bas Payne had told us of the variety of mammalian fauna and the changes that appeared to be taking place as he moved up the sequence. As each of the specialists made his or her report of preliminary observations, unit by unit in the sequence, a pattern began to emerge, a convergence of the various kinds of data that was extremely exciting.

Then it was Catherine Perlès's turn to report on her analyses of the lithics. Working, at the time, without access to field excavator's notebooks, or even final stratigraphic sections that showed superimposed units of excavation, she had noted flakes of obsidian in units that should have come from Mesolithic and

Palaeolithic deposits. Since some of those units also had very un-Palaeolithic ceramic sherds, she had assumed, initially, that the obsidian chips, like the ceramics, were drop-ins, accidentally knocked from higher up on the 30- to 40-foot, loose, friable scarps. As we went around the table, hearing about each other's work, she had noted which units had anomalous materials for other specialists, and what the superimposed sequence in the deepest Palaeolithic trench was. She told us she still had a number of superimposed units that included small flakes of obsidian and from which no other specialist had reported anomalous materials.

Obsidian is black volcanic glass and was used extensively in the Greek Neolithic, as elsewhere, for the finest chipped stone tools. The natural sources of obsidian in the Aegean area are in the Cycladic Islands, especially on the island of Melos. Tjeerd van Andel's work on prehistoric sea-level changes in the Mediterranean had shown that, among other things, Melos had been an island, separated by some distance from the mainland, even in Palaeolithic times. Thus, if obsidian flakes were found *securely stratified* in Palaeolithic deposits on the mainland, they would have far-reaching ramifications. Their presence in the Palaeolithic deposits at Franchthi would imply that people had been making sea voyages on the Aegean millennia earlier than we had ever imagined they had the technology and skills to do so.

As that realization sank in, I think the initial response of everyone around the table was skepticism. How could we claim the beginnings of seafaring based on a couple of chips of stone that were barely 5mm in maximum dimension, too small and simple even to have distinguishing typological characteristics? Something that small could so easily have fallen unnoticed from a scarp, or accidentally been left on a table after sorting one batch of residue and then picked up with a later batch sorted on the same table. How could we settle this—because the implications, if valid, were very far-reaching? What followed was certainly one of my most exciting experiences as an archaeologist. Everyone around the table pitched in with ideas and ways to test the hypothesis that the obsidian chips had been recovered *in situ*, that is, in a context that had not been disturbed since its original deposition. We looked at the pattern of occurrence of the obsidian chips: one flake in the lowest excavated unit in the series; one in the unit above that; none in the next unit up; then a few more units with, some without; and finally, a pattern of increasing frequency throughout the remaining deposits in the cave.[4] We looked at every other category of material from the same excavated units, on the assumption that it was highly unlikely that an obsidian chip, which was rare enough in superimposed deposits, would be the only thing to be knocked from a scarp, repeatedly. If the obsidian in the various Palaeolithic and Mesolithic units had been knocked from the scarps, there should be some other materials that were knocked with it, which would show up as equally out of place.

We looked carefully and critically at the stratigraphic sections, to see if there was any sign, any indication at all, of an intrusive pit, a rodent hole, or other disturbance. We reviewed the process of sorting residue, the sequence in which bags of residue from different contexts had been sorted, and by whom. Steve Diamant, who had excavated the deposits, thought he remembered finding a piece as he excavated, and confirmed that memory through reviewing the trench notebooks. And so we went on, checking every possible alternative explanation for the presence of the tiny bits of obsidian in apparently Palaeolithic and Mesolithic contexts.

In the end, we compiled sufficient, independent lines of evidence and reasoning to convince us all that the obsidian was indeed *in situ* and did, indeed, constitute evidence for Palaeolithic seafaring. Today, we take that conclusion as a given, although we and many other scholars are still working on the implications: the kinds of seagoing craft, the technology of their construction, the development of navigational skills, the impact of waterborne transport on the movements of people, goods, and ideas in the early prehistoric Mediterranean and elsewhere. We can't even keep track of all the studies and information, the excitement and interest that have followed on that discovery from the symposium. And it was a discovery made, not in the field, not at the side of the trench when an amazing, beautiful object was uncovered, but years after the excavation, from a series of unremarkable tiny chips of stone whose significance came entirely from their context. It was the result of carefully excavated and recorded, undisturbed deposits whose total environmental and cultural context is being thoroughly explored by rigorous, demanding, and patient scientists and humanists.

Similar painstaking analyses of the upper, Neolithic, deposits in the cave showed signs of considerable disturbance in recent times, possibly by looters looking for the showy, decorative pieces of pottery and other items that characterize the Greek Neolithic. Or perhaps, ignorant of its absence in early Neolithic sites, they sought the gold that is often assumed to be what archaeologists seek. These pits stop right at the boundary between Neolithic and Mesolithic, the point at which major items of potential interest to the antiquities market cease to occur. Had the diggers gone a few feet farther into the Meso- and Palaeolithic deposits, even if they had removed nothing, they would have destroyed the evidence of all the environmental materials, the bones, seeds, shells, pollens, and soils that gain their explanatory power entirely from their stratigraphic context. We might still be convinced that Palaeolithic people were ignorant of the sea. Who knows, however, what equally significant information about the Neolithic has been lost to those pits?[5] At least careful stratigraphic excavation, detailed record keeping, and subsequent analyses allowed us to separate the disturbed from the undisturbed and avoid misinterpreting the entire deposit as intact.

Stratigraphic excavation, detailed record keeping, rigorous questioning, painstaking analyses: these are what trained archaeologists bring to their endeavors and what makes archaeology work. These elements are lacking in the hasty digging of looters. Looters sometimes find beautiful and curious objects. They always destroy much more. Their efforts deprive us all of the chance to learn the meaning of and the story behind the beautiful objects and the small simple chips of stone.

Notes

1. James Rachels, *The Elements of Moral Philosophy* (New York: McGraw-Hill, 1993).

2. Ricardo J. Elia, A Seductive and Troubling Work, *Archaeology* 46(1) (1993):64, 66–69; Colin Renfrew, Collectors Are the Real Looters, *Archaeology* 46(3) (1993):16–17.

3. Helaine Silverman, (editor), *Archaeological Site Museums in Latin America* (Gainesville, University Press of Florida, forthcoming).

4. Catherine Perlès, *Les Industries lithiques taillées de Franchthi* (Argolide, Grèce), Tome I. Présentation Générale et Industries Paléolithiques (Bloomington, Indiana University Press, 1987).

5. Karen D. Vitelli, *Franchthi Neolithic Pottery*, vol. 1 (Bloomington: Indiana University Press, 1993); Karen Vitelli, *Franchthi Neolithic Pottery*, vol. 2 (Bloomington, Indiana University Press, 1999).

WHO OWNS THE PAST?

I

Archaeology and the Ethics of Collecting   I

ARLEN F. CHASE, DIANE Z. CHASE, AND HARRIOT W. TOPSEY

This article reviews various aspects of collecting antiquities and the related responsibilities of archaeologists and museums. It includes a brief history of the discipline of archaeology and how past actions and standards have contributed to present problems, the many responsibilities that follow from a commitment to a particular field project, and problems that stem from using unprovenienced objects in scholarly studies.

A MAJOR MAGAZINE RECENTLY RAN on its cover a photo of a handsome Maya jadeite mask, suggesting that the piece had originally been dug up by looters. The magazine also reported that the piece was for sale at an exorbitant price. The cover depicting this object and an article within the issue in defense of private collecting rocked the archaeological community, and underscored the growing rift between scientific archaeologists and art historians and epigraphers, who often use looted material in their research. The controversy also raised some ugly questions about the discipline of archaeology, the majority of them revolving around the deprivations caused by the intertwined evils of collecting and looting. It is important to ask, for instance, if the portrayal of a looted artifact on the cover of a national magazine raises its value on the illicit art market. Or is its appearance offset by educating the public about the serious problem of a burgeoning black market in looted antiquities? Even more controversial, however, is any stance sanctioning the collecting of illicitly recovered objects.

Some archaeologists feel strongly that every artifact shown publicly or used as a kingpin in arguments about ancient societies must have an archaeological pedigree—it must have been properly excavated. They must know precisely where it comes from to tell its story. Without any indication of its origins and context, it is deemed worthless by some, or at best unreliable. Many institutions, the Archaeological Institute of America among them, have taken strong stands against illegal traffic in antiquities and will not knowingly publicize looted objects for fear of increasing their market value.

The controversy concerns not only intent, but results. How can one defend, either directly or indirectly, the rape of the past? Doesn't buying the fruits of such an enterprise only make the collector an accomplice in the crime? Today's private collectors, however, usually point to the beginnings of archaeology to justify their attitudes.

In its infancy, the discipline was primarily concerned with collecting artifacts. A number of prominent individuals of the 1800s were indeed antiquarians or collectors. In that era, collecting was believed to be both a mode of science and a way to increase knowledge. But while the destructive excavation methods of the antiquarians may have been similar to those in use by looters today, even then antiquarians usually recorded at least some details about the context of their finds—something looters don't do.

By World War I, archaeology had grown out of this stage. Today, an archaeologist "collects data" and, more important, "collects" context. Collecting objects is not, in and of itself, scholarship. It is the collecting of information in a scientific way that characterizes archaeology. To liken the archaeologist and the looter to one another—as some have done—is to project a false and simplified version of what archaeology is all about. The ethical and moral responsibilities involved in carrying out archaeology are found in neither the world of the looter nor that of the collector. In fact, the looter and collector are so intertwined that neither could exist without the other. The case of the robbery of Mexico's National Museum of Anthropology on Christmas Eve 1985 serves as a grave warning. Here, the looters stole certain objects "on order," much as big-city car thieves steal a given make and model of auto. When people will rob an institution to satisfy the collector's greed, no cultural resource in the world is safe.

But where do these heated differences of opinion come from and who are the various parties that are concerned with ancient artifacts? Archaeologists, art historians, epigraphers, museums, government officials, collectors, looters and dealers each have their own concerns. But who are the rightful guardians of the past and what are the responsibilities that go hand-in-hand with such guardianship? Professional obligations cannot be ignored. Looted or fraudulent pieces have sometimes been made respectable by noted scholars, either through publications or exhibits. The authentication and valuation of non-pedigree pieces constitutes irresponsible behavior.

The archaeologists of today have inherited the consequences of the methods and attitudes of the researchers that went before them. The first big archaeological and anthropological museums developed out of the antiquarian attitudes of the 1800s. For them, amassing artifacts was one way to increase their prestige and reputation. They therefore sent out expeditions to collect large numbers of pieces. With the advent of foreign nationalism in the 1950s and with the beginning of scientific archaeology in the 1960s the traditional collection-related roles were redefined. Most archaeological and anthropological museums broke away from their previously mandated role. Now expeditions were sent out less to collect pieces than to make spectacular finds and collect data. By the early 1970s many museums openly discouraged looting and actively hindered unfettered collecting: they did this by refusing to purchase or acquire by donation collections devoid of archaeological context or pedigree. Yet even then these same institutions had not yet fully broken away from the collecting mentality. Once they had gained prestige by mounting a large long-term archaeological expedition that continually "collected" significant discoveries, many sponsoring institutions did not then go on to provide sufficient post-field support: they failed to process the mountains of collected data, or even to fully publish their findings in a timely manner. Archaeology may be defined as "controlled destruction": whatever is excavated must be fully recorded because it can never be precisely restored to its exact context. Full publication of archaeological investigations allows a recreation of this context. To put it simply, archaeologists do not and should not dig unless they can expect to fully record and then publish their findings. These go far beyond the pretty pots and objects that form the sole interests of the collector.

Not writing up and not publishing findings is irresponsible. However, non-archaeologists need to understand that for every day spent in the field, *at minimum* seven days are required for processing, analyzing and writing. Projecting these post-field rates, it is not surprising that it takes years for final reports to appear. If one's emphasis is solely on collecting, the rest of the data are expendable. Today's archaeologist and, indeed, today's responsible institution, does not take such a narrow view. Rather, whatever is collected needs to be placed into its context to be understood; this takes time and forms the basis of the scientific enterprise. The end result of this long-term procedure is a final report that not only deals with past ways of life and cultural processes, but also permits the reader to recreate the excavated archaeological record and cross-check archaeological interpretations.

Modern archaeologists have a series of commitments, contracts and responsibilities that they did not have in the past. Most often these ethics or rules of conduct are understood by working archaeologists, but the general public is largely unaware of them.

While the primary task of archaeology is to answer scientifically questions about ancient societies, through their research archaeologists become enmeshed in a wide network of relationships that involves not only their work but the plans and goals of their colleagues, the local public and the government. Once an archaeologist begins to work at a site, he or she has usually made a commitment not only to the collection of data from that locale, but also to the physical preservation of the site once excavation ceases. Preservation of a site is accomplished either through backfilling of all excavations, or consolidating the site for viewing by tourists, in conjunction with government offices in charge. Such a stabilization and reconstruction program is part of the ethical responsibility of modern archaeology.

Apart from responsibilities to the site being worked on, the archaeologist also submits published reports on his or her research to the government offices in charge of archaeology and to colleagues within the overall discipline. In a wider sense, this responsibility also extends to guardianship of data. Archaeologists recognize that they do not physically own any of the items they are digging up. Rather, these items generally form part of the patrimony of the country in which the excavation is taking place and they rightly belong to the people of that country. Likewise, the data collected through archaeology ultimately should be used by the wider profession and the public. These data, however, must remain fully in the hands of the archaeologist until full publication. Only then can such material be placed in a permanent archive, preserved for use by other scholars.

Perhaps the most obvious responsibility of modern archaeologists centers on the published articles, public lectures and museum exhibits that should result from their activities. For these are the only ways that archaeologists can fulfill their primary obligation to the public—in return for public funds. Still, major questions are currently being raised by archaeologists about just how to do this and how much to tell. Should all data be made openly available to everyone or should some finds be hidden? Does the open display of national treasures encourage looting and collecting? The archaeologist must attempt to educate the public concerning its collective responsibility to the past patrimony. This responsibility should involve the open sharing of data with non-archaeologists through lectures, exhibits and newspapers. Nothing found in or by archaeology should be intentionally hidden.

In certain countries there has been a recent trend in the opposite direction. Rather than fully educating the people as to their past, news of important finds made by archaeologists is sometimes suppressed from public dissemination. Pictures of rare finds are not shown in public forums and archaeologists make no mention of them.

Suppression of data can create a dangerous situation by making archaeologists and government officials untrustworthy in the eyes of the public. If the data are not made available, some might unknowingly ask how the archaeologist is different from a looter. And who is to know where these unpublicized finds might end up? A lack of openness or honesty is not in keeping with ethics of scientific archaeology. But still there is sometimes fear that increased knowledge will lead to even more looting and destruction.

In Belize, there is a concerted effort to educate all Belizeans as to the necessity for preserving the past. This effort is being carried forward by the Department of Archaeology, archaeologists working there and the Association for Belize Archaeology, a local group interested in prehistory. Major new finds are presented in public archaeological displays throughout the country's districts and archaeology is being taught in elementary school. This enlightened approach is raising the consciousness of the nation about the importance of preserving the past. As a result, the public is increasingly helpful in preserving both sites and artifacts.

Beyond the problems involved in excavation, analysis, preservation, and dissemination of information, the archaeologist is faced with another dilemma. Should looted pieces and collections be used side by side with carefully excavated material? Archaeologists who do not include unidentified objects in their interpretations share an outlook that embodies three major points: First, these looted or collected items do not provide the full story; they are not associated with other artifacts or a particular location that can provide a context.

Second, unprovenienced material originally derives from illegal excavation and using these objects indirectly legitimizes the artifacts and the looting from which they are derived. Professionals are concerned that the use of such objects may also drive up market value and increase looting.

Third, because of the high demand for archaeological objects in the public sector, many of the looted pieces on the art market today are either fakes or repainted vessels that bear little resemblance to the originals. There is no assurance that the interpretations made from them are valid. It is in fact often difficult to distinguish a fraud from the real thing.

Some collectors and art historians feel that a rich world of iconography and glyphs has been opened up by the collection of looted pots of unknown provenance. Any responsible archaeologist would question this assertion, for it is not known whether such materials are real or repainted. The use of iconography founded on unprovenienced vessels is likely to introduce false interpretations, for the modern forger is just as skillful and inventive as the ancient artist. Even if some of these vessels should prove genuine, a much richer world of iconography and associations has been destroyed by removing the vessels from their contexts. Archaeologists do not ignore or discard data that can be utilized by epigraphers and art historians, even though their goals are different. This collection of all data by the archaeologist leads, in fact, to the problem of lag time between data collection and full publication.

Epigraphers, by definition, are predominantly interested in hieroglyphic texts while art historians are primarily interested in single vessels and their iconography. Such information can be rapidly disseminated because it comprises such a small amount of the data recovered through archaeology. Yet hieroglyphics and single objects form only a part of the repertoire that the archaeologist seeks to publish.

Collecting is big business. Archaeology is not. Business ethics, in which the dollar is supreme, is not compatible with archaeological ethics, where contextual data are worth more because they provide a fuller picture of ancient peoples not discoverable solely from the iconography of decorated artifacts. These interpretations of prehistoric life are the goals of archaeological science. The collector of artifacts needs to be made more aware of the invaluable nature of archaeologically collected pieces—and of the fact that information gathered about the relationships and meaning of such items may be worth far more than the object itself. It would be far better if collectors could be persuaded to spend their time and money in support of legitimate archaeological research. Such work would not only produce beautiful objects, but would also result in the contextual data needed to make archaeological interpretations of the past. And more important, collectors could experience the thrill of discovery, and the multitudes of meaning, that can be derived from the accurate placement of objects in their context. This experience might prove far more satisfying than mere ownership of a looted pot.

Today, collecting and profit go hand-in-hand. The unfortunate truth is that if collectors were not willing to pay exorbitant amounts for artifacts, destructive looting would not be so rampant. Nor would fraudulent archaeological materials so often be introduced into the marketplace. The argument that collecting "saves the past" only clouds the issue. A looter is not salvaging materials. He is only helping to destroy the past—for a profit. Most sites are not in danger from any other source but the looter's pick. And untouched archaeological sites are rapidly becoming an endangered species. Private collecting simply encourages further looting and from an archaeologist's viewpoint it is wrong.

Some would argue that the responsibility for curtailing looting lies not with the collectors but with government officials. But many countries are only now realizing the invaluable nature of their past. Most countries have solid laws against such activity, but not the manpower to enforce them. The responsibilities to curb looting, however, go beyond enforcement and educating the nation's people. They also rest with the country to which the looted items ultimately go. The simple fact that customs checks are made when one is entering but not when leaving a country means that the country entered has more of a chance of detecting a looted piece than the country of departure. Beyond this, curbing of looting requires an educated public unwilling to purchase items not rightfully for sale.

The dispersal of looted artworks into the world is a direct result of the existence of an art market to support such activity. Responsible museums and individuals have recognized that their obligation to the public precludes the ownership, authentication, and valuation of such objects. It is now time for collectors, also, to realize their responsibility to the cultural patrimony of the world.

Discussion Questions

1. Is an artifact without a pedigree (i.e., archaeological provenience)[1] worthless? What, if anything, is lost if archaeologists refuse to include such artifacts in their research?
2. Why is the idea of stealing artifacts "to order" so offensive?
3. How might publicizing looted artifacts increase their market value? The AIA has recently modified its publication policy (posted on their website), to give the editors of the Institute's journals the option to permit first mention of unpedigreed objects if the editor thinks the aim of the publication is "to emphasize the loss of archaeological context." Why do you think they made this change and do you agree with their decision?
4. Do archaeologists have a legitimate claim to being the primary guardians of the past? What other groups might contest the claim?
5. Can you think of circumstances when authentication and valuation of non-pedigreed pieces might not constitute irresponsible archaeological behavior?
6. What should be done (and by whom) if an archaeological team cannot fully record and publish its finds with reasonable speed? What is "reasonable speed"? Why don't archaeologists publish more quickly? What could be done to speed up the process?
7. What are the complex obligations (and to whom) of an archaeologist engaged in fieldwork?
8. What are the archaeologist's obligations to public education in the locales of fieldwork?
9. What are the differences between archaeological and business ethics? (See Chapter 24: Conflict between the two is often cited as a major problem for archaeologists working together with underwater salvors). Between archaeological ethics and cultural property law?
10. Who do you think should be responsible for curtailing looting?
11. What responsibilities do collectors, including museums, have to the archaeological record? Do different kinds of museums have different responsibilities? What alternatives to major additions to their collections might museums consider?

Note

1. "Archaeological provenience" refers to the the place where an object was found: the site, location in the site, the object's association with other objects in an undisturbed context, etc. "Provenance" refers to the modern history of an object after it has left the ground: who has owned it, whether and where it has been exhibited and/or published, and the like.

Further Readings

Chippindale, Christopher, and David W. J. Gill. 2000. Material Consequences of Contemporary Classical Collecting. *American Journal of Archaeology* 104:463–511.

Colwell-Chanthaphonh, Chip. 2004. Those Obscure Objects of Desire: Collecting Cultures and the Archaeological Landscape in the San Pedro Valley of Arizona. *Journal of Contemporary Ethnography* 33(5):571–601.

Craib, Donald Forsyth. 2000. *Topics in Cultural Resource Law.* Washington, D.C.: Society for American Archaeology.

Hinsley, Curtis M. 2000. Digging for Identity: Reflections on the Cultural Background of Collecting. In *Repatriation Reader: Who Owns American Indian Remains?* edited by Devon A. Mihesuah, pp. 37–58. Lincoln: University of Nebraska Press.

Messenger, Phyllis M. (editor). 1999. *The Ethics of Collecting Cultural Property: Whose Culture? Whose Property?* 2nd ed. Albuquerque: University of New Mexico Press.

Pearce, Susan M. 1998. *Collecting in Contemporary Society.* Walnut Creek, CA: AltaMira Press.

Trafficking in Treasures

2

MARIA BRADEN

Collecting Indian artifacts has long been a part of life in rural America. In this article Braden chronicles the local traditions of collecting in Ohio, Indiana, and Kentucky and the extensive destruction done to sites when looted for profit. Objects for sale on the open market raise the problem of distinguishing fakes from authentic artifacts. While some legal remedies are used to combat looting, Braden explains why these are limited and why looting is still widespread.

ANN CRAMER CAN'T SHAKE THE MEMORY OF the huge crater strewn with bones. "There were bits of humans everywhere," says Cramer, forest archaeologist at the Wayne National Forest in Ohio. "It was hard for me to believe."

Looters had tunneled into a 2,000-year-old Hopewell mound on private land to collect burial goods, tossing aside human bones as though they were garbage. "All they care about is making money," Cramer says. "It's a never-ending problem. As long as there's a black market, it always will be."

Collecting artifacts is an entrenched part of the culture in rural areas of Ohio, Indiana, and Kentucky, where plowed fields and river banks yield arrowheads, spear points, bannerstones and gorgets by the hundreds. But looting is the dark side of collecting. Many responsible collectors want to preserve history; looters want to profit by it. The booming Native American artifact market has encouraged exploitation of this archaeologically rich region.

Looters have ransacked caves and rock shelters where millennia-old artifacts are preserved to an extent unusual in the Eastern Woodlands' highly acidic soils. They have carved out prehistoric mounds and other Indian earthworks in search of ceremonial burial goods, and have destroyed gravesites in the process. In one nightmarish Kentucky case known as Slack Farm, which occurred in late 1987, looters dug hundreds of holes into the vestiges of a large prehistoric village of wattle and daub houses—a prime Mississippian site from the time of European contact—and destroyed or disturbed nearly 1,000 graves.

Although there have been a number of successful prosecutions of looting cases in the Midwest, looters still pirate treasure wherever they can get away with it. Stepped-up enforcement on public lands appears to have diverted looters onto private property, where they're likely to face milder penalties if caught.

Archaeologists and others working to control looting in states such as Ohio and Kentucky, where state laws prohibiting it are limited or nonexistent, have their backs against the wall. Cramer, the national forest archaeologist, says she's beginning to feel she can't live up to the oath she took to protect archaeological resources. "We call our mounds doughnuts here," she said ruefully.

But Indiana, which has a tough archaeological resource protection law, is a different story. Looting continues, but not at the level it was at a decade ago. That was when one of the state's most egregious looting cases occurred. In the summer of 1988, collectors tunneled into a Hopewell mound on property owned by General Electric and hauled off extraordinary treasures: a copper celt wrapped with pearl-studded leather; spear points of obsidian, coal and rose quartz; silver-covered copper panpipes and ear spools; copper pins, nuggets and breastplates, cut and polished human jawbones; and pieces of leather and cloth.

Archaeologists know what the looters took because they were caught, convicted and forced to return their booty. Some of the artifacts had been remarkably preserved and archaeologists speculated that the organic and metal artifacts had some special placement within a tomb or pit that contained preservatives. But they'll never know for sure, because the complex ceremonial mound was heavily damaged and the artifacts reburied at the insistence of several Native American groups.

The convictions were the first under a provision of the Archaeological Resources Protection Act of 1979 for violations occurring on private land. The provision prohibits interstate trafficking in archaeological resources obtained in violation of state or local laws. Sentences for the five people convicted ranged from probation and fines from $1,000 to $5,000 to one year in prison and a $5,000 fine.

The robbery of such spectacular artifacts, desecration of graves, and subsequent conviction of several men helped pave the way for Indiana's law, which requires a state permit to dig on public or private land. Illegal digging still occurs, but nothing on the scale of the GE Mound, where looting continued intermittently over three months, says Bob McCullough, an archaeologist for the Indiana Department of Natural Resources Division of Historic Preservation and Archaeology. "It's hard to catch them in the act," he says, "but they don't come back."

Public outrage following the looting at Slack Farm caused Kentucky legisla-
tors to strengthen state laws in 1988, making the disturbing of archaeological sites
on public land and the destruction or desecration of archaeological graves on private land felony offenses. But archaeologists see room for improvement. David
Pollack, with the Kentucky Heritage Council, says he'd like to see Kentucky emulate Indiana's law, but efforts to pass similar legislation have failed.

In Ohio, no laws prohibit the removal of artifacts from private property so
long as the landowner gives permission. A looter could even dig up a mound and
graves on private land if he had permission. But in 1999, Ohio amended the
state's vandalism and desecration laws to include burial sites "that contain
American Indian burial objects placed with or containing American Indian human remains."

It's going to take more than laws to stop looting in this region, where collecting artifacts is a time-honored, multigenerational activity. Many responsible collectors fear that laws aimed at looters will keep collectors from pursuing a hobby
they are passionate about. Thousands of relics change hands at Midwestern artifact shows every weekend and thousands more are offered for sale on the Internet.
But it's virtually impossible to know whether an artifact was obtained illegally.
Once an artifact is out of the ground, it's anyone's guess whether it came from federal, state or private property—or whether it was a surface find or was hidden
deep within a burial mound.

"The easiest cases are where you catch someone looting an archaeological site,"
says David Tarler, who works with the National Park Service on archaeological resource protection. "If you go to a show, you can't say for certain if an illegal act
was committed."

And sometimes it's difficult to sort out the responsible collector from the
looter. Increased interest in owning Native American artifacts has created pressure
to illegally unearth marketable relics. But for every profiteer, there's a responsible
collector interested in the history and provenience of the objects he finds.

You can pocket a fistful of arrowheads for a dollar or two at any Midwestern
show, and be reasonably certain that they were surface collected. But rarer pieces
sell for thousands of dollars. Native American antiquities are eagerly sought by
collectors in Europe and Japan, and a rare clay pot or stone tool or ornament in
mint condition can reportedly bring in $100,000 or more on the black market.

Prices aren't as astronomical for Midwestern artifacts sold at shows or over the
Internet, but potential profits are high enough to encourage collecting and selling.
A seven-inch hornstone Adena point from Ohio with a slightly damaged tip is
priced at $500 on the Internet, for example, while the asking price for a banded
slate-winged bannerstone is $1,000. Unusual relics command higher prices: a slate
effigy of a snapping turtle, for instance, was sold for $2,400 by an Ohio collector.

Ceremonial burial goods plucked from ancient earthworks aren't openly displayed at shows or offered for sale on the Internet. In fact, it's rare to find a collector willing to talk about digging at all because the word is too closely linked with looting. Ask a collector at an artifact show where he got a piece, and likely he'll say one of three things: he picked it up in a field or a river bank; he traded for it; or he bought it at an auction or estate sale. "Everyone has the same story— I got these arrowheads and I don't know anything about them," says artifact dealer Greg Truesdell.

Many sellers offer "certificates of authenticity" for their pieces, but longtime collectors say such guarantees prove nothing if the seller isn't knowledgeable and honest since the market is flooded with forgeries. Truesdell, who runs Lends His Horse Gallery in Los Angeles, says forgeries are particularly rampant on the Internet. He purchases artifacts using the Web auction service eBay but, on average, sends back five out of six artifacts. "There are that many fakes," he says.

Artifacts are made to look authentic in a variety of ways: they may be steeped in manure, buried in the ground for a couple of years, boiled in a pot of hard water to leave mineral deposits, or even spritzed with glue and coated with fragments to look as though they are mineralized. Some archaeologists believe the abundance of fakes could ultimately be good for preserving archaeological resources because it may discourage people from buying and cause prices to drop. But that hasn't happened yet. "Prices are going up real fast," says Mike Barron, a Columbus, Ohio collector. "It's treated me better than the stock market."

Barron was showing his artifacts and helping others determine the value and authenticity of their collections last summer at the 20th annual Antique and Contemporary Indian Artifacts Show in Bowling Green, Kentucky, one of the largest shows in the country. The show is sponsored by the wife of Arthur Gerber, one of the five men convicted in the GE Mound case. "I've seen many a looter there," says Pollack.

Collectors from across the United States, Canada, and France displayed roughly 400,000 pieces in an exhibition hall larger than a basketball arena. Some spread out their glass-encased collections on several long tables, while others walked around showing off artifacts in wallet-sized cases as though they were baby pictures.

Looting isn't a new problem in the Midwest or in other areas, but public awareness of the social and cultural costs of looting is growing. Archaeologists and those who consider themselves responsible collectors, many of whom work closely with The Archaeological Conservancy, speak disdainfully of relic hunters who damage sites.

But a widely-held view among collectors in the rural Midwest is that archaeologists, lawmakers, and prosecutors are conspiring to keep amateurs from collecting, and that laws regulating collecting infringe on individual rights. "Folks really stare you down when they see you walking a field or even a river bank," Ron Michel, an Indiana collector, said in a message posted on the AACA (Authentic Artifacts Collectors Association) website.

The gap between archaeologists and collectors came into sharp relief earlier this year when a bitter debate erupted at the annual meeting of the 2,300-member Archaeological Society of Ohio. At issue was a proposed bylaw change that would have required officers to swear an oath supporting collecting, buying, and selling of artifacts—which would have effectively kept archaeologists from serving as officers.

Collectors took the opportunity to vent their frustrations about the array of laws they feel have hampered them. "This is a serious problem," says collector Mark Long. "Your freedom to collect, even to own them, is threatened. Your freedoms are being chipped away a little at a time."

At the society's meeting, Robert Converse, editor of its publication, *Ohio Archaeologist*, suggested to society members that it was not farfetched to imagine that collectors could be raided by the U.S. Park Service for simply taking their collections across state lines. Converse, author of a dozen artifact identification books, says it is ridiculous to assert that collectors are stealing history when they're actually saving it. The argument that collectors take artifacts out of context doesn't hold water either, he says. "It is out of context. It's plowed up by farmers. If it wasn't picked up by a collector, it would be broken up."

Not every collector is buying and selling. Many come to shows simply to display prized relics and to learn from each other. They wouldn't consider owning something they hadn't picked up themselves or that hadn't been handed down in the family. Many keep careful records of when and where they found artifacts. Take Robert Harness, who's been collecting artifacts on his farm south of Chillicothe for close to half a century. Harness doesn't buy or sell artifacts, and every piece in his collection is dated and its location noted. Archaeologists from institutions throughout the region have studied his collection, and he enjoys helping them learn more abut the mysterious people who built the mounds. "My intention is to share knowledge," he says.

Responsible collectors like Harness render a valuable service, according to Martha Potter Otto, curator of archaeology at the Ohio Historical Society. "There aren't enough archaeologists on hand to investigate every site," she says. "These people can rescue important information."

Cheryl Ann Munson, an archaeologist at Indiana University, uses amateur archaeologists in her field and lab work. But she says collecting is harmful if records of the findings aren't kept and safe storage of the artifacts provided. Researchers must also be given access to the artifacts.

She considers collecting, be it of artifacts or other items, to be inherently human, but she suggests several other ways to satisfy the urge to own a piece of the past: help The Archaeological Conservancy buy and protect sites; buy reproductions; fund archaeological research; or volunteer to help university or museum archaeologists on a dig.

Bridging the gap between archaeologists and collectors may prove to be the best defense against illegal looters, since state laws are inconsistent and there aren't enough law enforcement officers to protect archaeological sites. In Indiana, for example, where 200 conservation officers cover 92 counties, collectors prove invaluable. "Our eyes and ears are people who care about historical resources conservation and will report to us," says state archaeologist Rick Jones.

But getting people to work together to protect archaeological resources requires educating the public. In Indiana, Kentucky, and Ohio there are a variety of stewardship and training programs for people who want to learn to identify artifacts and protect sites; workshops are also held for children.

"The law can only go so far," says Tarler. "It is going to be a question of changing people's attitudes." People must realize there's no difference between someone stealing their grandfather's headstone and taking 500-year-old pottery from an Indian gravesite. "When people say it's socially unacceptable...," Tarler says, "that is going to provide the greatest protection to archaeological resources."

Discussion Questions

1. If the artifacts from the GE Mound had not been reburied, how might archaeologists have determined whether special placement within tombs and/or the use of preservatives were responsible for their excellent state of preservation?

2. Does your state have laws regulating archaeological excavation on private lands?

3. Have you ever gone artifact hunting with family or friends, or do you know anyone who has? Have you ever been to an artifact show or flea market where ancient objects were being sold? If so, were you aware at the time of the laws governing related activities? Do you think such laws are generally well known? If you should encounter someone at a flea market or elsewhere selling ancient artifacts, what would you say to them?

4. How would you distinguish between a "responsible collector" and a "looter"? What is the difference between looters and archaeologists?

5. How can sellers on eBay claim to provide "certificates of authenticity" if, as the gallery owner quoted here says, "five out of six artifacts" from that source are fakes? What is a "certificate of authenticity" and what does it

mean? How can you tell if an artifact is a fake? Does it really matter if fakes are common on the antiquities market?

6. Do you think that laws limiting digging for, or collecting archaeological materials on, private property with the owner's permission are an infringement of individual rights? Explain.

7. If collectors pick up artifacts from land that farmers have already plowed are they, in fact, saving the objects? Is this a good thing?

8. In the early 1990s professional archaeologists tended to say all collecting is bad because ultimately it destroys archaeological context and, therefore, knowledge. Now, in articles such as this one, we are seeing some distinctions drawn between "responsible collectors" and destructive looters. Why is this change in attitude taking place?

Further Readings

Dofman, John. 1998. Getting Their Hands Dirty? Archaeologists and the Looting Trade. *Lingua Franca* 8(4):28–36.

Fagan, Brian. 1988. Black Day at Slack Farm. *Archaeology* 41(4):15–16, 73.

Griffin, Gillett G. 1986. In Defense of the Collector. *National Geographic* 169(4):462–465.

Labelle, Jason M. 2003. Coffee Cans and Folsom Points: Why We Cannot Continue to Ignore the Artifact Collectors. In *Ethical Issues in Archaeology*, edited by Larry J. Zimmerman, Karen D. Vitelli and Julie Hollowell-Zimmer, pp. 115-128. Walnut Creek, CA: AltaMira Press.

Mallouf, Robert J. 2000. An Unraveling Rope: The Looting of America's Past. In *Repatriation Reader: Who Owns American Indian Remains?*, edited by Devon A. Mihesuah, pp. 59–73. Lincoln: University of Nebraska Press.

Renfrew, Colin. 2000. *Loot, Legitimacy, and Ownership*. London: Duckworth.

Sackler, Elizabeth A. 1998. The Ethic(s) of Collecting. *International Journal of Cultural Property* 7(1):132–140.

Guardians of the Dead

3

ROGER ATWOOD

Along the coast of northern Peru, local farmers used to occasionally unearth beautiful ancient pottery to decorate their homes. In the early 1990s, however, Moche pottery became highly desirable in the global antiquities market, and the small-time collecting turned into a substantial looting industry. Atwood documents this transition, the huge amounts of money involved, the viewpoints of Peruvian archaeologists, and the tension between those locals who are trying to prevent destruction and those who actively engage in looting. Atwood also provides a rare insight into the process of looting, as he accompanies a group of grave robbers on a midnight sortie.

A LEAN MAN IN HIS 50S WITH SKIN BURNISHED from a lifetime working in sugarcane fields, Gregorio Becerra remembers the days when his father used to bring home ancient ceramic pots to their home in the village of Úcupe. Birds, faces, fruits, animals—the whole pantheon of Moche pottery themes stood on their living room shelf, where his father would place the perfectly preserved vessels he and his buddies dug up. "Everyone had a few pots in his house. They were nice decorations," says Becerra.

But sometime around 1990, all that changed. "It became a business," he recalls. "Outsiders came. They came from the city, and you'd see them out in the hills digging up everything they could find. They'd take it all away and sell it."

And so the modern looting industry came to little Úcupe and a hundred villages like it up and down the coast of northern Peru. People who used to excavate pots as back-lot hobby or family activity at Holy Week, as much a part of local social life as fishing or football, watched first with bafflement and then anger as professional grave robbers descended on their lands to search for pieces to supply the international market for Peruvian antiquities.

Poor, neglected, hurt by the fall of sugar prices, these villages suddenly found themselves living literally on top of a commodity hotter than sugar ever was: Moche ceramics from the first millennium A.D. that, for a time, had collectors in their thrall, fetching prices in New York that for the best pieces could surpass $30,000.

Now Becerra is the leader of his village's *Grupo de Protección Arqueológica*, or *La Grupa*, a citizens' patrol armed with binoculars, a dirt bike, one revolver, and one shotgun but whose most important weapon is the eyes and ears of people living in the village's adobe houses. The brigade's mission is to stop people from occupying the land and plundering what lies beneath it. The patrol chases away bands of looters, or surrounds them, seizes their tools—shovels, poles, buckets—and ties up their wrists with rope until the police come.

Walter Alva, director of the new Museum of the Royal Tombs of the Lord of Sipán in the town of Lambayeque, 30 miles north of Úcupe, organized eight such patrols in the early 1990s in response to the phenomenal growth of commercial looting in the Moche heartland. In doing so, he took a cue from rural Peru's long tradition of ragtag peasant militias known as *rondas campesinas*, which have fought scourges ranging from cattle rustlers to Shining Path Maoist guerrillas. This time the enemy was looters prospecting for ancient art, and it was ironically Alva's own 1987 excavation of the tombs at Sipán that helped inspire the plundering.

On February 6 of that year, looters digging at Sipán's burial mound, or *huaca*, struck a tomb where a Moche lord had been buried around A.D. 300. They carried out about a dozen rice sacks full of gold and silver artifacts, somewhere between 200 and 300 objects in all, and smashed or discarded hundreds more either inadvertently or because they didn't think they were good enough to sell. Police stopped the pillage and notified Alva, who, under constant harassment from townspeople who wanted to ransack the site, began excavating where the looters had left off. He found a dozen more tombs, two as rich in artifacts as the looted one. Alva's excavations brought new insights into the social complexity of the Moche, who ruled the north coast from about A.D. 100 to 700.

Meanwhile the looted artifacts had already hit the market, whetting the appetite of collectors as never before. Once an exotic niche product, Peruvian artifacts became almost overnight one of the hottest items in the international antiquities trade. "It was a gold rush," recalls Alva. "It's been a constant struggle against looters ever since." More has been destroyed in Peru in the past 40 years than in the previous 400, he claims.

I had come to Úcupe because I wanted to see if what Alva and his followers were doing was actually effective in stopping the rampant looting.

Archaeologist Carlos Wester, who helped Alva and Alva's late wife, Susana Meneses, develop the patrols and is now acting director of the Brüning National Archaeological Museum in Lambayeque, led me to the top of an unmolested 1,800-year-old Moche *huaca* less than a mile from Úcupe. As such mounds go it was pretty small, maybe three stories high, overlooking the algarrobo trees, grazing goats, and the village in the distance.

"The patrols have really worked," said Wester. "If you come here to loot, they'll chase you out before the police even get here. People have become aware of the value of preserving the *huacas*. Inside this one, there are probably some good things. Someday we'll excavate it, but until we do it's well protected."

In Úcupe, Wester introduced me to Becerra and another patrol leader, Gilberto Romero. I returned by bus a few days later to see the patrol in action. The road to Úcupe passed through a moonscape of barren hills before reaching the lazy Zaña River where the women of Úcupe were washing clothes while children splashed among water lilies and goats nibbled weeds by the banks. The village itself is a collection of single-story brick and adobe houses along the main road; dirt streets lead away through farms and sand dunes to the Pacific coast a few miles away.

Romero met me at the bus stop. A man with a gravelly voice and a sleepy smile, his manner was so mild that I was surprised to learn he doubled as a security guard for the local sugar cooperative and, as such, was licensed to carry a gun. He is the only member of the patrol who regularly carries a weapon, although he told me that he had never shot directly at looters. "This isn't war," he said.

Becerra, Romero, and I hired a motorcycle fitted with a passenger seat wide enough for the three of us. With a young driver named Julio, we bumped along a rutted dirt road past fields of spicy red pepper plants and sugar cane. Now and then Romero would point out a bare hill and explain that it was not a hill. It was another *huaca*, weathered by many centuries of wind and sun. "We have virgin *huacas*, never been touched and known only to us," said Romero, shouting above the sound of the engine.

The Úcupe *Grupa* was created in July 1994, Romero told me. "There are about 20 of us active in the *grupa*, but directly or indirectly I would say 90 percent of the people in the town collaborate with us. There are always a few who still want to dig up pots to sell, but we keep an eye on them. If we see somebody looting, we call the [Brüning] museum, and it calls the police. If the police can't get here fast enough, we hold them ourselves. A month ago we detained three looters and their tools. We let down our guard for an hour and before we knew it they were digging. It's like that here. You go to lunch and you come back, and there they are, digging. It's always people from outside, mostly from Cayaltí."

The market town of Cayaltí, with a population of about 10,000, lies 12 miles northeast of Úcupe. It is built around a rambling, wooden plantation mansion with peeling yellow paint. In the late 1960s, a left-wing government confiscated the house and the surrounding sugar plantations and turned them over to a workers' cooperative. Thirty years later the cooperative went bankrupt, and residents say the town has been struggling ever since. "No jobs here. Nothing to do," said a young man in the town square.

Cayaltí is known throughout the region as a looting center, a town where plundered antiquities are bought and sold with impunity. It's a busy town of woodworking shops and stands selling pirated videos, where fruit sellers and prostitutes in clingy black pants stand in the street and little cafes sell sandwiches and warm Cokes. One day as Wester and I drove into town, he pointed to two men walking beside a horse-drawn cart. "The older one, he's been arrested several times for looting," he said. "We know who he is."

Social hierarchy in Cayaltí is no longer based on sugar but on loot, with grimy tomb-diggers at the bottom, small-time dealers above them, and at the top, antiquities traders who sell to Peruvian and occasionally European collectors who come to town to buy. Two carpentry shops serve as fronts for the antiquities business. A taxi stand at the edge of town is known as a distribution center.

I wandered alone through Cayaltí, posing as a buyer and asking around for *antiguedades*. It didn't take long before a dealer led me to an alley behind his house, where he offered me point-bottomed Inka pots, a broken Moche portrait vessel, and an exquisite little ceramic jar no bigger than a perfume bottle in the shape of a spondylus seashell. All freshly dug up, he told me. (I bought an Inka pot and the broken portrait vessel for the equivalent of $3 each and took them to Alva at the National Museum in Lima, where he confirmed they were authentic. I donated them to the museum.) The dealer wanted to know if I was a museum director. Like loot sellers everywhere, he boasted that he sold his best pieces to museums. The son of the late owner of Lima's Gold Museum, he told me, occasionally came to town in a big black car to see what he had to offer.

The hills outside Cayaltí are pockmarked with holes left by looters and strewn with human bones, empty water bottles, and worthless bits of ancient textile. "*Aquí todo el pueblo huaquea*" (everybody loots here), the dealer told me, including the former president of Cayaltí's sugar cooperative, who was arrested in 1996 along with four other men for looting.

The people of Úcupe speak with disgust about places like Cayaltí. "No respect for their ancestors," an Úcupe woman told me as we waited for a bus. Archaeologists and the brigade have made the people of Úcupe more aware of their cultural heritage. "When I was a boy, people knew nothing about the importance of these objects we found," said Becerra. "We didn't know what the pre-Columbian cultures were. Moche, Chimú, Chavín, we'd never heard those names. Now everyone knows them. They teach them to the children in school."

Úcupe and Cayaltí are also divided by a bitter land feud. Farmers in tranquil Úcupe fear that Cayaltí people will descend on their lands and then petition a judge for legal title. Whole towns are born this way in Peru. Squatters take over idle private land by the light of the moon, and months or years later they ask that their settlement be incorporated as a town.

"People come from Cayaltí saying they want to work on the farms," said Romero. "Some of them have family members here. But to us, everyone who comes from Cayaltí is a looter." Becerra added, "We have extinguished looting in this area, because after the looters come the cattle rustlers, the thieves, and the land invaders. All the bad elements."

Some 350 people are now actively involved in the brigades. Alva calculates they have seized about 3,200 objects from looters. He also knows their efforts have pushed the problem elsewhere. Partly because of police and *grupa* pressure, and partly because the tastes of international collectors have changed, the professionals are moving south.

"It's tough working in the north these days. You can get arrested," says 23-year-old Robin. In Italy he would be a *tombarolo*, in Guatemala an *estelero*; in Peru he's a *huaquero*, a professional grave robber who has been digging up tombs almost every night since his early teens. He loves his job and lives in a small brick house with his wife and two daughters in a town north of Lima. He earns a little money on the side driving a taxi.

Robin and his buddies now work mostly in the Cañete area south of Lima, where there are no citizens' patrols, less police interference, and abundant ancient textiles of the kind that bring big bucks on the international art market—$10,000 for good ones, a quarter of a million for the very best. I met Robin and his colleagues through a collector friend. It took some persuading but he finally agreed to take me along on a nighttime raid. I told him I wouldn't buy anything or join in the digging. I just wanted to watch and take notes. They agreed.

We met late in the afternoon and took a bus south. There were four of us: Robin, two other looters named Remi and Harry, and me, a 39-year-old American reporter who drew a lot of stares as we crowded onto the bus with armfuls of shovels and tools. We got out at an empty stretch of highway some 80 miles south of Lima and walked for nearly an hour across cotton fields illuminated by moonlight. A few dogs barked but we encountered no one as we walked. Eventually we came to a tree. Sitting on its gnarled roots, we chewed coca leaves. About 100 feet away rose the Inka-era *huaca* they were about to assault.

The looters drank cane liquor and talked about strange and beautiful things they had found over the years—perfectly preserved pots, color-spangled weavings, piles of human bones and skulls. Robin told of a weaving that bore the image of a huge condor with outstretched wings.

They also talked about the fickle spirits of the dead. The *huaca* was a living force, with jealousies and resentments, moments of generosity, and fits of spite. "If you act greedy, the *huaca* won't give you anything," said Robin. "You take too much, and it will close up and never give you anything again."

"But it warns you," added Remi. "When the coca leaf tastes sweet, the *huaca* is about to give you something."

The looters particularly liked this *huaca*; it was relatively untouched, and they knew, having dug into it before, that the tombs within were not too deep. But, unusual for the south coast, there was some police presence here. Police had chased them away before, and Robin only barely escaped arrest one night at a burial site in the area. They told me the ground rules: no flash pictures (the flash might attract police), make as little noise as possible, and if you must talk, whisper.

I followed them to the *huaca* and sat on the chalky surface as they began their work. Shaped like a kidney, it stood about 40 feet high and stretched a quarter of a mile end to end. First they plunged metal poles into its smooth, bald surface to locate tombs. When they hit nothing but sand, they moved on. If the pole suddenly met no resistance, that meant they had hit an empty pot, probably within a tomb. And if the pole made a certain muffled crack, that meant they had hit human remains. The excruciating crack of metal hitting bone made me recoil.

After an hour of sinking their poles and making mental notes of where they had hit bodies, they began to dig—fast. In 15 minutes, they excavated a hole six feet deep; in half an hour, they had broken into tombs ten feet down. These seemed to belong to Inka commoners, simple graves with gourds containing peanuts or bird bones, woven bags, and coils of string. There were knitting instruments, broken ceramics, a child's tiny bone flute with a string attached. I looked at all this in the moonlight, fascinated, disgusted and saddened. They couldn't sell this stuff, and they were throwing it into heaps of debris.

"We know what people are buying and what they don't want," said Robin. "We leave a lot of stuff because we can't sell it. It's hard to sell ceramics these days. Too much of it is on the market. These days buyers want textiles and more textiles." They often get specific requests relayed from collectors through middlemen—customized looting.

Within a few hours they had ripped into half a dozen tombs and the remains of adults and children who had lain together for 500 years were scattered all over the *huaca*. The looters grasped human skulls by the hair and chucked them out like basketballs. They shoveled out bones, some with bits of desiccated human tissue still attached.

At about 4 a.m. they found what they wanted—an Inka weaving. At the bottom of a hole nine feet deep, using a flashlight, they could see the fabric wrapped around a bundle that surely contained human remains. In the light they could see the deep red and ocher of the fabric. "Look at those colors! We've got a good one," said Robin. "I'm going to dig around the sides, carefully so as not to damage the weaving. If you rip it out, you'll destroy it." Another half-hour of digging and he pulled the weaving free and clambered out of the pit. He held it up to the flashlight and shook it, releasing a cloud of dust. It was indeed a lovely piece, a design of red, yellow, blue, and beige diamonds. It was a shirt, almost perfectly intact, with a hole for the head and two for the arms. It probably belonged to a boy or a young man. The bones of the body it had wrapped lay at the bottom of the pit: a femur, a spine, a skull gazing up at the stars.

"This is the best thing we've found in two weeks," said Robin. They were all the more lucky because the pole had not pierced the fabric. They gathered their tools and put the weaving in a knapsack. As we walked back across the fields, they anxiously discussed how much money the textile might bring them. A thousand dollars, maybe $1,500.

As the sun came up we flagged down a bus making the all-night trip from Cuzco to Lima. Back in the small house where Remi lived, the men spread out the weaving on the dirt floor. They were tired but excited as they made calls with Robin's cell phone to find a buyer. By 9 a.m., they had one, a smuggler they knew only as Lucho, and asked him to come see it. "Believe me, it's a good piece, *una belleza*," said Robin. "We're not going to bring you all the way down here for something that's not worth it."

That was when I had to leave. I could not be present at the deal because Lucho might not like it. Would he be armed? I asked. No, he does not carry a weapon, but he is an important buyer and might feel uncomfortable having someone he doesn't know present, Robin explained.

The looters told me later that they asked for $1,500, but Lucho bargained them down to $1,000. The weaving would be on a plane out of Peru within days.

I had asked the looters how they felt about digging up bodies. "When you first start doing this, it makes you nervous," Remi said. "Digging up bones, you think you're going to incur a curse. But after a while it becomes easy. You don't even think about it."

"But," I inquired, "doesn't it bother you personally? I mean, how would you like it if someone dug up your grave and stole everything your family had put in it?" They looked at each other nervously, and then at me as if suddenly they wished I weren't there. Then Remi said, "Around here there is no other kind of work."

Discussion Questions

I. Explore the relationship between significant archaeological discoveries and the growth of looting for the commercial market in various parts of the world. Do archaeologists bear some responsibility for looting that follows on their discoveries? If so, what could they do to prevent the problems?

2. If looting is rampant in an area and archaeologists know where the mounds and important sites are, why don't they just excavate them now rather than creating patrols of local villagers to try to protect them?

3. Was it ethical for the author of this chapter to buy even a small artifact in the course of doing research for the story? To go on a looting expedition with the *huaqueros?* Why do you think the *huaqueros* agreed to have him come along and write about their work?

4. Do you think that being able to teach the local children in school about their heritage is a fair exchange for having to give up the old family outings to collect artifacts? Do you think the villagers find it a fair trade?

5. Explore the looters' answers to the reporter's questions about their emotional response to the work they do. Are there keys here to changing the situation?

Further Readings

Atwood, Roger. 2004. *Stealing History: Tomb Raiders, Smugglers, and the Looting of the Ancient World.* New York: St. Martin's Press.

Church, Warren B., and Ricardo Morales Gamarra. 2004. Tomb Raiders of El Dorado: Conservation Dilemmas on a "New" Archaeological Frontier in Peru. *SAA Archaeological Record* 4(1):24–28.

Howell, Carol L. 1993. Daring to Deal with Huaqueros. *Archaeology* 45(4):3, 15–16, 73.

Matsuda, David. 1998. The Ethics of Archaeology, Subsistence Digging, and Artifact Looting in Latin America: Point, Muted Counterpoint. *International Journal of Cultural Property* 7(1):87–97.

The World Wide Web of Antiquities   4

ELAINE ROBBINS

After drug dealing, money laundering, and arms trading, antiquities and art trafficking is the fourth-largest illegal pursuit in the world. With the emergence of the Internet in the late 1990s, the Web now serves as a major conduit for illicit trades. The boundless nature of the Internet, however, makes these exchanges incredibly difficult for law enforcement to tackle.

ARCHAEOLOGIST JONATHAN LEADER JOLTED out of his reverie and stared at the computer screen, where some items were being offered for sale on eBay. Leader clicked one at a time on the six high-quality photos—a breastplate, buttons to an overcoat, belt buckles, a cartridge box, shoe leather. As he read the descriptions of the items, he suspected that they were looted from a Civil War burial.

It wasn't the first time that Leader, the state archaeologist of South Carolina, found pieces of his state's heritage for sale on the Internet. In fact, he has followed the Internet's impact on cultural resources from its beginnings. "When I first came to South Carolina in 1989, there were already list-serves where people were swapping material for sale, discussing where to go dig them up, setting up flea markets," he says.

After watching with growing alarm, he decided to take action. Joining forces with the lead archaeologist from the South Carolina Department of Transportation and the State Historic Preservation Office, he formed a sort of archaeological SWAT team. On weekends the threesome descended on gun shows and flea markets. Whenever they heard a dealer publicly claim that artifacts came from burials or public lands, they filed a complaint.

Although they got few convictions in South Carolina, their presence had a chilling effect. "The dealers started shifting to on-line," he recalls. "So we started monitoring eBay once a week. I would do a search for 'dug,' 'excavated,' and 'relic.' I was finding an average of 300 hits under these key words for South Carolina alone." Although many of the items offered were obvious fakes, they found about 50 to 100 authentic South Carolina artifacts for sale each year. "Most were from the Civil War," he says. The items included "buttons, belt buckles, bullets, personal effects, wedding rings, slave tags." By exploiting the demand for artifacts, archaeologists say the Internet has hastened the devastation of archaeological sites. "A lot of Southwestern sites are beginning to look like moonscapes," says Alex Barker, chair of the ethics committee of the Society for American Archaeology. "Is it new? Well, no. There's been looting going on since the beginning of Southwestern archaeology. Some would argue that's the way it started. But because the prices commanded by some of the artifacts are getting ridiculous—certain kinds of Southwestern vessels are being sold for thousands of dollars—it is driving looting in a way that it might not have done if it was less lucrative."

Looters now hit once-overlooked sites throughout the country because they know they can find buyers for even mundane objects. "We're seeing a lot of the same looters, but I think we've added a lot more of them because of the Internet," says John Fryar, who investigates cultural resource cases as a special agent for the Bureau of Indian Affairs. "We've seen all different types, from the mom-and-pop types to the commercial looters. We see a lot of local people who claim this is their God-given right to do this."

This trend has popularized what was once a secretive, word-of-mouth business. Before the Internet, collectors had to show up at weekend artifact shows and flea markets—or visit Park Avenue dealers or elite auction houses. Now anyone with a taste for antiquities can purchase Mimbres pottery or Civil War belt buckles from the comfort of his home. While the big on-line auction sites are the most visible manifestation of this trend, some archaeologists say that a greater threat is the proliferation of websites of private dealers, some of whom traffic in illegal artifacts. Type "arrowheads," "Anasazi pottery," or "Civil War artifacts" into a search engine, and you'll get thousands of responses for dealers who specialize in everything from Caddo pottery to Clovis points.

Sold in Cyberspace

According to Interpol, the international law enforcement agency, art and antiquities trafficking is the fourth-largest illegal activity in the world, after drug dealing, money laundering, and arms trading. Since the rapid rise of the Internet in the late 1990s, much of that trafficking has shifted to the Web. While experts acknowledge the problem, the actual volume of Internet trafficking is hard to measure.

One reason is that most sites offer a hodgepodge of legal and illegal items. When students at Indiana University attempted to count the number of antiquities for sale on eBay, for example, they found approximately 4,000 items that were categorized as such. "About 60 to 65 percent are immediately obvious as not antiquities," says archaeologist Kaddee Vitelli, who directed the study. "They include books on ancient art, tourist items, and reproductions, antiques, and collectibles. So maybe 1,400 to 1,600 items on any given day are potentially of archaeological origin. Closer examination reveals that some of these are, in fact, offered as reproductions. How many of the remainder are authentic is anyone's guess."

Indeed, experts say that the Internet is littered with fakes. "Hobbyists can make stone tools that are virtually indistinguishable from prehistoric ones," says Ann Early, the state archaeologist of Arkansas. Even for an expert, it's often difficult to tell a real arrow point or chipped-stone tool from a fake. The certificates of authenticity offered by many sellers are no insurance against such fraud. But these facts rarely stop eager buyers. "Unfortunately," says Early, "human beings often become so passionate about collecting something—whether it's marbles or Mercedes or Indian pots—that good sense sometimes gets lost in the excitement of acquiring something that is attractive and special. It's like buyer's hysteria. But when you buy a mink coat out of the back of a pickup truck, you're risking a lot."

The on-line commerce may be just the tip of the iceberg. "Many of the dealers do a lot of their business off the Internet once the contact is made," says Early. "People are invited to call or e-mail if they have special requests or things of special interest to them. So the impact of the Internet buying and selling is not just that it has made the market for local artifacts global, but that it provides linkages between people who may continue to buy and sell off the website itself." Therefore the extent of the traffic may be significantly greater than it appears to be.

Internet trafficking is posing a challenge to state and federal law enforcement effort, experts say. According to Tim McKeown, the head of the National Park Service's Native American Graves Protection and Repatriation Act (NAGPRA) program, of the 21 cases convicted under NAGPRA since the law was enacted in 1990, none involved Internet commerce—this despite the fact that Native American human remains show up with disturbing frequency on eBay and other sites. "The problem is there are not many people out there investigating and prosecuting these types of crimes," says Fryar, who is investigating about a dozen Internet-related cases. "We just don't have the manpower."

When hundreds of artifacts from the world's oldest civilization started showing up for sale on the Internet after the U.S. invasion of Iraq, it served as a wake-up call to the FBI. However, investigators are challenged by the speed of Internet transactions. "It's a brave new world, investigative-wise," says Lynne Richardson, Art Theft Program manager at the FBI. "An item will go up for sale, and in a few days it's gone." Her department has just begun working with the agency's Cyber division to find new ways to investigate these types of cases. "Whether it's stolen computers or stolen artwork, we're going to have to find ways that we can respond quickly to these sorts of things."

Circumstances make these cases hard to prosecute. The primary law, the Archaeological Resources Protection Act (ARPA) of 1979, requires proof that an item offered for sale was stolen from federal or Indian lands. Items taken from private land must be done so without the permission of the landowner and then be offered for sale in other states and countries. (Offering cultural items for sale via the Internet constitutes such a violation.) This is difficult to prove short of catching a looter in the act.

NAGPRA, by contrast, doesn't have such arduous provenience requirements. It is illegal to offer for sale Native American human remains regardless of where they're taken from. If cultural items taken from federal or Indian lands are offered for sale, that's also a violation of NAGPRA. But if these same items are taken from private land and offered for sale, the act may violate ARPA, as well as other federal laws concerning mail and wire fraud, or state laws, but not NAGPRA.

"There almost has to be a statement saying, 'We potted this off some geezer's land without his knowledge, and we're pretty sure it's from this tribe, and we sure hope they don't find out about it,'" says Barker regarding the difficulty of convicting someone who has taken archaeological items from private land. "Unless you have a statement that's that direct, it's very difficult to get any kind of legal action." For example, when the South Carolina Civil War burial items showed up for sale on eBay, the seller wrote about how he paddled his canoe in the middle of the night, stole onto private property, and started digging in a spot where he knew a battle had taken place. Although Leader alerted the South Carolina State Law Enforcement Division, which prepared a case, a lawyer told them that the only way to successfully prosecute would be to catch the looter in the act.

The way some courts are interpreting ARPA poses another challenge. In 2000, the U.S. Court of Appeals for the Ninth Circuit in San Francisco overturned the felony plea of a man who had been convicted under ARPA for taking a human skull from a national forest in Alaska.

The court determined that, in order to convict the man under ARPA, the prosecution had to prove the man knew or should have known that the skull was at least 100 years old, the age at which the law deems it an archaeological resource. "ARPA was never designed as a specific intent crime," complains Fryar. "Now we're having to get into people's minds to find out if they think this thing is over 100 years old or not." He adds that the statute of limitations under ARPA is five years, which is too short given that sometimes these crimes are discovered years after they've taken place.

Though ARPA has shortcomings, it also has teeth. Due to the Internet's global nature, anything illegal sold on it automatically becomes an interstate sale of stolen property—a federal violation under Section 6C of ARPA. "If I steal a pot from state trust land in Arizona, I have violated state law by stealing it," explains Martin McAllister, managing partner of Archaeological Resources Investigations, a Missoula-based consulting firm. "Now if I offer it for sale on the Internet, I'm also in violation of federal law." ARPA decrees that personal property used to carry out the crime, such as vehicles and computers, can also be forfeited to the government or tribe that is victimized by the crime.

In 2002 the Federal Sentencing Commission promulgated new sentencing guidelines that increased the chances of violators going to jail. "I think it's just starting to have an impact," states an Assistant U.S. Attorney who has prosecuted both ARPA and NAGPRA cases. "I think they're effective," he says of the laws governing antiquities, but he also thinks they should be made stronger. Legislation is pending in Congress to increase the penalties under these laws up to 10 years for a felony offense. Currently, a felony offense under ARPA carries a maximum penalty of two years under ARPA and five years under NAGPRA.

Auctioning Our Past

A few years ago the Society for American Archaeology, along with the Society for Historical Archaeology and the American Anthropological Association, launched an educational campaign to halt illegal antiquities sales. Their first move was to ask Amazon and eBay to curb the sale of illegal archaeological items on their websites. Their efforts met with little success. While eBay's official policy prohibits sales of illegal artifacts and grave-related items, the company argues that it can't possibly police its site. "There are 24 million items available on the site at any given time, and 3.5 million new listings are added every day," says eBay spokesperson Hani Durzy. "So it would be impossible for us to completely eliminate anything that might fall under the illegal category from ever appearing on our site." Instead, eBay says it depends on law enforcement officials to alert them when illegal artifacts are offered for sale on their site. "We're not experts over here. We don't have core competency in Native American artifacts," says Durzy. While eBay has been unresponsive when archaeologists point out suspect offerings, it has been quick to pull a questionable listing when contacted by law enforcement officials. It also cooperates with investigators when they request information about buyers and sellers.

But archaeologists want the auction sites to do more. While eBay posts its policies on "Artifacts, Grave-Related Items, and Native American Crafts" on its site, most buyers never see those policies unless they search for them. "We'd like to at least get to the point that when antiquities are being advertised, there's the statement that says, 'here are the things you should be concerned about,'" says Barker. Some experts advocate that the auction sites require proof of legal ownership of the items being sold.

Barker urges a war on two fronts. While law enforcement needs to shut down the websites of illegal dealers, the SAA hopes to continue to educate the Internet auction sites. It also endeavors to educate the buying public and local law enforcement officers, many of whom aren't aware of antiquities laws.

There is also the issue of self-education. "Archaeologists have to understand what it takes to prosecute a case," Early notes. There is much more involved than merely informing law enforcement officials of a violation. "It doesn't do any good to call the cops if the prosecutor isn't on board," she adds, meaning that archaeologists have to supply evidence sufficient to win a case in court.

"Are we, as a community, doing enough?" asks Barker. "The answer is no. Now we need to figure out what tools we've got and how much will we've got in the community to do something about it."

Discussion Questions

1. Spend an hour or two searching the Internet using the keywords "dug," "excavated," and "relic" (or substitute similar words related to your own area of interest). Can you recognize fakes? Did you find sellers explaining where their objects had been found and under what circumstances? Did they offer "certificates of authenticity"?

2. Spend some time comparing the offerings of artifacts on eBay and those on some of the small dealer sites. Do you agree that the smaller sites present more of a threat to site preservation than the big auction houses?

3. While the Web makes it easier for more people to buy and sell antiquities, it also makes it possible for archaeologists to track these sales more easily than was once true. You might try dividing up responsibilities to monitor, over a period of several weeks or longer, the actual sales of (some category of) artifacts on eBay, to see what prices people are actually paying, compared to asking prices; what categories of artifacts are most frequently bought; whether materials from war-torn areas are showing up at auction; whether sources of objects are indicated; whether scholars are cited as authenticators; whether you see signs that sellers are simply luring buyers to their brick and mortar shops; and any number of other possibilities.

4. See if you can develop additional ideas to help the Cyber Division of law enforcement to investigate cases of potential illegal Internet sales of antiquities.

5. What additional suggestions can you make for controlling the sale of illicitly acquired artifacts or, at least, increasing awareness of the issues involved in collecting antiquities to potential buyers on the Internet?

6. What could your class do to make Internet users more aware of these issues?

7. What role does U.S. tax law play in the antiquities market? Could tax laws be used to reduce the damage caused by the market?

Further Readings

Barker, Alex W. 2000. Ethics, E-commerce, and the Future of the Past. *Society for American Archaeology Bulletin* 18(1):15.

Bruhns, Karen Olsen. 2000. www.plunderedpast.com. *Society for American Archaeology Bulletin* 18(2):14–15, 17.

Vitelli, Karen D. 2000. E-commerce in Antiquities. *Society for American Archaeology Bulletin* 18(4):4–5.

Faking Biblical History   5

NEIL ASHER SILBERMAN AND YUVAL GOREN

Since the very beginning of archaeology as a discipline, scholars have attempted to find physical evidence of the stories and people recounted in the Christian Bible. In 2002, a major press conference was held to announce the first definitive proof of Jesus' existence—a small chalk ossuary, or bone container, with the carved Aramaic inscription Yaakov bar Yoseph, Achui de Yeshua, "James, son of Joseph, brother of Jesus." But after much publicity and controversy, as Silberman and Goren recount, the ossuary was discovered to be nothing more than a fake.

TWO CENTURIES OF INTENSIVE ARCHAEOLOGICAL ACTIVITY in the land of the Bible—surveying, digging, and frantic antiquities buying and selling—have yielded only a handful of artifacts that can be directly connected to specific biblical personalities. Yet since the beginning of the great search for archaeological proof of the scriptures, those personalities have loomed large in virtually every debate. Were the Patriarchs—Abraham, Isaac, and Jacob—genuine historical characters? Did David and Solomon really rule over a vast united kingdom? Was Jesus of Nazareth a real figure who lived much as he is described in the New Testament?

Archaeology has done a great deal to clarify the general social background and historical context in which the Bible was written, but scholars are still divided, often acrimoniously, about how much of the scriptural narrative is historically accurate. That is why the stakes were so high when two astounding discoveries recently surfaced in Jerusalem that, if authentic, would have offered convincing, perhaps even irrefutable, archaeological evidence of the historical reliability of two important biblical events.

But the story that began with trumpet blasts of spiritual triumph was destined to end as an embarrassing farce. Indeed, the pious self-deception, shoddy scholarship, and commercial corruption that accompanied these relics' meteoric rise and fall as media sensations offer an instructive Sunday school lesson to anyone who would, at any cost, try to mobilize archaeology to prove the Bible "true."

The Greatest Discovery of the Century?

The story first exploded into the headlines on October 21, 2002, with the beginning of a skillfully orchestrated publicity campaign. At a Washington press conference jointly sponsored by the Discovery Channel and the Biblical Archaeology Society, Hershel Shanks, publisher and editor of the popular *Biblical Archaeology Review*, presented a large audience of reporters and TV crews with photographs and background supporting what he called "the first ever archaeological discovery to corroborate biblical references to Jesus." The discovery in question was a small chalk ossuary, or bone container, bearing the Aramaic inscription *Yaakov bar Yoseph, Achui de Yeshua*, "James, son of Joseph, brother of Jesus." According to Shanks, the ossuary belonged to an anonymous Tel Aviv antiquities collector who, having become aware of its significance, was now willing to allow news of its discovery to be made public.

Authenticated as dating from the first century A.D. by renowned Semitic epigrapher André Lemaire of the Sorbonne and by some laboratory tests carried out by scientists at the Geological Survey of Israel (GSI), the ossuary caused a worldwide sensation. No previous artifacts had ever been found that could be directly connected to the gospel figures Jesus, Joseph, or James—yet here was one that might have held the very bones of Jesus' brother. In the following days, excited reports about the "James Ossuary" appeared on NBC, CBS, ABC, PBS, and CNN and in the *New York Times*, the *Wall Street Journal*, the *Washington Post*, and *Time*. *Newsweek* suggested that "Biblical archaeologists may have found their holy grail."

The initial studies of the ossuary had indeed produced some dramatic conclusions. Lemaire reported that even though the ossuary seemed to be undecorated, its inscription was truly remarkable. He dated the distinctive forms of the inscribed letters to the period A.D. 20 to 70 and made a mathematical calculation about the possibility that this was in fact the container that had once held St. James's earthly remains. Relying on estimates of first-century Jerusalem's population (around 80,000) and the frequency of name combinations appearing on ossuaries from that period, Lemaire suggested that "it was very probable" that this was the burial box of James, who, according to the ancient Jewish historian Flavius Josephus, was executed by the order of the high priest Ananus in A.D. 62.

Shanks immediately understood the potential significance of this find to his magazine's conservative Christian readers. In recent years, the literal reliability of the scriptural descriptions of Jesus' early life and ministry has been challenged by a significant number of biblical scholars. Shanks's publications *Biblical Archaeology Review* and *Bible Review* have covered the controversy in detail. And ever keeping his ear to the ground to learn of recent finds that might influence the course of the debate, Shanks solicited and received a manuscript from Lemaire describing his conclusions about the James Ossuary, to be published as a world exclusive in *Biblical Archaeology Review*.

A cautious lawyer by training, Shanks sought second and third opinions from other world-renowned experts in ancient Semitic epigraphy: Kyle McCarter of Johns Hopkins University and Joseph Fitzmyer of the Catholic University. Though McCarter detected two handwriting styles (and therefore two scribes) in the first and last parts of the inscription, both he and Fitzmyer agreed that the Aramaic letters were authentic and dated to the first century A.D.

Next, Shanks turned to hard science. Amnon Rosenfeld and Shimon Ilani of the GSI carried out microscopic and chemical tests on the ossuary. Their results provided another seeming confirmation of the ossuary's authenticity: its stone is of the type commonly used in Jerusalem ossuaries and the patina that covers it "has a cauliflower shape known to be developed in a cave environment"—suggesting that it was naturally formed in a rock-cut burial chamber over hundreds of years. In sum, Rosenfeld and Ilani concluded in their report, "No evidence that might detract from the authenticity of the patina and inscription was found."

The archaeological value of this potentially unique and precious relic was also plagued by nagging uncertainties about the date and place where it was obtained. According to current Israeli antiquities law, only artifacts that were discovered prior to 1978 can be privately owned or sold by officially licensed antiquities dealers. All subsequent finds belong to the state. In his October press conference, Shanks reported that the ossuary had been found "around fifteen years ago," which would therefore make it subject to confiscation by the Israel Antiquities Authority (IAA). But the collector, with whom Shanks was in close contact and whom he called "Joe" to preserve his anonymity, issued a clarification. "Joe" claimed he had obtained it as a sixteen-year-old—at a Jerusalem antiquities shop (but which one he could not exactly remember)—just a few years after the 1967 war. It was one of his earliest acquisitions and he had kept it at his parents' Tel Aviv apartment for many years. It was only fifteen years ago that he brought it to his own apartment. And why had the self-professed owner of "probably the largest and most important private collection of its kind in Israel" never recognized the ossuary's significance? Shanks quoted "Joe" as innocently admitting in one of their many conversations that "I never thought the Son of God could have a brother!"

The November/December 2002 issue of *Biblical Archaeology Review* carried Lemaire's exclusive cover story on the ossuary with the bold headline "Evidence of Jesus Written in Stone." But this was only a part of a far wider publicity campaign.

Shanks teamed up with Simcha Jacobovici, a Canadian film producer who believed the "James Ossuary" could be a huge media sensation all over the world. A deal was concluded with the Discovery Channel, which would air a nationwide prime-time documentary special during the Easter weekend. Negotiations also got underway with mass-market publisher Harper-Collins for a book that Shanks would coauthor with Ben Witherington III of the Asbury Theological Seminary in Kentucky, a staunch defender of the historicity of the gospels and an occasional columnist for Shanks's other publication, *Bible Review*. And as if that were not enough of a media overkill for a humble white bone box from Jerusalem, Shanks proposed (with the willing and by now enthusiastic cooperation of "Joe") that the ossuary would be the centerpiece of a highly publicized public exhibit at the prestigious Royal Ontario Museum (ROM) in Toronto, coinciding with the annual meetings of the Society of Biblical Literature.

Before the media uproar of the October 21 press conference, "Joe" reportedly insured the ossuary for $1 million and obtained routine approval for the temporary export of an inscribed ossuary from the IAA. On October 25, while the media was still humming with excited speculation about the significance of the bone box, William Thorsall, ROM director and CEO, proudly announced in an official press release that the "ROM is honoured to receive the James Ossuary such a short time after its discovery," and that "we are delighted to be the first museum to display it and bring forth the various theories regarding its significance and archaeological history."

Yet for all the ballyhoo, hosannas, and lucrative negotiations, the journey of the James Ossuary to Toronto was ill-starred. When it arrived at the Royal Ontario Museum and was removed by the curators from its cardboard shipping box and bubble-wrap blanket, it was found to be severely damaged by a network of deep cracks. Desperate to recover from this public-relations debacle and launch their exhibition on time, ROM conservators began feverish work to repair the damage—discovering, in the meantime, carved rosette decorations on the side opposite the inscription that had apparently been overlooked by Lemaire. In the meantime, the identity of the owner was revealed by a reporter for the Israeli daily *Ha'aretz*. He was Oded Golan, a 51-year-old engineer, well known on the Israeli antiquities collecting and dealing scene.

The IAA, for its part, was criticized (and embarrassed) by the ease with which it had issued the export permit. It demanded that Golan return the ossuary to Israel after the conclusion of the exhibition so that its legal status could be resolved and it could be examined by IAA experts. The whole affair of the James Ossuary was in danger of becoming a comedy of errors. But so many people were now caught up in the enthusiasm of the "first discovery that proved the historical existence of Jesus" that almost everyone forgot to laugh.

Or almost everyone. From the start there were some skeptical voices. In an op-ed piece in the *Los Angeles Times*, Robert Eisenman of University of California-Long Beach, a well-known, controversial scholar who had written extensively on James, termed the discovery "just too pat, too perfect." He suggested that the names of Jesus, Joseph, and James together "is what a modern audience, schooled in the Gospels, would expect, not an ancient one."

With the ossuary glued back together and dramatically illuminated in a main exhibit hall of the Royal Ontario Museum, the best possible light was cast on the celebrated discovery. Even proud owner Oded Golan had flown over to Toronto to be at the festive opening of the exhibition and to participate in the public lectures held in connection with it. Lemaire, basking in the media attention and scholarly acclaim of the moment, firmly defended his original conclusions about the inscription at a special session of the Society for Biblical Literature. Standing at the lectern, he angrily dismissed claims that it was a modern forgery, misdated, or even written by two people. As a scholar of unquestioned reputation, Lemaire icily questioned the professional qualifications and expertise of those individuals who had come forward to challenge his reading.

Following Lemaire, in an impassioned rhetorical tour de force worthy of a skillful summation to the jury, Shanks also belittled the critics of the inscription as far less credible than the famous scholars who supported its authenticity. Addressing critics who found fault with the promotion of a privately owned artifact whose provenience was so uncertain, he railed against those who opposed the antiquities trade, suggesting that there are "bad" collectors who hoard their treasures and "good" collectors who share them with the world. Oded Golan was, by that definition, certainly good.

The doubters had been at least temporarily humbled. The sheer weight of skillful promotion, museum prestige, media attention, and scholarly reputation had lined up in favor of the authenticity of the James Ossuary and discouraged most from taking a closer look at the emperor's clothes.

Another Amazing Artifact

Hardly had Christmas come and gone when, in January, another amazing and unprecedented archaeological find, the so-called "Jehoash Inscription," was revealed to the world. It was rumored to have come from the construction rubble of recent, controversial building activities by the Muslim authorities on the Temple Mount in Jerusalem. According to another version, it was found lying face down, in the Muslim cemetery, down slope from the Temple Mount. Bearing fifteen lines of Hebrew-Phoenician script, this cracked gray stone slab was dated nine hundred years older than the James Ossuary and described repairs to the Temple in

Jerusalem apparently overseen by Jehoash, son of King Ahaziah of Judah. It described how the ancient king of Judah collected contributions from his subjects and obtained the precious materials:

> When the generosity of the men from the land and from the desert, and all the towns of Judah, was filled, to give much hallowed money to buy quarried stones, cypresses, and copper, meant to do the work faithfully. And I repaired the benches of the Temple and the walls around, and the gallery, and the fences, and the spiral stairs, and the niches, and the doors. And this day would be a testimony that the craftsmanship would endure. May the Lord bless his people.

This language was strikingly reminiscent of the account in 2 Kings 12. And at a time when the date of composition of the Hebrew Bible, like that of the Gospel accounts, had become a matter of disagreement among biblical scholars, the Jehoash Inscription offered a lapidary reply to those who would deny that the Hebrew Bible contained a reliable record of events. According to archaeologist Gabriel Barkay of Bar-Ilan University, this find, if authentic, would be "the most significant archaeological finding yet in Jerusalem and the Land of Israel. It would be a first-of-its-kind piece of physical evidence describing events in a manner that adheres to the narrative in the Bible." And Shanks, by now a familiar TV and newspaper presence when it came to assessing the significance of biblical discoveries, asserted that if authentic, the inscription would be "visual, tactile evidence that reaches across 2,800 years."

Photographs and feature stories about this find were quickly flashed around the world by a media hungry to relive the excitement of the James Ossuary. The circumstances of its discovery and ownership over the previous years were even murkier. Published reports in the Israel dailies *Maariv* and *Ha'aretz* suggested that it was owned by a Palestinian Arab antiquities dealer in Hebron. He had offered it for sale to the Israel Museum, which had declined. The museum had no comment. But the Jehoash Inscription had an additional, explosive effect in the turbulent world of Middle Eastern politics. It intensified an already fiery rhetorical battle between the Muslim religious authorities on the Temple Mount and those who sought full Israeli sovereignty there, at the site where the ancient temple stood.

The right-wing Israeli group The Temple Mount Faithful quickly posted photographs of the Jehoash Inscription on their website, declaring it "completely authentic" and noting that "people feel that the timing is no accident and that it is a clear message from the G-d of Israel Himself that time is short, the Temple should immediately be rebuilt. . . ." A few days later, Abdullah Kan'an, secretary-general of Jordan's Royal Committee for Jerusalem Affairs, issued a press release asserting that extremist factions in Israel were using the claims of the discovered tablet to support their bid to destroy the Al-Aqsa Mosque and rebuild the Temple, and further warned that "if that happened, God forbid, a holy religious war will definitely inflame the whole region." This was dangerous territory for an archaeological artifact to be drawn into.

The process of recognition and authentication of the Jehoash Inscription seemed to duplicate the story of the James Ossuary in at least two important ways.

Once again the object had reportedly languished in a private collection for years until its true value was recognized. Its owner—though this time lacking a cute nickname—insisted on remaining anonymous and was represented in public by a prominent lawyer who zealously protected his anonymity. And once again Rosenfeld and Ilani of the GSI provided support for the artifact's authenticity through a series of seemingly conclusive scientific tests. Together with Michael Dvoracheck, another geologist, Ilani and Rosenfeld prepared a dramatic article for the GSI's scientific periodical, *Current Research*. Not satisfied with providing mere geological data, they also translated the inscription and—even though none of them was a trained historian, archaeologist, biblical scholar, or linguist—opined on its epigraphy, historical background, and biblical significance.

They identified the stone as arkosic sandstone, most likely originating in the area of southern Israel or Jordan. The chiseled letters seemed to be weathered (and thus most likely ancient) and the patina that covered the stone was produced over centuries by a natural process. Most intriguing, they found microscopic gold globules in the patina, which were not present in the stone itself. In addition, they noted that a carbon-14 dating of carbon particles within the patina performed by a laboratory in Florida had yielded a date of the third century B.C., by which time, it was suggested, the stone lay buried in the rubble around the Temple Mount.

The three geologists' interpretations were presented in a style more dramatic and speculative than usual for a geological journal. For example, they connected the presence of gold globules within the patina with the intense fire that melted the gold-lined walls of Solomon's Temple at the time of the Babylonian destruction of Jerusalem in 586 B.C.

A volunteer editor employed by the Geological Survey was so excited by the "discovery" that she shared galley proofs of the article with her son, a reporter at *Ha'aretz*, Nadav Shragai. Shragai broke the story in two headline-grabbing articles, and a new international media frenzy began.

Yet this time one important thing was different. The critical murmurings were earlier and louder than they had been with the James Ossuary—and they were from sources that could not be easily dismissed. In 1998, historian Nadav Na'aman suggested in a scholarly article that the text of the Books of Kings could have been based at least in part on public inscriptions. After he had first read the Jehoash Inscription in press reports, Na'aman told Ha'aretz, he assumed "one of two things—either I hit the nail on the head, and my theory was confirmed fantastically, or the forger read my theory and decided to confirm it."

Famed epigrapher Joseph Naveh of the Hebrew University subsequently revealed to the IAA and police investigators that he had secretly met with the owner's shadowy representatives in a hotel room in Jerusalem to evaluate the stone's authenticity. He immediately recognized it to be a crude forgery, haphazardly combining ninth-century Hebrew letter forms with seventh-century Aramaic and Moabite. And perhaps the most highly esteemed Semitic epigrapher in the world, Frank Cross of Harvard (who had been widely quoted as saying that if the James Ossuary was a forgery, "the forger was a genius") offered quite a different opinion about the Jehoash Inscription. He noted numerous errors of spelling, syntax, and terminology and declared without hesitation that it was a fake.

In the meantime, co-author Yuval Goren of Tel-Aviv University decided to confront the scientific conclusions of the GSI head-on. Through a controlled laboratory experiment, he demonstrated how it might be possible to manufacture a biblical relic like the Jehoash Inscription and obtain the same test results that Ilani and Rosenfeld had. After selecting an appropriate stone, incising the letters, and "weathering" them artificially by means of an abrasive airbrush, it was possible, Goren suggested, to cover it with an authentic-looking but totally artificial patina. If a modern forger ground some of the stone into powder, mixed it into a soup with microscopic gold globules and ancient charcoal samples, he or she could paint this "patina" over the entire surface and fix it with heat.

So a negative verdict on the Jehoash Inscription was nearing. The present whereabouts of the stone were unknown—as was the owner's identity. But the James Ossuary was still capturing the world's attention. Startling developments would suddenly link the two together—and challenge the idea that the world's greatest, most celebrated scholars could infallibly distinguish valuable ancient inscriptions from worthless modern fakes.

A Storehouse in Ramat Gan

While Hershel Shanks and Ben Witherington III were about to embark on their cross-country authors' tour for their newly published book, *James, the Brother of Jesus*, proclaiming the spiritual and historical importance of the James Ossuary, the case of the Jehoash Inscription was finally on its way to being solved. *Maariv* correspondent Boaz Gaon reported that several months before, in response to rumors of an impending plot to defraud a wealthy collector in London by selling him a faked artifact, the IAA's Theft Unit had focused their attention on the Jehoash Inscription as possibly being the expensive bait for the impending sting.

Following a trail of leads to determine the identity of the shadowy "representatives" who had met with Professor Naveh in a Jerusalem hotel room, the investigators linked a phony business card and a scribbled phone number to a Tel Aviv private detective who, confronted with some aggressive questioning, admitted that his employer was none other than Oded Golan—the innocent "Joe" of the James Ossuary saga. He said that Golan had hired him to bring the Jehoash Inscription to Naveh. Yet Golan repeatedly denied, in television and newspaper interviews, that he was the owner of the stone. He consistently claimed that the real owner was a Palestinian Arab antiquities dealer who lived in an area controlled by the Palestinian Authority and whose identity he had promised he would not reveal.

Then a stunning break in the story hit the headlines in Israel. A March 19 article in *Maariv* by Gaon reported that a court-authorized search warrant had been obtained by the police and Golan's apartment, office, and rented storage space were thoroughly gone over, yielding incriminating documents and photographs showing Golan posing proudly beside the Jehoash Inscription—which he still insisted he did not own. Reportedly, the police questioning continued for several days; Golan's offer-under-pressure of information about the stone's location in exchange for complete immunity from prosecution was refused. A surprise court-ordered search was then carried out by the police and by IAA investigators at a storage space Golan had rented in Ramat Gan (but that he had not voluntarily revealed to the police).

Gaon's *Maariv* article reported the discovery of some truly damning archaeological evidence: scores of artifacts of unclear provenience, forged ancient seals and other inscriptions in various stages of production, epigraphic handbooks, engraving tools, and labeled bags of soil from excavation sites around the country. Handcuffed and taken to his parents' apartment for further questioning, Golan reportedly broke down and asked the police and the IAA officials to stop. He agreed to hand over the Jehoash Inscription to the proper authorities the following day.

Gold Dust and James Bond

And so, in March 2003, the James Ossuary and the Jehoash Inscription were finally together, now the subjects of an intensive, official examination by a multidisciplinary team of specialists gathered by the IAA and divided into epigraphic and scientific committees.

The Israeli Minister of Culture, Limor Livnat, had personally mandated the work of the scientific commission. She noted, particularly with regard to the Jehoash Inscription, that if it were found to be genuine, it would be "the most important archaeological discovery ever made in the State of Israel." Now both artifacts would be studied under controlled conditions, without personal ties to the owner or under the pressure of an upcoming museum exhibition.

The verdict of the epigraphers with regard to the Jehoash Inscription was unanimous: the numerous mistakes in grammar and the eccentric mixture of letter forms known from other inscriptions made it clear that this was a modern forgery. The James Ossuary was a different matter. The epigraphers were divided about the authenticity of the first part of the inscription but in light of the results of the patina committee, they unanimously agreed that the entire inscription must have been modern. In the case of the James Ossuary, it was geochemical and microscopic analysis, rather than scholarly erudition, that uncovered the truth.

Examination of the chalk from which the ossuary had been carved indicated that it was from the Menuha Formation of the Mount Scopus Group, consistent with the hundreds of other ossuaries found in the Jerusalem area. But the earlier geologists and the ROM conservators had mentioned only a single kind of "cauliflower"-shaped patina. Goren and Avner Ayalon of the GSI, however, identified three distinct coatings on the surface of the ossuary: (1) a thin brown veneer of clay and other minerals cemented to the rock surface, presumably rock varnish created by living bacteria or alga over prolonged periods of time, (2) a crusty natural coating of patina (this was the "cauliflower") that formed over the rock surface due to the absorption or loss of various elements and minerals, (3) the "James Bond," a unique composite material nicknamed by Goren since it was bonded onto the incised letters of the James Ossuary inscription but wasn't found at any other place on the ossuary surface—or on the three authentic inscribed ossuaries that the commission members had sampled for comparison.

The varnish covered large areas of the ossuary surface and the patina had burst through the varnish in many places. Both varnish and patina coated the rosettes on the other side of the ossuary. But microscopic analysis showed that the letters of the entire inscription "James, son of Joseph, brother of Jesus" were cut through the varnish, indicating that they were carved long—perhaps centuries—after the varnish-covered rosettes.

Strangest of all was the "James Bond," the chalky material that coated the letters. It contained numerous microfossils called coccoliths, naturally occurring as foreign particles in chalk, but not dissolved by water. Hence it was clear that this was not a true patina formed by the surface crystallization of calcite, but rather powdered chalk that was dissolved in water and daubed over the entire inscription. Thus, the forger's technique was apparent: the James Ossuary was an authentic, uninscribed artifact, on which decorative rosettes originally marked the "front" side. At some time long after the natural processes of varnish and patination in a damp cave environment had been completed, someone carved a series of letters through the natural varnish on the ossuary's "back" side. Then he or she covered the freshly cut letters with an imitation "patina" made from water and ground chalk.

Ayalon's study concentrated on a telltale clue to the nature of authentic ancient patina: its isotopic ratio of oxygen provides a distinctive indication of the qualities of the water with which the patina was produced.

Calcite (calcium carbonate, $CaCO_3$) is the primary component of naturally formed patina on buried archaeological artifacts in calcareous areas, such as the Jerusalem region. This is because calcite dissolves in ground water. With the loss of CO_2 from the ground water by evaporation, the calcite crystallizes again on the stone's surface (just like the "stone" that collects inside a tea kettle). The oxygen within this re-crystallized calcareous coating—the patina—has the same isotopic ratio as the water from which it was produced. And that value can even be used to determine the temperature at which the crystallization took place.

Ayalon determined in his analysis that while the calcite of the patina from the uninscribed surface of the James Ossuary, and indeed the surfaces and inscriptions of other authentic ossuaries that he examined, had ratios that were normal for average ground temperature of the Jerusalem vicinity (64–68 degrees Fahrenheit), the ratios of the "James Bond" suggested that its crystallization took place in heated water (about 122 degrees), not the "cave environment" that the earlier geologists had claimed. The evidence pointed to an intentional faking of the patina over the letters of the "James, son of Joseph, brother of Jesus" inscription—and nowhere else.

And what of the two styles of handwriting on the James Ossuary that had been discerned by some early critics? The physical examination showed that the entire inscription was carved at the same time, so two different hands seemed unlikely in an inscription of only five words. An examination of the very same catalog of ossuaries that Lemaire had used as comparison for the letter forms in the James Inscription, L.Y. Rahmani's (1968) *A Catalogue of Jewish Ossuaries in the Collections of the State of Israel*, now seemed possibly to be their source. In an age of readily available scanning software it is entirely possible to make flawless copies of ancient letters as they appear on genuine artifacts. For example, taking the word "Jacob" (from catalog #396); the words "son of Joseph (from catalog #573); "brother of" (from catalog #570); "Jesus" (common enough to have many examples) and resizing them and aligning them with Photoshop or PageMaker can create a puzzlingly authentic template for a faked inscription, that seemed to be carved by more than one hand.

In the case of the Jehoash Inscription, the geological verdict was as damning as the epigraphic one. The original GSI geologists had even misidentified the rock type. It was not arkosic sandstone from southern Israel or Jordan but low-grade metamorphic greywacke of a type found commonly in western Cyprus and areas still further west.

Once again, there was a dramatic difference between the patina on the uninscribed back and sides of the stone from that found within and between the chiseled letters. Unlike the siliceous deposit everywhere else, this material was soft and made of pure clay mixed with powdered chalk. Within this artificial mixture were a few micron-sized globules of metal as well as carbonized particles. The isotopic ratios of oxygen for the calcite in this "patina" indicated again the crystallization was produced in hot water, not in the ground. Most obvious, the "patina" could be easily rubbed off the letters, revealing unmistakably fresh engraving marks.

Based on these results and a combination of epigraphic and historical considerations, the commission concluded in a packed press conference in Jerusalem on June 18 that both inscriptions were modern fakes, engraved on authentic artifacts and covered with a carefully prepared mixture to imitate patina and to make them look centuries old.

Lessons to Be Learned

The principal supporters and promoters of the dubious biblical relics quickly mounted a counterattack. "I am certain the ossuary is real," Oded Golan told *Ha'aretz*. Accusing the committee of having preconceived notions, Golan also asserted his confidence that the Jehoash Inscription was genuine.

Shanks, who had reaped enormous publicity for himself and his magazine from the promotion of the James Ossuary, was likewise reluctant to retreat. In a broadside quickly posted on the Biblical Archaeological Society website, he explained "Why I Am Not Yet Convinced the 'Brother of Jesus' Inscription Is a Forgery." He once again summoned up the authority of the famous paleographers he had consulted, the results of the initial GSI examination, and the conclusion of the Royal Ontario Museum. He accused the IAA of stacking its committee with laymen who, according to Shanks, had all been convinced to come to their conclusion by Yuval Goren. He also launched a personal attack on IAA director Shuka Dorfman, suggesting that Dorfman's eagerness to see the James Ossuary declared a forgery was because Dorfman "hates antiquities collectors, antiquities dealers, the antiquities trade, and would like to put Israeli antiquities dealers out of business."

But the keystones of this hastily constructed stone wall quickly began to crumble. On June 22, Amos Bein, director of the GSI, discredited the results of the initial ossuary examination by Rosenfield and Ilani, expressing confidence in Ayalon's new results, and stating unequivocally that it was "the official view" of the GSI that "the carbonate oxygen isotopic composition of the 'Jeoash Tablet' [sic] and the 'letters patina' of 'James Ossuary' reveals that the patina could not have formed under natural climatic conditions (temperature and water composition) that prevailed in the Judea Mountains during the last 2000 years."

Two days later, on June 24, even the epigraphical support, such as it was, seemed on the verge of collapse. Although Lemaire remained adamant that his original evaluation was correct, the biggest heavyweight in the world of ancient Semitic scripts, Harvard's Frank Cross, circulated a letter to colleagues around the world regretting Shanks's "continued persistence in making claims" for the authenticity of the James Ossuary, and declared that he now stood "wholly and unambiguously with those who believe the ossuary inscription to be a forgery, a good forgery, but a forgery."

As this article went to press, the affair of the biblical sensations was finally reaching its conclusion. The most important unresolved issue was the decision of the IAA Fraud Unit and Israel Police as to which of the principals would be subjects of further criminal investigations—and which would be granted immunity as witnesses for the state. But this case was more than an instance of science and justice triumphing over charlatanism; it was something more like the passing of an age. In an era of digital scanning, even a teenager with average computer skills and the right software can resize and reproduce an ancient script more precisely than an expert scholar ever could do by hand. The age of the great sages of epigraphy with magnifying glasses and drawing paper would now have to give way to statistical studies of letter-form characteristics and detailed chemical and geological analysis.

There would also have to be a great change in the way that biblical finds are publicized and valued. The cases of the James Ossuary and the Jehoash Inscription showed that what was at stake is not mere collecting or celebrating relics but rather the integrity of archaeology itself.

Put simply, it is time for scholars to stop dealing with unprovenienced antiquities and work to outlaw the private antiquities trade. The respected scholar who publicizes or publishes a private artifact of dubious provenience is boosting its potential market value—and contributing to the general inflation of antiquities' monetary worth. The very serious question of the historicity of the Bible—with all its powerful implications for religious belief and identity—is not the sort of thing to be decided by staged public presentations of isolated artifacts from dubious sources. It is only by adopting a strict and uncompromising standard of evidence and rejecting temptation to simplistically trumpet a headline-grabbing relic or promote a high-visibility museum exhibition that our understanding of the Bible—and indeed all of the human past—will be advanced.

Sadly, the whole affair of the "greatest" archaeological discoveries of the century had precisely the opposite effect its passionate promoters intended. It made scholars outside the circle of true believers more skeptical of ever finding literal proof of the historicity of the Bible. And it made the wider public—to the extent that they were still paying attention—more doubtful that the biblical experts and university professors interviewed on TV about their latest sensation could ever be believed. The least that any of us concerned with the future of archaeology can now do is to persistently and aggressively attack sensational claims about artifacts of dubious origin, not help to construct them, and to recognize how dangerous and ultimately misleading this modern form of relic worship can be.

Discussion Questions

1. How could highly regarded scholars such as Lemaire, McCarter, and Fitzmyer have been so wrong in their evaluations of the ossuary and its inscription? How could the scientists at GSI have made their mistakes?

2. What early hints might have suggested that something was amiss with the claims made for the ossuary and the Jehoash Inscription?

3. How can a buyer/owner of an ancient artifact prove (e.g., in a court of law) that an object was in his/her (or someone else's) possession prior to a specific date?

4. Explore the role of the media, museums, and conservators in cases such as these. How might all have been more responsible in their participation? Do your local museums have mission statements or exhibition codes that would have prevented them from making the mistake of the ROM?

5. Examine Shanks's interests and contributions to this whole story. You might review on his web pages some of the other archaeological stories he has published and discussed in his journals. Is he making a positive contribution to the debate?

6. An editor leaked the report of the GSI findings on the Jehoash inscription to her son, a reporter. Archaeologists often see similarly exciting ideas when reviewing grant proposals for their peers. What are the ethical issues for scholars in talking about or sharing such information?

7. It would appear that a crude forgery is relatively easy to identify, but how does one "prove" an object is authentic? How do forgeries affect the marketplace? How do they affect scholarship?

8. Considering the potential political ramifications of certain kinds of archaeological materials, what responsibilities do scholars, media, and other authorities have when making claims about the origin and authenticity of those objects?

9. Is the detailed explanation of the scientific methods and arguments used to determine the authenticity of these pieces likely to deter future forgers—or merely tell them what they have to do to avoid detection by these means?

10. Discuss Shanks's attack on Shuka Dorfman, as hating "antiquities collectors, antiquities dealers, the antiquities trade" and wanting to put them all out of business. Is this a bias that interferes with scientific objectivity?
11. How does this case call into question "the integrity of archaeology itself"?

Further Readings

Brent, Michel. 2001. Faking African Art. *Archaeology* 54(1):27–32.

Muscarella, Oscar White. 2000. *The Lie Became Great: The Forgery of Ancient Near Eastern Cultures*, vol. I. Studies in the Art and Archaeology of Antiquity. Groningen, the Netherlands: STYX Publications.

Whittaker, John C., and Michael Stafford. 1999. Replicas, Fakes, and Art: The Twentieth Century Stone Age and Its Effects on Archaeology. *American Antiquity* 64(2):203–214.

Anasazi in the Backyard　　　　　　　6

ANDREW CURRY

Indian Camp Ranch in southern Colorado is touted as "America's First Archaeological Subdivision," a unique development of 31 lots that encourages buyers to study the ancient ruins on the land with the assistance of professional archaeologists. In this article, Curry explores the debate over whether Indian Camp Ranch provides a model for combining the interest of private landowners and those of archaeological preservation or represents a "throwback to a darker time in American archaeology."

WHEN CALIFORNIA REAL-ESTATE DEVELOPER Archie Hanson bought a 1,200-acre ranch in Cortez, Colorado, in 1989, he took the unusual step of commissioning an archaeological survey of the property before subdividing it. An archaeology enthusiast, he thought that, with luck, he might have a couple of dozen ruins.

His optimism wasn't unfounded. Cortez sits in an archaeological hot spot, with an estimated eighty thousand sites in surrounding Montezuma County alone. Hanson's ranch is next to the 165,000-acre Canyon of the Ancients National Monument. From Hanson's front door, it's a half-hour drive through winding canyons to Mesa Verde National Park. And just down the road is Crow Canyon Archaeological Center, a nonprofit organization that teaches thousands of people a year about the Native American cultures that have peopled this corner of the Southwest for millennia.

Even so, the survey results were a surprise. Hanson's land had more than two hundred individual sites on it, the densest concentration of ruins on record in the state of Colorado. "I could recognize five or six ruins as an amateur. When we found out we had 210 ruins, it became apparent we had a responsibility," Hanson says. "What would you do as a private individual if you found out you had something of worldly importance? How would you treat it?"

How Hanson answered that question has kept the archaeological community in and around Cortez buzzing ever since. After dividing the ranch into thirty-one high-end lots, Hanson wrote up rules governing how prospective buyers were expected to treat any ruins found on their land. It was an unusual step. In Colorado, as in most of the American West, property rights are paramount. Building permits are rarely required, and it's up to the owner what to do with ruins and artifacts found on private land.

Hanson had a higher standard in mind. According to the covenant, residents could only excavate under the supervision of a trained archaeologist, who had to write up a report from the data gathered. Anything dug up—pottery sherds, bone or stone tools, and the like—could be kept and even displayed in the owner's home but not sold. When the owner moved or died, any artifacts had to be donated to a museum Hanson planned on building.

The result: Indian Camp Ranch, which Hanson proudly calls "America's First Archaeological Subdivision." His dream was to gather a collection of homeowners dedicated to preserving and exploring the archaeology of the region, with responsible excavations in each backyard. For Hanson, the years since he announced his plans in 1989 have been an often rocky learning process.

"Has Archie created a furor? Absolutely," says Stephen Glass, an Indian Camp Ranch resident who serves as the subdivision's chief archaeologist. "When he announced this, field archaeologists were just aghast that anybody could place an economic value on cultural resources, and that he might even make a profit. But protecting cultural resources costs money, and if that can be done through private means, all the better."

To Hanson and his supporters, Indian Camp Ranch is a model for how archaeology and preservation can meet the interests of private landowners. To others, the idea of wealthy hobbyists indulging in extensive excavation for their own amusement is a throwback to a darker time in American archaeology. Even those who approve of Hanson's concept are scrutinizing everything he does, disapprovingly noting each perceived departure from the rules he's set for himself.

Indian Camp Ranch is in the middle of a landscape rich in archaeology. Montezuma County is the southwestern tip of Colorado, and the tiny town of Cortez is about thirty miles as the crow flies from the Four Corners. Driving across the area's rugged terrain—full of deep canyons, soaring mesas, and broad expanses of scrubby desert—it's easy to forget that eight centuries ago this area was home to a thriving population. Some scholars think the area around Cortez once supported twice as many people as it does today.

Archaeologists call the people who once lived here ancestral Pueblo, in deference to the modern tribes who consider them their forebears. To the general public, they're still known as the Anasazi, a sophisticated culture most famous for the spectacular cliff dwellings and elaborate complexes they built throughout the Four Corners area.

The centuries of human habitation here left an abundance of archaeological evidence unrivaled in the United States. Just walking across Hanson's property means crunching across painted potsherds that litter the ground like gravel. Rubble mounds dot the area, the remains of mud-and-stone buildings that collapsed in on themselves long ago. At nearby Mesa Verde, the National Park Service excavated a string of ancestral Pueblo sites in the 1960s and 1970s. In tourist season, the mesa top is jammed with visitors eager to see the cliff dwellings and the kivas, or circular underground chambers, that these early architects left behind.

But for sheer crowd appeal, Mesa Verde has nothing on Hanson's backyard. Jutting out from the side of his house, a 175-foot-long corrugated steel roof covers a virtual outdoor museum: three kivas and what may be the base of a tower, surrounded by the foundations of room blocks—twenty-eight rooms altogether. The roof structure alone, built in keeping with Hanson's insistence that any excavated sites be protected, cost more than $100,000. Unlike the Mesa Verde sites, which were stabilized when excavation was complete and then left alone, Hanson has taken his project one step further. Using stones found at the site, he's hired a mason to partially reconstruct what he thinks the complex may have looked like. "This was just a great big mound when I got here," says Hanson. "My mission is to put the buildings together to show how they really lived." As far as he's concerned, the meticulous reburial professional archaeologists conduct when they're done researching a site is a shame. "Archaeologists cover it all up when they're done every year. It's hidden history. I am giving you something you can see and touch and feel."

Those who know him describe the seventy-eight-year-old as a force of nature. Clomping around "Hanson Pueblo" in muddy boots and a leather jacket, cigarette dangling from his lips, he leaps from thought to thought with the energy and enthusiasm of a child. It's easy to see how he could rub archaeologists—who require vast reserves of patience and focus during seemingly endless digs and data entry sessions—the wrong way. "Archie doesn't have to follow the paradigms we're used to, and what he's doing isn't what some people would think of as standard archaeological technique and reporting. But he's doing a lot better than a lot of private people have," says Jerry Fetterman, who did the original survey of Hanson's land and supervised much of the excavation at Hanson Pueblo.

Fetterman, a contract archaeologist who has worked in the Four Corners area for twenty-five years, says Hanson's enthusiasm has been a breath of fresh air: "We as archaeologists use academia as our client, and we're primarily focused on data and analysis and academic research. We're taking something as inherently interesting as human behavior and producing sleep aids. In some ways Archie has opened my eyes to archaeology."

But as an example of where Hanson's romantic notions conflict with standard practice, Fetterman points to the reconstruction of the pueblo's kivas, which he says originally had earthen walls, and which are now lined with stone. "Archaeologists dig it up and rebury it. Archie wants to make it come alive," he says. "His contention is that the romance has been lost. He's not the National Park Service, he's not vested with any responsibility to do anything. It's his deal."

Part of Hanson's problem is that many archaeologists see even rigorously controlled excavations as problematic. "When I got into archaeology thirty years ago, we didn't have some of the techniques we have now," says Meg Van Ness, the Colorado Historical Society's staff archaeologist. "The big thing now is not to excavate unless you have to, and if you do, to leave things for future generations to study." As a result, most modern digs are done with surgical precision: Researchers will excavate only a fraction of a kiva's hearth, for instance, and then rebury it. The idea of a Hanson-style dig runs counter to everything students today are taught.

Stephen Glass, a trained archaeologist with experience in cultural resource management surveys, dismisses this notion as excessive. "What does 'excavate only as a last resort' mean? If nobody excavated, there would be no science," he says. "As far as I'm concerned, archaeology is the ability for someone using scientific discipline to satisfy their curiosity about the past." There are, of course, some who take issue with any excavation, period. In the last decade, professional archaeologists have, sometimes reluctantly, come to respect the concerns of Native Americans, many of whom still regard archaeologists as glorified grave robbers. The Native American Graves Protection and Repatriation Act (NAGPRA), passed in 1990, requires federal agencies and federally funded museums to return human remains and sacred objects to lineal descendants and culturally affiliated Indian tribes.

Ernest M. Vallo, Sr., an Acoma Pueblo elder and retired engineer who serves on Crow Canyon Center's Native American Advisory Group, has visited Indian Camp Ranch, although not Hanson's site. "What he's doing is going too far," says Vallo. The Pueblo consider the Anasazi their direct ancestors, and want their resting places left alone. "The research has already been done," says Vallo. "If an individual wants to learn more, go check out a book and read about it."

As a private landowner, Hanson is free to ignore concerns like Vallo's. He says data from his sites could be crucial to the controversial field of Anasazi archaeology, which is roiled with a debate about whether the ancestral Pueblo people practiced cannibalism. Hanson is willing to make human remains discovered on his property available to researchers who want to use the latest scientific techniques. "NAGPRA killed DNA research," he claims. "But I'm not under NAGPRA. We could break archaeology wide open with our stuff."

Hanson's enthusiasm for the history of the region and the discoveries he's made in his backyard is plain. Following the rules—his own rules—has cost him tens of thousands of dollars, for everything from hiring professionals to do the work to building the extensive structure that shelters his pueblo. And one thing people on all sides of the debate are quick to point out is that when looked at in context, Hanson's dig is an incredible improvement over what usually happens to cultural resources found on private land in the West. "Most sites on private land are simply looted—quarried for pots with no regard for context or preservation," says Ricky Lightfoot, Crow Canyon's president.

Archaeologists in and around Cortez all have similar stories: Farmers clearing their fields by bulldozing entire rubble mounds into ravines, or charging enterprising pothunters hundreds of dollars a day in digging fees. Here, property rights trump all. "On private land, just about anything is legal unless there's an unmarked human grave. If there aren't any graves, it's not up to us," says Van Ness, whose agency handles archaeological resources on Colorado state land as well as occasional reports of unmarked burials. "Some people don't recognize what they have, and through neglect and ignorance things get destroyed. Then there are people who just don't care, and would just as soon charge people to dig there."

Their motivations aren't always that hard to understand. As far as area farmers are concerned, the increase in property value an intact archaeological site might bring is worse than useless. They're not selling any time soon, and higher property values bring higher taxes. In Lightfoot's words, most local landowners are "land-rich and cash-poor." Compounding the problem, many in the area view archaeologists with deep distrust. "People are afraid of them," Hanson says. "Around here, archaeology is seen as an arm of the U.S. government, and people don't allow archaeologists on their property." In this light, Hanson's strict rules for the protection of sites on the subdivision seem like a decent middle ground.

A casual visitor to Indian Camp Ranch might be forgiven for thinking the ancient past is mainly decorative. A faux pueblo ruin greets visitors at the subdivision's front gate, and scattered across the property are Southwestern-style signposts marking the sites discovered in the original survey. Hanson's house, which he designed, is faced with stones recovered after a local farmer bulldozed a pueblo ruin. The thirty-one thirty-five-acre lots originally sold for $120,000 and are now going for $250,000; only three are left.

For all the hype, only two people have actually done any digging at Indian Camp Ranch: Hanson, and his neighbor Bob Greenlee, a retired radio-station owner and a former mayor of Boulder, Colorado. When he bought his land, Greenlee was told it had nine sites on it. He hired a contract archaeologist to help him excavate a kiva and a small group of room blocks three hundred feet from his house. He and his wife, Diane, were part of the crew. "It was a great experience," says Greenlee. "We learned the basics, and learning from the resources there heightened our awareness of the land and its history."

In accordance with the subdivision's bylaws, the site was partially reburied, with the kiva pit itself covered by a solid roof that includes a plexiglass window so visitors can look inside. A report on the excavation was filed with the state of Colorado. Greenlee is still curious about the other sites on his property, particularly a huge rubble mound down the hill. His hope—echoed by Hanson—is that an enterprising graduate student will take the project on as a thesis. Neither are particularly optimistic. "There's always this division between professionals and amateurs, and I think academics don't like people like me and Archie stepping on their turf," Greenlee says. "Some people are not in favor at all of what Archie has done. He's been honest and upfront, but hasn't had a lot of acceptance."

Predictably, his staunchest defenders are other Indian Camp Ranch property owners, a close-knit community of wealthy people, mostly retired, who share a common interest in exploring and preserving the region's past. Less predictable is how few of Hanson's neighbors share his enthusiasm for digging. "You can be thrilled you're protecting resources and still not be driven to see what's under the ground," Glass says. "Archie drew people interested in archaeology, but most of us just don't share his interest in excavation." One casualty of this lack of interest has been the subdivision's planned museum, which few other owners are interested in funding. How the objects already excavated on the property will be stored and curated for the long term remains to be seen.

Though Hanson and Greenlee have been the project's lightning rods, by all accounts Jane Dillard is more typical of the subdivision's residents. Her lot has thirteen documented sites, and she is convinced she may have found one more. Just south of her house is a pueblo complex with a kiva and room blocks. When she bought the property in 1993, she had a vague notion she might like to do some digging. "I thought I'd go out with a trowel on days when I was bored, but of course that's not how you do archaeology," she laughs. "But I do like having sites on my property."

Since moving here permanently in 2001, she hasn't had the urge to do anything more than walk and reflect among the foundation stones barely visible above the ground. "It's fascinating for me to just go out and sit and look. That's all I have done, and all I want to do," she says. "There's a spiritual context to the whole thing. The archaeology's just icing on the cake."

Discussion Questions

1. Try answering, as honestly as you can, Hanson's question: "What would you do as a private individual if you found out you had something of worldly importance? How would you treat it?"

2. Is it ethical for professional archaeologists to direct excavations under the rules Hanson has set up for his community? Why or why not? How

would working as an archaeologist on Hanson's lands differ from doing CRM work for the government? Do you see any problem with a graduate student doing dissertation research excavating one of the sites in Indian Camp Ranch?

3. Divide into groups to debate whether Indian Camp Ranch provides a model for combining the interest of private landowners and those of archaeology and preservation, or whether it represents a "throwback to a darker time in American archaeology." Feel free to introduce the interests of other groups in such an arrangement.

4. Stage a similar debate on reburying an excavated site vs. reconstructing buildings "to show how they really lived."

5. Many places outside the United States have a concentration of artifacts and sites comparable to or greater than those around Indian Camp Ranch, yet, because their national governments claim ownership of all archaeological remains, an Indian Camp Ranch could never happen there. How do private property owners in other countries respond to the presence on their property of significant archaeological remains?

6. Do you agree that, while academic archaeologists work carefully and precisely, they often produce "sleep aids," and that, without the responsibilities of an archaeologist, Hanson's approach makes the past come alive?

7. Why are archaeologists today trained to leave sites un-dug for future generations, especially when sites on private land can be dug or destroyed freely by the landowner?

8. How might the lack of direct cultural affinity with the buried past for most (i.e., non-Indian) Americans contribute to the looting of prehistoric sites here? Compare the situation in the United States with that in other countries.

9. Is it ethical for Hanson to ignore the concerns raised by Native Americans about their ancestral sites? Why or why not?

Further Readings

Burström, Mats, Birgitta Elfström, and Birgitta Johansen. Serving the Public: Ethics in Heritage Management. In *Swedish Archaeologists on Ethics*, edited by Håkan Karlsson, pp. 135–147. Lindome, Sweden: Bricoleur Press.

Pwiti, Gilbert. 1996. Let the Ancestors Rest in Peace? New Challenges for Cultural Heritage Management in Zimbabwe. *Conservation and Management of Archaeological Sites* 1(3):151–160.

Vitelli, Karen D., and K. Anne Pyburn. 1997. Past Imperfect, Future Tense: Archaeology and Development. *Nonrenewable Resources* 6(2):71–84.

Celebrating Twenty-Five Years of Preservation   7

KATHLEEN BRYANT

For those dedicated to preservation and land stewardship, the past 25 years has not been all frustration and loss. On the contrary, a number of organizations have been dedicated to building programs that successfully preserve places of the past. The Archaeological Conservancy, based in Albuquerque, New Mexico, has established 300 archaeological preserves in 39 states, conserving them for future generations.

WHAT DO THE FOLLOWING HAVE IN COMMON: a Civil War battlefield near the Mississippi River, a Mesa Verde Anasazi pueblo complex, the remnants of a sixteenth-century barrio in Arizona's Sonoran Desert, and a Pleistocene-era bison bones site in north-central Oklahoma? Though the items on this list might sound as alike as oranges and orangutans, you've probably guessed the common thread that links them all is The Archaeological Conservancy. They are among the nearly 300 archaeological sites the Conservancy has preserved, all of which contain valuable information about our country's past.

Battery D, near Helena, Arkansas, marks the location where Confederate troops struggled unsuccessfully to capture a Mississippi River port from Union defenders. The Joe Ben Wheat Site Complex in Colorado's Montezuma Valley includes 90-plus rooms and 14 kivas dating to the thirteenth century. The Carrio de Tubac is the southern portion of Arizona's first permanent European settlement, established by Spanish colonists in the 1750s. Among the Pleistocene bison bones uncovered at the Burnham site, archaeologists found flakes of stone that could be tools made by humans as long as 40,000 years ago—a discovery that could affect the First Americans debate, one of the most controversial topics in American archaeology.

Preserving the rich and varied past of our continent, from Paleo-Indian campsites to historic battlefields, has been The Archaeological Conservancy's focus for the past 25 years. It all started when a small group of people working together to enact the Archeological Resources Protection Act of 1979, which empowers federal agencies to prosecute people who loot publicly-owned sites, decided to take their success even further.

Inspired by The Nature Conservancy, they formed The Archaeological Conservancy in 1979, with the goal of protecting cultural resources on private land. The Ford Foundation and Rockefeller Brothers Fund contributed start-up grants, and by the end of 1980, the Conservancy acquired its first sites, including the Hopewell Mounds near Chillicothe, Ohio. That acquisition is now part of Hopewell Culture National Historic Park, which is administered by the National Park Service. According to co-founder and president Mark Michel, the Conservancy's mission is "to preserve a good sample of all archaeological sites left in the U.S. so that future generations are ensured a research base of various kinds of cultures that have existed on this continent for the past 13,000-plus years."

Preserving a varied research base is like building a portfolio of archaeological stock, leveraged to gain from advancing technology. Michel cites as a "classic example" the Borax Lake site in California, first excavated by archaeologist Mark Harrington in 1941. Harrington unearthed large, fluted obsidian points he attributed to the Folsom culture.

When Harrington declared the site to be at least 10,000 years old, others scoffed at the idea of human presence in northern California that long ago. In the 1950s and again in 1964, archaeologists returned to Borax Lake, testing Harrington's findings as well as their own. They used a new technology, obsidian hydration, that was introduced as an archaeological dating method in 1960. Eighty obsidian hydration readings obtained from man-made tools found at the site confirmed Harrington's dates, shifting perceptions about how early human populations expanded in the New World.

Obsidian hydration, now relatively common, continues to be refined as even newer technologies emerge. Borax Lake, a Conservancy site since 1989, continues to be preserved and studied. And as past meets future, archaeologists using emerging technologies may glean even more from Borax Lake and other sites, answering questions that continue to concern humanity today such as plant uses, social structure, population pressure, or climate change, to name a few.

Archaeologists conducting research on Conservancy sites employ some of the most sophisticated technologies, such as remote sensing and laser scanning. Three-dimensional computer models were used to produce a CD-ROM that allows people to "tour" Sherwood Ranch Pueblo, an Arizona preserve, even though the great majority of its approximately 100 rooms have been backfilled.

"One of the main reasons I wanted to make sure sites were preserved was because of the technologies being developed over new generations," says Conservancy co-founder and board member Jay Last. No stranger to changing technology, Last helped start industry-shaking Fairchild Semiconductor, which developed the first practical integrated circuits.

Important research is routinely conducted on Conservancy preserves. A four-year limited excavation at Albert Porter Pueblo in southwest Colorado by the Crow Canyon Archaeological Center yielded new information about the relationship between the Mesa Verde and Chaco Canyon Anasazi. At the Barton site in northwest Maryland archaeologist Bob Wall has discovered a hearth and stone tools that may be approximately 16,000 years old. Should further research confirm these findings, Barton would be one of the oldest known sites in the country.

It still surprises Last "how quickly major sites are on the verge of disappearing." He decided to do something about it, launching one of the Conservancy's most successful ventures, the Protect Our Irreplaceable National Treasures program or POINT. In fall 2000, Last pledged a million-dollar challenge amount for emergency acquisitions, specifically for those projects in which having cash on hand would make the difference between preserving a site or losing it to development. For example, the Smokes Creek site, a seventeenth-century Iroquois village south of present-day Buffalo, New York, would have been swallowed by suburbia if cash-poor developers hadn't agreed to a deal with the Conservancy. Today, thanks to POINT funds, the village is a seven-acre preserve surrounded by homes.

POINT acquisitions can proceed very quickly. Consider, for example, the De-Prato Mounds site, purchased in 2004. According to Michel, someone driving through the countryside around Ferriday, Louisiana, spotted a hand-painted "FOR SALE" sign and turned down a lane to investigate. The advertised home stood atop a mound site. After a phone call to the Conservancy, a deal to purchase the property was sealed within the week.

The DePrato site is part of a five-mound complex on a natural river levee, incorporating features that date from A.D. 400 to 800. It's an acquisition that especially pleases Vin Steponaitis, a University of North Carolina archaeologist, who has a longstanding interest in the archaeology of the Lower Mississippi Valley. Steponaitis, who also directs the archaeology research laboratories at the university, has been a member of the Conservancy since its early days. He joined the board in 2000, delighted to be associated with an organization he terms "essential." He now serves as the Conservancy's chairman.

Steponaitis explains, "On both state and federal levels, the legal structure in the U.S. is set up to protect sites on public lands. In the face of development pressure, the only way to save sites on private land is to purchase the land."

Though the POINT program has added speed and maneuverability to the Conservancy's acquisitions, slow and steady sometimes still wins the race. Andrews Ranch, a Chacoan outlier about 25 miles south of the great houses along Chaco

Wash, was acquired in 1993 after nearly 13 years of negotiations, proving that persistence pays.

So does diplomacy. The most complex acquisitions, according to Michel, often involve multiple owners who don't get along. More than once, the Conservancy has played a peacemaker role among family disputes. Conservancy staffers also know tax and property laws, and occasionally need to resolve challenges that are less about legalities and more about logistics.

One site, a Mississippian village mound in eastern Arkansas, was inhabited by a small community. The presence of people and homes on top of the mound actually preserved it over the years, keeping it from being looted. Lot by lot, the Conservancy acquired the mound site.

One owner, however, was particularly reluctant to sell her home despite Michel's many visits, featuring hours spent rocking on the owner's front porch and talking to her about the site. "You know, I don't think there's anything here," she concluded. At last, she agreed to sell, with one condition—that the Conservancy relocate her . . . and her house. "The house needed to be moved across a big field, and it got stuck in the mud," Michel remembers. "It was touch and go for awhile, but it worked out well in the end for everyone."

The former owner still lives in her beloved home, now located in town across from a community center for seniors. When archaeologists began working at the site where her house once stood, they recovered burials containing two effigy pots shaped to resemble human heads.

"That was an interesting project," Michel says, "and one of my favorite in that we were able to acquire the land for a park 30 miles from Memphis." The 17-acre site, likely the village of Casqui mentioned in Hernando de Soto's 1541 expedition records, is known today as Parkin Mound Archaeological State Park. The park, which now serves as a research station of the Arkansas Archaeological Survey, also includes an interpretive exhibit area.

Acquiring sites can be the result of careful planning or of fortuitous opportunity. The Conservancy's vice president and director of the Southwest regional office, Jim Walker, describes the systematic acquisition process, used in the mid-1980s to acquire Sinagua culture sites in the rapidly growing Verde Valley area of central Arizona. "The Conservancy begins by asking archaeologists working in a region or state to provide a list of what they consider to be significant sites on private land," he says.

Based on this, the Conservancy will create a priority list of as many as 20 sites and begin researching ownership. Property owners are contacted and asked if they are aware of the archaeological resources on their land. The Conservancy will then request a meeting and go out on the property with the landowner to view the site. "When I see a feature or resource that has been undisturbed for the last 20 or 30 years, I know that property owner has thought at least once about who will protect the resource after he or she is gone," explains Walker. "These are the landowners I really like to meet."

Walker joined the Conservancy in 1981, with "a newly minted" MBA, an undergraduate degree in anthropology, and experience selling real estate. "I didn't understand then the motivation of those people who'd been protecting sites on their land. I was surprised the first time a landowner donated property. Now I'm surprised when they don't." Most of the Conservancy's 300 acquisitions in 39 states have been partial or total donations, the "perfect solution," according to Walker, for those who want to see their legacy of protection continued.

Sometimes acquisitions are the result of opportunity rather than planning. The Conservancy often works with developers who've discovered archaeological resources and who need solutions that will help them satisfy federal permitting requirements, or who seek alternatives to mitigation through excavation. "I can prove to a developer that if he is dealing with a complex site, one with habitations or other features, it is cheaper to donate the property for preservation than it is to excavate," says Walker. The solution is often creative and innovative—preserving a site as part of the rough in a golf course, for example. For developers who hesitate, Walker jokes that he keeps a copy of Steven Spielberg's movie *Poltergeist* in his briefcase.

Typically, the Conservancy will enter into a one- or two-year-option agreement with the landowner, and then seek funding. Where option agreements aren't possible, POINT funds are used. Once a site is acquired, the property is fenced. If there is existing damage, the site is mapped and backfilled to protect it. The cost is hours, weeks, sometimes even years of work, and of course, money.

The Conservancy's annual budget runs about $3 million. "This is not a whole lot of money as far as things go," Michel says. "We pride ourselves on getting a lot done with the resources we have. Of course, with more funding, we could accomplish a great deal more."

Funding comes mostly from member contributions. The Conservancy also receives support from a wide range of foundations all over the country, and from government sources. Much of this money is targeted for specific projects. Raising needed money during the past couple of years has been tough, Michael admits, and yet the Conservancy continues to expand.

From a small group of people with a common purpose, the Conservancy has grown into "a large, stable, widely recognized organization, reflecting a lot of hard work on the part of many," says Last.

The Conservancy currently has regional offices in Sacramento, Atlanta, Albuquerque, Columbus, and Washington, D.C. The board encompasses business leaders, professional archaeologists, and conservationists, including Stewart Udall, Secretary of the Interior under presidents Kennedy and Johnson. Udall says that he has watched with "delight and amazement" the Conservancy's growth from a small, Southwestern-based organization to the national organization it is today, adding, "I don't think anyone predicted how strong the response would be in other parts of the country."

Membership, now more than 20,000, tripled since the debut of *American Archaeology* in 1997. The magazine publishes articles about archaeology in North America as well as the Conservancy's latest acquisitions and research taking place on its preserves. The magazine also has information about archaeological tours—ranging from Mississippian mound complexes to Maya cities to Peruvian tombs—that the Conservancy organizes and leads.

During its early years, The Archaeological Conservancy managed to preserve about four sites annually. Recently it's saved about 30 sites a year. "We hope to expand that in the future. Over the next 10 years, we'd like to more than double the number of sites under our protection, adding 500 or more," says Michel. "While we will continue to add sites in the Southwest, we are adding emphasis to other parts of the country." The plan is to target areas where the Conservancy's presence isn't yet felt, particularly the Plains and New England states.

In 2004, the Conservancy added its first site in North Dakota. The Biesterfeldt site is an eighteenth-century village believed to be Cheyenne, though researchers have noted Mandan and Arikara influences, including a large ceremonial lodge. Because the site's future is now assured, archaeologists will be able to investigate how and when the Cheyenne, a settled horticultural Eastern Woodlands tribe, pushed west and took to hunting bison.

The peopling of this continent, from Clovis hunters to Plains tribes to Euro-American settlers to African American slaves, is a story that continues to unfold. The Conservancy is determined that that story be told.

Discussion Questions

1. What other lessons might those interested in the preservation and management of cultural heritage learn from environmental groups? How might cultural and environmental groups collaborate to their mutual benefit? With what other groups would those concerned about cultural heritage have a natural affinity, and how might this be developed to mutual advantage?

2. Had you heard of The Archaeological Conservancy before reading this chapter? If so, in what context? If not, how could they become better known? See if you can come up with some good fund-raising ideas to share with the Conservancy.

3. Do you agree that (in the United States) the "only way to save sites on private land is to purchase the land"? Do you know anyone who has protected an archaeological site on his or her property and who might consider donating it to The Archaeological Conservancy?
4. Most towns in the United States have had an experience with conflict between development and archaeological resources. Look into those in your area and explore how the conflict was resolved. How might more developers be made aware that it "is cheaper to donate property for preservation than it is to excavate"? Isn't it cheaper still for developers to just ignore and pave over archaeological sites?
5. How do U.S. tax laws affect the protection of cultural property within the United States? Could these laws be used more widely and effectively to protect America's archaeological heritage?

Further Readings

Green, William. 1998. Cultural Resource Management and American Archaeology. *Journal of Archaeological Research* 6(2):121–167.

Mills, Barbara J., and T. J. Ferguson. 1998. Preservation and Research of Sacred Sites by the Zuni Indian Tribe of New Mexico. *Human Organization* 57(1):30–42.

VanderVeen, James M. 2004. Site Preservation or Self Preservation? The Issue of Stewardship and Control. *SAA Archaeological Record* 4(1):30–33.

ARCHAEOLOGY AND (INTER)NATIONAL POLITICS

II

The Race to Save Afghan Culture   8

KRISTIN M. ROMEY

War has long ravaged the people and places of Afghanistan. World-wide attention returned to the be-
leaguered nation-state in 2001, first when the ruling Taliban ordered the destruction of all icons,
including the giant Buddha statues of Bamiyan, then when looting became rampant after the Amer-
ican invasion. Romey details this destruction, and highlights the work of Paul Bucherer-Dietschi, a
controversial Swiss architect hoping to save Afghan's cultural heritage. Afghanistan, and Bucherer's
work, inspires fundamental questions about what individuals, nations, and the international com-
munity should and can do during times of war and political unrest.

ALONG THE MAIN HIGHWAY BETWEEN ZÜRICH AND BASEL, chemical plants
and lumberyards are slung across the hills, and the occasional nuclear plant
sends roils of steam along the treetops. In this unlikely Swiss landscape is
an even more unlikely museum, housed in a white, three-story compound off the
main street in the village of Bubendorf, population 4,400. It's discreet among the
centuries-old wooden buildings and stuccoed taverns clustered around it, and unless you catch a flash of an elaborately embroidered caftan in a window—almost
riotously creative against the clean, orderly lines of the village—you'll pass right
by the Afghanistan Museum.

The low profile of this museum, established under a most unusual agreement
between the Taliban and the Northern Alliance in 1998, is deceptive, for its mission presents a direct challenge to the international heritage community's near-
sacred policy of keeping objects of archaeological and cultural importance in their
country of origin, regardless of the depths of chaos and destruction that country
has fallen into.

The force behind the museum is Swiss architect Paul Bucherer-Dietschi, who,
despite criticism from scholars and reluctance from international organizations,

refused to ignore entreaties from Afghan political leaders and archaeologists to find a safe haven for the country's cultural treasures while the country fell apart during decades of war. The destruction of the Bamiyan Buddhas in March of 2001 has swung popular opinion to Bucherer's side, and organizations like UNESCO, which did not initially endorse the idea, are re-evaluating their policies on safeguarding cultural heritage.

The events in Bamiyan were just the culmination of 12 years of systematic looting and destruction of ancient sites and objects that have left Afghanistan bereft of most of its earlier Greek, Buddhist, Mongol, and early Islamic heritage. When Bucherer first arrived in Afghanistan more than 30 years ago on a personal quest to research what he calls a "never-colonized country," tourists were flocking to the Bamiyan Valley and admiring exquisite Gandharan and Bactrian sculpture in the renowned Kabul Museum. When, in 1975, he established the Fondation Bibliotheca Afghanica, an Afghan library and research institute near Basel, he stocked its shelves with guidebooks, catalogs, and reports from foreign teams excavating in the country. Following the Soviet invasion in 1979, Bucherer researched human rights violations for the UN, and, through his personal contacts with Afghanistan's power brokers, led ultimately unproductive talks on transferring power from the hands of Soviet-backed President Mohammed Najibullah to mujahideen leaders in the early 1990s. The country quickly plunged into civil war, and by the time the Taliban came to power in 1996, the Kabul Museum was all but an empty shell, with most of its contents blown away or sold to foreign collectors (Museum Under Siege, *Archaeology*, March/April 1996).

When, at the request of U.S. officials, Bucherer returned to Afghanistan in early 1998 to negotiate a political settlement between the Taliban and the Northern Alliance, the only common ground the warring sides could find was the need for a safe, neutral location outside the country to store what cultural treasures remained until they could be safely returned to Afghanistan. "They saw that if things continued like they did, their culture would fall through their fingers like sand," recalls Bucherer. "I asked them, with all of this misery around, with all of this sickness and hunger, how can you care about culture? And both sides told me 'There will die 100, there will die 500 children. Within one month double the number of children will be born. But if one cultural item gets lost, it will never be reborn.' So this became the common link between them, and we took the charge to make the museum."

The Afghanistan Museum is open to the public on Saturdays and to private groups by appointment, and on a Friday in late January Bucherer is busily wrapping up an interview with a Swiss newspaper while dealing with a carful of wooden furniture that an Afghan donor dropped off that morning. Silver-haired and impeccably groomed, with a beard more Amish than mullah, he interrupts his labors to answer his cell phone with crisp Swiss efficiency: "Afghanistan Museum. Bucherer." His Afghan counterpart, engineer Zemaray Hakimi, appears with a package of photographs taken during their trip to Afghanistan two weeks earlier. Hakimi, who was in charge of crafting the museum out of an old villa and warehouse, is Bucherer's antithesis: a short, quiet man in a rumpled jacket who, even in the darkened rooms of the museum, looks like he's permanently squinting into the sun.

The exhibits are laid out in a series of small, white rooms bordered with the black, green, and red colors of the Afghan flag. In part to discourage looting and the black-market trade in antiquities, everything in the museum must be an unconditional donation, as mandated by a 2001 agreement between the museum, the Swiss government, and UNESCO. The majority of items on display are ethnographic—elaborately carved wooden chests, silver jewelry, old photographs, embroidered textiles, legal documents decorated with lavish calligraphy. Many of the donors are Europeans and Americans who purchased the objects while working or traveling in the country over the last few decades and are now, in Bucherer's words, "paying back a little bit of their emotional debt to Afghanistan." Some donations have come from antiquities dealers and collectors. Everything is carefully presented with a label identifying the object, when and where it was purchased, and the name of the donor in large print. Some items have been smuggled out over the years by Afghans concerned for their fate—their labels simply list point of origin.

This is not to say that the Afghanistan Museum is simply a host for assorted tourist bric-a-brac. Archaeological items of considerable importance have been donated to the enterprise—including 2,300-year-old bronzes from Aï-Khanum, the easternmost of Alexander the Great's cities, and a few of the gracefully carved first-century-A.D. Begram Ivories—but they are not on display. Bucherer is tight-lipped regarding the objects and their donors, which include the late Northern Alliance commander Ahmed Shah Massoud and several European dealers. "They're being kept safely in a bank vault. What's important is everything here gets back to Afghanistan safely," he explains, then adds: "Display is secondary, but showing that items are here, are safe, is a great counterweight to all of the bad news."

While there exists historical precedent for Switzerland safeguarding another country's cultural heritage—Spain shipped the contents of the Prado there during the siege of Madrid in 1937, and had them returned following World War II—the Swiss government was reluctant to support the proposed museum without the approval of UNESCO, the preeminent global heritage organization. While a member of UNESCO, Afghanistan has yet to sign one of its most important conventions for protecting cultural heritage—the 1970 Convention on the Means of Prohibiting and Preventing the Illicit Import, Export, and Transfer of Ownership of Cultural Property, which prohibits, among other things, the removal of artifacts from their country of origin without approval of that country's government (UNESCO member Switzerland has also not signed the 1970 Convention). Still, UNESCO could not be expected to support an enterprise that encouraged the removal of cultural objects from Afghanistan without the express approval of the Afghan government. The problem in 1998 was that the internationally recognized government of Burhanuddin Rabbani was powerless within most of the country, operating from the five- to ten-percent of Afghanistan held by the Northern Alliance.

Undaunted, an Afghan delegation that included representatives of the Northern Alliance and the Taliban toured possible sites in Switzerland for their museum. Perhaps making it even more unpalatable to the heritage establishment, the delegation refused a suggestion to move the objects to Zürich's prestigious Rietberg Museum, which specializes in Asian art. Bucherer recalls them saying, "We want our own museum, we don't want to be mixed up with the Indians or the Chinese. We're Afghan."

Buoyed by the alliance between warring factions, in February 1999 the Swiss local government went ahead and approved a donation of $350,000 for the purchase and construction of the museum. A promising meeting was held two months later between the government and the director of the UNESCO's World Heritage Center, Mounir Bouchenaki, to discuss the idea of a museum-in-exile. "[Bouchenaki] was extremely positive about the idea and declared it a pilot project to safeguard cultural objects in times of conflict," says Bucherer. "He was obviously thinking about what had happened in Yugoslavia." In 1991, the National Library in Sarajevo and Dubrovnik's old city were destroyed during the country's civil war. The International Council of Museums (ICOM) also began discussions with Bucherer, but, like the Swiss government, was reluctant to endorse the idea without UNESCO's backing. The establishment of the museum was announced in the press in November 1999, but by the end of the year, UNESCO had yet to establish an official position on it.

The consensus within the international heritage community was that cultural heritage helped to build and strengthen national identity, and should remain in its country of origin. UNESCO, chastened by the extent of looting and smuggling within Afghanistan in the 1990s, was beginning to think outside the box. According to Lyndell Prott, director of UNESCO's Cultural Heritage Division, a "special" policy was instituted: "When there is serious danger to the survival of a heritage, at the request of the recognized government of the country concerned, UNESCO will arrange safe custody of objects donated to it for the purpose of eventual return to the country concerned when the situation will allow." The policy enabled the organization to support a similar Afghan cultural heritage safeguarding program sponsored by UNESCO goodwill ambassador Ikuo Hirayama in Tokyo, as well as the activities of the Society for the Preservation of Afghan

Cultural Heritage (SPACH), which was purchasing back artifacts stolen from the Kabul Museum that had surfaced on the black market.

Bucherer's relationship with UNESCO was difficult at best. In an attempt to raise money and donations, the Swiss architect spoke freely of his plans with the press, which may have drawn unwanted attention to UNESCO and its policies. "Activities by such organizations have generally been most successful where there is a certain amount of discretion," says Prott. Without UNESCO's official support, Bucherer was left open to accusations from scholars that he was stealing Afghanistan's heritage, accusations that he blithely writes off to jealousy. "These experts, they would ask, 'Who is this architect making this museum? We're the ones with the training to do this.' But I knew I had the support of the Afghans. I made it work."

Bucherer scouted the area around Basel—where his family has lived for more than 900 years—for a suitable space for the museum, and the property in Bubendorf was purchased and renovated beginning in January 2000. The buildings at the time were in such a state of disrepair that Rabbani joked on a visit to the village that they looked "like Afghanistan." Bucherer and Hakimi, with the assistance of a group of expatriate Afghan architects and craftsmen, worked day and night for ten months to renovate the space at a cost of $1 million.

When Taliban forces took Kabul in 1996, it appeared that the rampant looting and destruction of cultural institutions and archaeological sites might cease. Over the years, Taliban leader Mullah Omar had issued decrees prohibiting the illegal excavation of archaeological sites and promising to punish anyone caught with items stolen from the museum. Reports coming out of the country by 2000, however, were contradictory: local commanders were ignoring Omar's decree, looting was rampant in certain areas, and the black market in Afghan antiquities was booming. At the same time, the Taliban culture minister supported, at least in theory, the idea of the Swiss museum (although the Taliban officially contributed very little, if anything, to the enterprise). The regime was also renovating the Kabul Museum, and even opened it for a month in the summer of 2000 until it was shuttered by hard-liners scandalized by the "idols" on display. Christian Manhart, Asia program chief for UNESCO's Cultural Heritage Division, began talks with the Swiss museum around this time, later telling the New York Times that "For [Bucherer], things went too slowly, but we are bound to the 1970 Convention, and this made things very complicated." But the situation was already becoming critical; a report by the International Committee on Monuments and Sites that year called Afghanistan a country "whose entire cultural heritage is endangered most directly by arbitrary acts of destruction."

The death knell for Afghanistan's heritage was ultimately being sounded not just by hard-line Taliban, but by the increasingly influential al-Qaeda forces in the country who bankrolled them. For Bucherer, the final realization came on a trip to Kandahar with Omar's assistant Jalil Ahmad in December 2000. "We went somewhere to take photographs—I had written permission from the Taliban to do so—and when I pulled out my camera a bunch of al-Qaeda people appeared with Kalashnikovs and made us leave. Then I knew that the Taliban were no longer masters in their own house." Al-Qaeda, under increasing pressure from the United States following the 1998 embassy bombings in Africa and the attack on the USS *Cole*, was keen on strengthening its grip on the country. Afghan nationalism, reflected in the stone monuments and elaborate sculptures going back thousands of years, was getting in the way.

Afghan archaeologists in Kabul knew what the future held, and on that same December trip—a little more than two months before the destruction in Bamiyan and Kabul commenced—they pleaded with Bucherer to spirit whatever artifacts remained in the Kabul Museum and various storerooms out of the country. "I had to tell them that I couldn't do it without the official agreement of UNESCO. Even if I had their agreement, I now doubt whether the Afghans would have managed to bypass al-Qaeda [and get the materials out]. But at the time. . . ." He trails off, frustrated, then uncharacteristically pounds his fist into his palm. "Rabbani, the recognized president of Afghanistan, gave written permission in May 2000 to bring the materials here to Bubendorf and this was not acceptable to UNESCO. The president of a country is responsible for the belongings of his nation, and if his request is not accepted, I do not know what else can be done."

But to others, the situation was not as clear-cut. "There's a lot of fury in hindsight," says Nancy Hatch Dupree, an expert on Afghan history and culture and member of SPACH, "and it's easy to pontificate on 'principles' in Paris or London when you have no idea of the realities on the ground. But the reality isn't that simple, for the basic fact is that cultural heritage is inevitably bonded to national honor." According to Dupree, SPACH had also explored the option of removing museum collections to a safer area, but while many Afghan officials enthusiastically endorsed the idea, those at the top often demurred, saying that it would make them look weak and unable to protect their cultural heritage. This was also the situation Bucherer encountered back in 1991, when Najibullah asked him to find a safe place in Switzerland for the fabulous Tilya Tepe treasure, over 2,000 Bactrian gold objects excavated by the Soviets in 1979. The Afghan government couldn't reach a consensus, however, and the treasure was eventually locked away in a vault beneath the presidential palace. Massoud was equally reluctant to move objects, including the Tilya Tepe treasure, out of the country when he held power in Kabul between 1992 and 1996, but gave his full support to the Swiss museum after being ousted by the Taliban. In the last interview before his assassination in September 2001, Massoud told *Newsweek* that he regretted the fact he didn't move the contents of the Kabul Museum to a "safer place" when he had the chance. The fate of the Tilya Tepe treasure remains unknown; that fact obviously haunts Bucherer, and perhaps helps to fuel his work at the museum today.

By the time UNESCO established official guidelines with the Afghanistan Museum in July 2001, says Bucherer, "there was hardly anything left" in the country. In his office, he pulls out a photograph of a storeroom in the basement of the Ministry of Information and Culture in Kabul. "Here's 18 cubic feet of primarily Gandharan and Bactrian artifacts from the Kabul Museum, in pieces no bigger than my little finger. The Taliban came in the morning, hammered until prayer time, paused, hammered again, paused for tea, then hammered for the rest of the day. And this," he says, pointing at a photograph of a large hole in a rock face, "is what they did to the Buddhas in Bamiyan. Afghan Taliban refused to do the job, so Mullah Omar sent in foreigners—Arabs, Chechens, Sudanese—to blow them up. These guys were experts. They drilled holes four, five, six feet into the rock and stuffed them with explosives."

Bucherer is pragmatic about the fact that so many of the objects in his museum were once part of private collections; he argues that anything that can help sustain or resurrect the cultural traditions of a country ravaged by 20-odd years of war, where one in five children is born in a refugee camp, is worth a place in the museum. In his opinion, the essence of Afghan culture lies in the continuity of its traditions: "In Afghanistan, it's the highest compliment to say that you made something that looks hundreds of years old. Look at Afghan embroidery, for example. Grandmother teaches granddaughter, who teaches her granddaughter, and that's the way that styles are retained for centuries." The museum displays reinforce this idea by juxtaposing similar objects separated by hundreds, even thousands of years. Before a display of some 30-odd oil lamps manufactured in Afghanistan over the centuries, Bucherer asks a visitor to guess which lamp is more than a thousand years old. After the putative artifact is selected, he consults a carefully detailed catalog and chuckles. "Actually, that one was made from a bicycle axle."

Bucherer isn't an archaeologist, he's an Afghanophile, and while clothing, furniture, and other unprovenanced ethnographic material may help to build awareness for Afghan culture both among Westerners as well as Afghans born in the tumult of the past two decades, many officials concerned with looting and destruction in the region are skeptical about the museum's success in preserving Afghanistan's more ancient legacies. "If Bucherer can motivate others to give [artifacts] to his museum then that's wonderful," says Dupree, who as a SPACH representative has received criticism for buying back items plundered from the Kabul Museum. "I'm all for it, but I have not heard of any great rush [to donate] from collectors or dealers." Neil Brodie, coordinator of the Illicit Antiquities Center at Britain's McDonald Institute for Archaeological Research, supports the idea of a safe haven in theory, but believes the donation initiative will be hamstrung by a lack of provenience. "Who can know whether a particular piece has been removed from Afghanistan or Pakistan, or whether it's fake or genuine?" he asks.

Under its agreement with UNESCO, the museum agreed to accept only unconditional donations of objects from Afghanistan. Bucherer's count now stands at around 3,000 objects from Afghans, foreign visitors, and dealers and collectors. Everything must be inventoried and nothing may be used for commercial purposes. UNESCO will consult with specialists and organizations like ICOM to decide what items should be returned to Afghanistan and where they should go; UNESCO will ultimately decide when.

"When" is the big question. Bucherer and Hakimi, who was responsible for rebuilding Kabul University and several hotels in the mid-1990s, agree that the current Kabul Museum site—actually six miles outside of the Afghan capital in Darulaman—is unsuitable. Even if the museum were completely rebuilt, there's the problem of the high water table, which would preclude the construction of secure underground vaults, and location. "Darulaman is only convenient for tourists," says Bucherer. "The museum should be in the center of Kabul, where schoolchildren and locals can easily visit it." Even if museum construction began this year, they estimate it could take at least six to eight years before a properly staffed museum could reopen. Assuming, of course, that peace finally comes to Afghanistan.

As Bucherer steps out of the room for the umpteenth phone call ("Afghanistan Museum. Bucherer"), Hakimi begins to discuss his own plans in rapid Dari- and Swiss-accented German. "We need two museums in Kabul," he says. "One for the antiquities—for what has happened in the far past—and one to remember what has happened in Afghanistan for the past 22 years. To show what al-Qaeda, what Pakistan and Iran have done to our country." Hakimi recalls his recent trip home with Bucherer: "Everyone is hopeful that things will get better in the next five or six months. But it's similar to when I was there in 1996. The same people are in government, I know all of the new ministers. You see a lot of foreigners with guns. But now, instead of Pakistanis and Saudis, it's Germans and Brits. Not much has really changed," he jokes ruefully.

Hakimi's family, which fled Afghanistan with the rise of the Taliban and now lives in Bubendorf, helps make money for the museum by preparing lavish Afghan dinners for visiting groups. The income from these meals, along with an annual contribution of $10,000 from UNESCO, Bucherer's speaking fees, and a five-franc entrance fee (about $2.50) paid by the approximately 200 visitors a month who hear about the museum from newspaper reports or by word of mouth, are all what keep the museum functioning.

Could anyone outside the country really have anticipated the unimaginable destruction that occurred in Afghanistan in the spring of 2001? Even if someone did, the sad fact of the matter is that nonprofit groups and international cultural organizations are ultimately powerless to stop an unrecognized government hell-bent on destroying its cultural heritage. If there is a silver lining to the destruction of the Bamiyan Buddhas and the resultant international outcry, it is that scholars and institutions that would not have previously endorsed the removal of cultural objects from their country of origin are accepting the fact that extraordinary sit-uations require unorthodox solutions. "The notion that cultural heritage belongs to all humanity must replace the idea of national cultural heritage," wrote UNESCO consultant Michael Barry in the April 2001 UNESCO *Courier*. Now that the idea of the museum-in-exile has been breached, however, the international community must engage in a serious discussion over the details.

Dupree lists some concerns: "What principles will apply regarding the pur-chase of artifacts; who will determine provenance and authenticity; which institu-tion will be designated as a depository; how will legal issues be resolved with countries in which objects are obtained. How is the sovereign right of a nation to maintain control over its heritage properties to be defined?"

When asked about the future of the small museum in Bubendorf, Bucherer manages a small smile. "We're living hand to mouth," he says, and adds that its fu-ture is uncertain. "We started this idea, but we don't know how it will develop. We have to adapt to developments in Afghanistan. If the Afghans want everything back, it goes back. If it's better for the Afghan cause to keep this museum alive, then we'll find a way to do it. Ultimately, it's not up to us [Europeans], it's not up to UNESCO, or anyone else in the outside world. It's up to the Afghans."

Discussion Questions

1. Why has the international heritage community been determined to keep important archaeological and cultural objects in their country of origin, even during the direst of times? Why do you think a change in attitude is beginning to appear? Discuss the pros and cons of each position.

2. Why did the Swiss government, the International Council of Museums, and others think it was so necessary to have UNESCO approval for the Afghan museum in Switzerland?

3. Was it a good idea for SPACH to purchase back artifacts that had been stolen from the Kabul museum and had shown up on the black market? What alternatives are available for recovering objects stolen from a country during wartime and illegally exported?

4. What is the International Committee on Monuments and Sites (ICOMOS), and what do they do? (Find their website.)

5. Discuss, in the context of this and other chapters, the implications of the statement "cultural heritage is inevitably bonded to national honor."

6. What options does the international community have when, during a time of serious warfare or political unrest, the cultural heritage of a people is clearly under threat of major destruction and the local government is unable or unwilling to stop that destruction (or, as in the case of the Bamiyan Buddhas, is the party responsible for the destruction)?

7. Does Bucherer's museum in Switzerland support the contention of private collectors that they are, in fact, "saving the past" by, e.g., providing a safe place for objects out of their countries of origin, which are often subject to civil unrest? Does the art market, in fact, preserve materials that would otherwise be destroyed by modern warfare, postwar development, neglect, and the like?

8. What do you think of Bucherer's argument that a new national museum should be in the center of Kabul? What are the important considerations in determining the location of a new archaeological museum, national or otherwise, in any country?

9. Do you agree that "the notion that cultural heritage belongs to all humanity must replace the idea of national cultural heritage"? How do the provisions of legislation such as NAGPRA (see Section IV) fit in with this concept?

10. Discuss the questions raised by Dupree in the penultimate paragraph of this chapter.

11. Some observers have suggested that Bucherer is just grandstanding, looking for publicity, and taking advantage of the emergency to criticize UNESCO. What do you think? What should be the role of outsiders such as Bucherer during national crises?

Further Readings

Bosco, David. 2005. Waking the Buddha. *Archaeology* 58(1):18–23.

Colwell-Chanthaphonh, Chip. 2003. Dismembering/Disremembering the Buddhas: Renderings on the Internet during the Afghan Purge of the Past. *Journal of Social Archaeology* 3(1):75–98.

Dupree, Nancy Hatch. 1996. Museum Under Siege. *Archaeology* 49(2):42–51.

Fitschen, Thomas. 1996. Licit International Art Trade in Times of Armed Conflict? *International Journal of Cultural Property* 5(1):127–132.

Jones, Schuyler. 1975. Afghan Cultural Heritage Threatened by Art and Antiquities Traffic. *Cultural Anthropology* 16(3):443.

Meskell, Lynn. 2002. Negative Heritage and Past Mastering in Archaeology. *Anthropological Quarterly* 75(3):557–574.

The War within the War $\qquad$ 9

MICAH GAREN

In March 2003, American and allied forces invaded Iraq. While the Iraqi army was quickly defeated, in the ensuing power vacuum, disorder ruled. Looters found museums and archaeological sites unprotected—easy targets. Garen discusses the inability of American and allied forces and Iraqi archaeologists to stem the tide of destruction and despoliation.

THE RIDE OUT TO UMMA, a third-millennium-B.C. Sumerian settlement northwest of Nasiriya, is grueling. I spend much of the trip trying to remain in the military truck, which knocks me about as it rattles over dirt roads. I am accompanying the Carabinieri, the Italian national police, as they patrol archaeological sites in southern Iraq. Since the autumn of 2003, the Carabinieri, a part of the coalition force, have been conducting random patrols on the ground and by helicopter, as well as aerial reconnaissance to photograph and document the damage from looters. These forces have special training in site protection. Checking just three sites can take up to ten hours.

As we turn off the long canal road on a stretch west of Umma, a small truck approaches. The Carabinieri stop and surround the vehicle, guns drawn, to check for stolen artifacts. They find only a sheep and some bales of wool.

At Umma, modern Tell Jokha, a new but empty guard tower stands sentinel near a devastated landscape. Today there are no looters at work, but last year, shortly after the U.S.-led invasion, thieves ravaged Umma by digging hundreds of trenches in their search for salable artifacts. A coalition raid led by U.S. Marines in May 2003 resulted in the arrest of a hundred of them and seems to have put an end to large-scale illegal excavations. Looting continues, however, on a smaller but still destructive scale. A single guard with a rifle for his own protection wanders the site. He complains that the patrol needs to come at night—that's when the looters come. He points to a new trench ten feet deep, only two days old. We have to move on; while evidence of looting is everywhere—broken fragments of inscribed clay, shattered pottery, pieces of bones—the looters themselves are not, and the goal of the patrol is to catch them. The Carabinieri are eager to get to other sites before any looters can escape.

A few miles northwest of Umma is the site of Fara (modern Shuruppak). As we approach, the Carabinieri spot through binoculars what they believe are a few looters in the distance. By the time we arrive at the site, they have disappeared into the desert. The Carabinieri fan out into the surrounding scrub land with guns drawn, but after ten minutes they give up the search. With only a few minutes' lead time, the looters have easily escaped.

The invasion in March 2003 has had a significant impact on archaeological sites in Iraq. Satellite photographs of the region from 2000 show there was already extensive damage from looters, but Abdul-Amir Hamdani, director of antiquities in Dhi Qar Province, where Umma is located, says there was as much looting in the south in the first three months after the invasion as there was in the previous ten years. Watching the looting, Hamdani says, made him feel "like a man who lost his lover in a great sea and stood waiting on the shore looking for her."

In the area south of Baghdad between the Tigris and the Euphrates rivers more than twenty different tribes control the more remote areas where most sites are located. In the power vacuum created by the war, both local and professional looters, who had been attacking sites regularly for the past decade, moved to the region in great numbers and began working on an unprecedented scale. While there has been some looting in the north since the invasion, the south fared much worse because of a long history of poverty and neglect.

Until the autumn of 2003, there was no plan to protect these sites. It was then that former Italian ambassador Mario Bondioli-Osio, the senior advisor for culture to the Coalition Provisional Authority (CPA), came up with a plan to train seventeen hundred guards from the Iraqi-staffed Facility Protection Service, or FPS, to act as caretakers with radios rather than police with guns. (FPS guards are generally stationed at governmental buildings and facilities, utilities, and ports.) Equipped with radios and guard towers, they are supposed to report looting activity to the local police, who then are to come out to the site and arrest the looters.

Yet it's hard to see how an unarmed FPS guard is going to get the necessary support from the overtaxed police, let alone defend himself against the heavily armed looters. Many of the sites are remote and take hours to reach. Colonel Abas Fadil, who is in charge of training the FPS archaeology guards, characterizes the support from the CPA so far as limited. As of this April, only three hundred guards had been trained, and no communications equipment, vehicles, or uniforms had arrived. "Guards are still not authorized to carry weapons or make arrests," says Fadil. "It is better if they [CPA] let us do it alone."

He wants to create an independent antiquities police. "One hundred guards with guns in each province would do it," he estimates. I ask him why the FPS guards stationed at oil assets around the country were equipped with uniforms, guns, and vehicles long ago, while the archaeology guards still go without. He laughs and answers, "You will have to ask George Bush and Paul Bremer that question."

John Russell, who became CPA senior advisor for culture following Bondioli-Osio's April departure, would like to expand the plan to deal with the poverty, lack of education, and the black market that lure people to loot. So far $750,000 has been committed by the Packard Humanities Institute and $1 million by the CPA for site protection.

The 1980s war between Iran and Iraq destroyed many archaeological sites along the border, and after the Gulf War in 1991, widespread looting began, peaking in 1994 and 1999. Saddam Hussein publicly promoted Iraq's archaeological heritage, going so far as to have his name inscribed on a plaque next to Nebuchadnezzar's at Babylon and, in 2000, had ten Iraqi businessmen executed live on television for illegally selling Assyrian artifacts. But looting was also a kind of graft for government higher-ups and others cozy with the deposed dictator, according to Burhan Shaker, director general of Investigations and Excavations at the State Board of Antiquities. "Saddam's regime gave members of the Baath party and their relatives thousands of acres of land throughout Iraq, including areas with important antiquities," he says. During the 1990s, Shaker, then an excavator, says he watched helplessly as precious objects he had excavated and brought to the museum in al-Kut were taken by members of Saddam's regime.

Ali Majed—better known as Chemical Ali for gassing thousands of Kurds—built a huge palace right on top of Tell Al-Ward, a second-millennium B.C. site. ("And now the Americans are occupying it," Shaker adds as an afterthought.) Arshad Yasin, an officer in the Special Guard and Saddam's brother-in-law, organized and financed much of the looting in the south in the 1990s. The archaeological destruction during that time was to some degree an extension of Saddam's war with the Shiites in southern Iraq. Hamdani says there was a clear plan by the Baathists to destroy the culture of southern Iraq. There is also speculation that Saddam turned a blind eye to looting—a lucrative business for impoverished tribesmen—to maintain the support of tribal leaders.

Shaker says the ongoing neglect of the region and looting of archaeological sites is exacerbated by "weak security, no jobs, poverty, and lack of education." Taufiq Abed Muhamed, head of antiquities and sites for Muthanna Province in southwestern Iraq—where Uruk, an ancient city-state dating from the fourth-millennium B.C., lies—shows me letters requesting assistance that he has written to

Paul Bremer, the U.S. administrator of Iraq. He's yet to receive a response. Muhamed is frustrated by the lack of progress. "The security situation belongs to the coalition troops. They should protect these sites, not us," he asserts. "We have no guns, no guards. How are we supposed to protect the sites? The coalition will arrest guards for carrying guns." He says the Dutch forces in the area have only lent assistance on two patrols.

Just north of Muthanna, in the province of Al Qadisiyah, where the Sumerian city-states of Nippur and Isin lie, the situation is no better. The Marines stationed there immediately after the invasion didn't protect the sites, and a number of them, including Isin, were heavily looted. Spanish coalition forces, who were in charge of Al Qadisiyah until, following the Madrid train bombing, their government ordered them to withdraw in mid April, didn't see protecting archaeological sites as their mission. As of press time, U.S. troops were slated to replace the departed troops in Al Qadisiyah, but it was unknown if securing the province's archaeological sites was on the agenda.

Despite this bleak picture, Hamdani looks to the future with a surprising sense of optimism. He eagerly shows photographs from a site recently discovered in the marshlands on the Iraq-Iran border where the Tigris and Euphrates meet. It's one of about twenty-five dating from the third dynasty at Ur (2113–2004 B.C.) that emerged when, after the Gulf War, Saddam Hussein cut off water to the marshes to suppress an uprising by the "Marsh Arabs." When the water levels dropped, the sites became visible. After Saddam's fall, the CPA began to rehabilitate the region. Fifty percent of the marshes have been re-flooded, and the former inhabitants, who had been forcibly relocated, are returning. Hamdani has done a GPS survey to document the archaeological sites. He says he needs to excavate before the re-flooding continues.

But logistical problems like these pale before deadlier realities. In April, as Iraqi insurgents fought coalition troops and the security situation worsened, Hamdani returned with the Customs Police to Umma, where they found evidence of new digging. Soon five trucks loaded with looters toting Kalishnikovs and grenade launchers surrounded them. After a half-hour gun battle, Hamdani and the police fled. They were attacked again on the road back to Nasariyah but made it to the city unharmed. Their vehicles, however, riddled with bullet holes, bore wounds from a fight that is far from over.

Discussion Questions

I. The extensive looting in Iraq, reported here and in numerous other articles and media reports, presumably means the artifacts are leaving the country and entering the antiquities market. Do you find evidence of this in the Internet auctions? At any of the Internet antiquities sales sites?

2. Is the instant access to news from all the world's trouble spots making it easier for the international art market to exploit situations in which it can be assumed that authorities will be paying relatively little attention to cultural heritage protection?

3. What legal restrictions, international and national, exist to protect cultural property during wartime? Why do they seem to be having so little effect in stopping the looting in Iraq and elsewhere?

4. In the United States, the Archaeological Institute of America was particularly active before the war in Iraq began, trying to prevent the destruction in the national museum and the extensive looting of sites and local museums that has, after all, occurred. Explore their efforts, what they did and continue to do (see their website), what went wrong and why. What role should archaeologists, museum curators, and other scholars play in protecting the cultural heritage of their own and other nations during and after a war?

5. Why are works of art a desirable target in wartime? Should (and can) works of art, cultural monuments, and archaeological sites receive special protection in times of war? Realistically, how might this be done? What can field archaeologists do to secure their sites, storerooms, and records against political turmoil?

6. Was the infamous toppling and breaking up of the statue of Saddam Hussein different in kind from other acts of iconoclasm, e.g., blowing up the Bamiyan Buddhas? Is it acceptable to destroy contemporary monuments, but not acceptable to destroy ancient ones?

7. Do you think it is the responsibility of invading nations such as the United States to protect sites and museums? If so, what could the U.S. military have done differently? What role might archaeologists have in this process?

8. Is, after all, a free and open market in antiquities the best hope for preserving the world's cultural heritage?

Note
Marie-Hélène Carleton and Munawar Zubeidi contributed to this article.

Further Readings
Brodie, Neil. 2003. Spoils of War. *Archaeology* 56(4):16–19.

Chapman, John. 1994. Destruction of a Common Heritage: The Archaeology of War in Croatia, Bosnia and Hercegovina. *Antiquity* 68:120–126.

Farchakh, Joanne. 2003. The Specter of War. *Archaeology* 56(3):14–15.

Sandler, Lauren. 2004. The Thieves of Baghdad. *Atlantic Monthly* 294(4):175–181.

Simpson, Elizabeth (editor). 1997. *The Spoils of War: World War II and Its Aftermath*. New York: Harry N. Abrams.

Beirut Digs Out

10

MARILYN RASCHKA

For 15 years, between 1975 and 1990, civil war wreaked havoc on Lebanon. At least 150,000 people were killed. When the country finally achieved peace, a $2.4 billion rebuilding project began on close to 300 acres in downtown Beirut, an area rich in archaeological remains. This project, which often contentiously pitted locals, politicians, developers, and archaeologists against one another, raises important questions about the process of cultural resource management, especially during postwar reconstruction.

ACCORDING TO LEBANESE FOLKLORE, Beirut was destroyed and rebuilt seven times during its 5,000-year history. When the recent civil war ended in late 1990, the Lebanese army took possession of the downtown or "old city," where much of the fighting had taken place. As a journalist, I was invited to document the city's eighth destruction.

When I first moved to Lebanon in 1970 to do graduate work in linguistics at the American University of Beirut, the city's huge Martyrs' Square, honoring those who had rebelled against Ottoman rule in 1915, teemed with vehicles, people, goods, and produce, and the din was deafening. In those days I gave little thought to the city's venerable buildings, captivated as I was by the color and energy of Beirut's commerce. The old city center was only a stage. By 1990 that stage, along with the social fabric of Lebanon, was in ruins, its historic churches, mosques, and public buildings ravaged by 15 years of war during which 150,000 people were killed, one-third of the population fled their homes, thousands were maimed, and thousands more simply disappeared. Survivors of the war were horrified at the destruction. "God what a loss," they would say, adding "*Inshallah* [God willing], we will rebuild." Some talked about a unique opportunity to excavate ancient Beirut, to locate its Phoenician roots and Roman past. Where were the city's Bronze Age ramparts? Where was the famed Roman law school mentioned by the eminent theologian Gregory Thaumaturgus in A.D. 239? For two centuries the law school flourished, and the reputation of Beirut's jurists spread through the provinces. Others spoke of the pressing need to create a city that once again would be the pride of the eastern Mediterranean. Last January, having been on family business in the United States for a year, I returned to Beirut to see firsthand how both sides, archaeologists and developers, were progressing.

I found both conservation and rebuilding in full swing. (Israel's bombing of targets on the outskirts of Beirut and brief blockade of the city's harbor had little effect on the rebuilding.) The battered facade of Lebanon's National Museum had been restored. The repository of the country's most prized antiquities, the museum had stood at the worst of all possible places—the city's Green Line, the infamous divide between warring factions (see *Archaeology*, Jan/Feb 1994). During the war the museum had to be abandoned. Smaller treasures were packed and hidden in safe houses such as the Central Bank of Lebanon. Cases of pottery and terra-cotta figurines were secured in the museum behind sealed doors. Statues and sarcophagi too heavy to be moved—a second- or third-century A.D. statue of Hygeia, a goddess of health, and the thirteenth-century B.C. sarcophagus of King Ahiram of Byblos—were encased in concrete blocks and cement. Today they have been freed from their protective casings and await the museum's reopening.

I asked Helga Seeden of the American University of Beirut about her excavations. She told me of her finds in the extensive market or *souk* area of downtown Beirut: 3 to 4 million potsherds, 2,000 Roman lamps, some 7,000 coins of the Hellenistic through Ottoman periods, nearly 1,200 square yards of mosaics from both private and public Byzantine establishments, and 110 pounds of glass fragments from Roman to Ottoman times. She had also unearthed evidence of a flourishing silk industry: seven basins where the silkworm cocoons had been washed and threads reeled. According to nineteenth-century documents, Ottoman Beirut was surrounded by mulberry trees on whose leaves silkworms fed. Seeden cleaned several of the basins for preservation in place while others were sacrificed as she dug deeper, exposing mosaic floors of Byzantine residences. Nearby she found Byzantine shop porticoes with alphabetic addresses worked into their mosaic floors. The "alpha" shop was found first. Beta, delta, gamma, and epsilon soon emerged.

At one point Seeden was approached by an onlooker with more than the usual curiosity. "I can help you when you excavate there," he said, pointing to where his own shop had once stood. In the 1960s he and his neighbor had found two Roman column drums while digging a basement storage room. One provided a convenient foundation for a wall; the other was put down an old well, where Seeden did find it.

In 1990 bulldozers clearing debris near this site uncovered the domed shrine of an eminent Mamluk religious scholar, Ibn 'Iraq al-Dimashqi, dating to 1517.

A square, brick, arched sanctuary, it served as a hostel or inn for the followers of the scholar and as a private religious school, according to the sixteenth-century Arab historian Ibn Tulun. Today it is the only standing late Mamluk monument in Beirut. The Mamluks, an elite military corps, had overthrown their Egyptian masters in 1250 and ruled over Egypt and its territories, including Lebanon, until they were overcome by the Ottomans in 1517. Other buildings, constructed during Ottoman times, had hidden the shrine. Here Seeden also found elaborately constructed Ottoman water and drainage systems, neatly fitted ceramic pipes so efficient that some had remained in use until they were demolished during recent reconstruction work.

The war-ravaged area being rebuilt covers 282 acres of downtown Beirut. Another 114 acres of reclaimed land on the seafront will also be developed. To do this efficiently, the Lebanese Parliament in 1992 created the Lebanese Company for the Development and Reconstruction of Beirut Central District, or SOLIDERE, the French acronym for the giant real estate company. First on SOLIDERE's list of priorities was to clear out the rubble of war and raze hundreds of condemned buildings. Some 308 structures will be restored because of their architectural, historical, or religious significance, including ornate buildings from the French Mandate (1919–1943) and the Omari mosque (1291), a converted twelfth-century crusader cathedral. In November 1994 a contractor began working on new infrastructure—water mains, sewers, electricity and communications lines, and underground parking lots—part of SOLIDERE's vision of Beirut as a carefully planned modern city. In doing so the contractor dug into the city's ancient past.

I spoke about archaeology and the rebuilding program with Michel Eddé, Lebanon's minister of higher education and culture, whose ministry's responsibilities include making decisions about archaeological work in Beirut and throughout the country. A politician from a wealthy, well-connected family, Eddé has life-or-death power over the city's cultural heritage. Naturally he attracts his share of complaints. Critics say he wants control of the archaeology and credit for the finds but cannot finance much beyond exploratory excavations. He told me how no one had expected such important discoveries so soon in the downtown digs and how excited the Lebanese press and people were about their patrimony. His greatest pride, he said, was reserved for "our young archaeologists who will be the most wonderful product of the archaeological work." When asked who was responsible for protecting archaeological remains, he responded that his country's antiquities laws, instituted under the French mandate in 1933, require archaeology before development. He described his dealings with SOLIDERE as "hard, hard discussions," adding "I told them, 'You have such an investment here, so if you want it done more rapidly you will have to pay for the archaeological survey and excavation.'"

To date SOLIDERE has spent $4 million for archaeological work. It has paid for backhoes and bulldozers to clear the modern rubble, for foreign archaeology teams, and for computer systems and programs with which to record the sites and finds. It has financed exhibits and publications, including a brochure called "Paths of History" that is given free to the many visitors the downtown project attracts. SOLIDERE has three guides who conduct tours of downtown archaeology for schools and the public. According to the Master Plan, on display at a kiosk downtown, sizable areas will be turned into archaeological parks. Parts of parking garages and building lots are earmarked for displaying finds in place. A museum dedicated to the history of Beirut is being discussed.

The entire project is to be completed by the year 2018, when SOLIDERE's 25-year charter from the government expires. Its cost has been estimated at $2.4 billion, of which the $4 million expended on archaeology is a mere 0.17 percent. (In Athens, the Greek government spent about $19.5 million for salvage archaeology in advance of the city's new subway.) SOLIDERE raised most of its money through a sale of shares, which netted $650 million.

When SOLIDERE contracted out the huge infrastructure part of the project, it set a four-year deadline, placing archaeology and development on a collision course. To make matters worse, it offered a 20 percent bonus if the work was finished in three rather than four years. SOLIDERE hired Dutch archaeologist Hans Curvers to work on site, communicating with its in-house archaeologist, Harith Boustany, via two-way radio. If archaeological remains were found in the path of demolition equipment, Curvers would evaluate the finds, determine how much delay, if any, to impose, and make final decisions with Boustany about excavation, preservation, or destruction of the site.

The UNESCO representative in Lebanon, Kacem Bensalah, like Eddé, assured me that archaeology takes precedence over development, and that "excavating Beirut will help change the mentality of the Lebanese" and heal the wounds of the war by restoring a sense of national unity. He recalled, however, a report issued after a visit by UNESCO secretary general Federico Mayor in 1995, which concluded that the archaeological "work was of good quality, but the overall plan was insufficient" to cope with the magnitude of the site.

As of last January some 50 sites, from Phoenician to Ottoman, had been identified. When I visited Helga Seeden's site I was astonished to find that the Mamluk shrine was there but everything else was gone. No cocoon basins, no reused Roman columns, no walls, no hint of the Ottoman drainage system whose pipes had appeared on the cover of a SOLIDERE-funded brochure on downtown archaeology. All had been bulldozed during infrastructure work. Nearby a team of archaeologists was removing the Byzantine alpha shop mosaic. They said they were seven days behind schedule. Whose schedule? The contractor's. Delay was costing him money. As if to spur them on, a backhoe tore at the earth just yards away. A few days later I returned to the site. No trace of the shops remained. The bulldozers had been given the go-ahead.

Only one site had enjoyed immunity from this fate—the area thought to contain the Roman law school and dug by Muntaha Saghieh of Lebanese University. Funding for its excavation has come from SOLIDERE, UNESCO, and Prime Minister Hariri. A well-preserved set of Roman Corinthian columns was found in the 1950s in this area, a short distance from historic Greek Orthodox and Greek Catholic churches. It was here that one of the main Roman thoroughfares, the *cardo maximus*, was discovered. The archaeology here is meticulous—urban archaeology at its finest. If anything remains of Beirut's once-famous fifth-century A.D. law school, it will be found here. The high quality of the remains—columns, a Roman *cryptoporticus* (removed last fall to make room for an underground parking lot), and a Roman-Byzantine basilica excavated in 1927—suggests buildings of consequence. In 1906 a funerary monument with an inscription naming Patricius, a sixth-century A.D. professor at the law school, was found here. Artifacts are stored on site in a secure building, and information on the finds is archived on computer data bases as fast as the students can feed it in. Warned in advance of the existence of major sites, SOLIDERE is glad to have them remain as archaeological parks. But just yards from this model site is a pile of Roman column shafts yanked from the earth during infrastructure work. When I asked about them, the archaeologists working at the site only shrugged their shoulders.

The location of Bronze Age Beirut, near the modern port, has been known since the 1950s, when the foundation was dug for the first multistory department store in the downtown area. At the time four Canaanite rock-cut tombs were unearthed by bulldozers, studied and then destroyed. The Bronze Age city lies nearby and is being excavated by Leila Badr, curator of the Archaeological Museum of the American University of Beirut. Finds there include huge amounts of pottery, murex shells from the purple dye industry, Canaanite and Phoenician city ramparts, a Bronze Age tomb, and the remains of a crusader fortress. Winter rains were pounding sections of a 3000 B.C. mud-brick wall found near the site when I visited. Little time, money, or energy is available to maintain and preserve exposed remains. One section of wall had been covered with plastic sheeting that tore loose in the first winter storm. Obviously heritage management is more than plastic sheeting, but the question of who will manage and finance this aspect of Beirut's archaeology has gone unanswered. Happily, the Canaanite-Phoenician city site was given protected status this past April. No further urban work will be done on the site and SOLIDERE's Master Plan will be amended to preserve it in place.

Early this year the seawall of the Ottoman port was uncovered by bulldozers as they dug a trench for more infrastructure. Only salvage archaeology was carried out there, and the wall was later demolished. The Canaanite (Bronze Age) and Phoenician (Iron Age) city walls on George Haddad Street suffered a similar fate. The street appears on old maps as two blocks long and running through the red-light district. SOLIDERE's Master Plan called for a highway connecting the city with what will be the new sea front, and George Haddad Street was chosen as the route. In November 1994 bulldozers dug a trench as they worked their way from the sea toward the street's original two blocks, cutting into large wall-like structures. Digging stopped but was resumed in February by which time Lebanese University archaeologist Naji Karam had been assigned to the site. On February 24 at 2:30 p.m. archaeologists left the site, having told the bulldozer operators not to come close to the wall they were excavating. Representatives of both UNESCO and the Department of Antiquities reiterated the warning, which was in accordance with the law. When the archaeologists returned the next morning they found that a 20-foot stretch of the Canaanite wall had been destroyed.

The finds in Beirut have been fantastic, providing an unbroken archaeological record of the city's past. A proposed City of Beirut Museum may one day house a Canaanite jar burial with the skeleton of a young girl wearing a necklace of gold and carnelian beads; local Canaanite pottery and ancient imports, including an Egyptian jar with the name of Ramses II; a Hellenistic sculpture thought to represent a deity; a bronze coin of Roman Emperor Galerius Maximianus (A.D. 305–311); Byzantine pilgrim flasks for holy water; and Mamluk and Ottoman glazed pottery.

But the losses have been staggering. Crusader fortress walls were bulldozed even though the site was earmarked as a candidate for preservation in place. Ten Iron Age shaft tombs, two of which were found intact, stand in the way of infrastructure and will be removed. Archaeologists have found piles of crushed murex shells, industrial waste from Phoenician purple-dye extraction. The stone chute where the crushed shells were thrown after processing was excavated but will now be bulldozed. Groups of young student archaeologists talked to me in private about their concerns, but not until the day before I left did I hear criticism from anyone directing excavations. Naji Karam had written an article in the Arabic daily An-Nahar on January 17, 1996, criticizing the government for letting SOLIDERE, a private company, take over the downtown area, and accusing SOLIDERE of rushing the work to increase its profits. "The endless struggle between the developer and the archaeologist," he wrote, "has been faced by other countries before us and was solved in an acceptable way. More than once SOLIDERE has told us that the archaeology that they have come across is not of a high enough cultural quality, and that archaeologists will not be allowed to put up obstacles to development. We must condemn archaeology by bulldozer...." Karam called for a temporary halt to the development work to provide adequate time and resources for archaeologists to conduct proper excavations, and to allow the Master Plan to be redesigned to preserve more sites and monuments in place.

It is unlikely that anyone will pay much attention to Karam. After the infrastructure is complete, individual developers will buy lots and begin building. While Eddé and others insist that archaeology will come first, the reality is that politics and money are playing a disproportionate role in the rebuilding of Beirut, and will continue to do so.

Discussion Questions

1. What, if any, lessons might the experience of archaeology and postwar reconstruction in Beirut provide for reconstruction in Afghanistan, Iraq, and elsewhere? Where do funds for such work come from? Do foreign archaeologists have a legitimate role to play in postwar archaeological activities? Who decides?
2. Lebanon's Minister of Higher Education and Culture suggested that the massive salvage work preceding reconstruction would produce a generation of wonderful young archaeologists. What other opportunities are presented in such a context?
3. Were the economics and politics of reconstruction in postwar Beirut terribly different from what CRM firms in the United States and elsewhere regularly encounter? You might invite a practicing CRM archaeologist to talk to your class about similarities and differences.
4. What do you think about SOLIDERE hiring a non-Lebanese archaeologist to evaluate and make decisions about whether to excavate, preserve, or destroy archaeological sites encountered in the course of development?
5. Can archaeological excavation done under the pressure of a developer's deadline be good archaeology? Defend your position.
6. We can't save every archaeological site and monument. How should choices be made—and by whom?

Further Readings

Naccache, Albert Farid Henry. 1998. Beirut's Memorycide: Hear No Evil, See No Evil. In *Archaeology Under Fire: Nationalism, Politics, and Heritage in the Eastern Mediterranean and Middle East*, edited by Lynn Meskell, pp. 140–158. London: Routledge Press.

Silberman, Neil A. 1989. *Between Past and Present: Archaeology, Ideology and Nationalism in the Modern Middle East*. New York: Henry Wolf.

Wiseman, James. 2000. Beirut in Transition. *Archaeology* 53(5):8–11.

Flashpoint Ayodhya

11

KRISTIN M. ROMEY

Disputes over the origins and cultural affinity of Ayodhya in India caused serious violence between Hindus and Muslims. (Ironically, "Ayodhya" in Hindi means "a place where there is no war.") Archaeologists played a difficult role in the crisis, at times using ambiguous evidence for political ends. Romey investigates the genesis of this tragedy and encourages us to reflect on how archaeologists should handle their research in potentially volatile situations.

O N THE MORNING OF DECEMBER 6, 2003, the leader of Ayodhya's Hanuman temple assembled the town's Hindu holy men for a *shanti yagna*, a peace chant, repeating the name of the monkey god Hanuman a thousand times before a blazing fire. Hard-line Hindu nationalists from around India had gathered in town to celebrate the destruction of a historic mosque torn down in Ayodhya more than a decade earlier. Ayodhya's Muslims raised black flags on their houses of worship and shuttered their shops in protest and mourning. As the chanting rose with the morning sun, hundreds of paramilitary police warily paced the dusty streets, determined to keep a peace that the *shanti yagna* couldn't guarantee.

In Hindi, "Ayodhya" means "a place where there is no war." But peace has been hard to come by in this northern Indian town since December 6, 1992, when a 75,000-strong mob, fueled by the belief that the town's sixteenth-century Babri Mosque was erected atop a razed temple marking the birthplace of the Hindu god Ram, tore down the three-domed stone structure. They were determined to correct a historical injustice by rebuilding the Ram temple where it supposedly once stood. More than a thousand people died in the communal rioting that rocked India in the following days.

The destruction of the Babri Mosque was the most visceral expression of an extreme nationalist ideology, Hindutva (literally, "Hinduness"), which preaches a revival of Hindu pride and honor its followers feel were violated over five centuries of Muslim rule in northern India. The event laid bare simmering tensions between the country's Hindu and minority Muslim populations, and several thousand people have lost their lives in violence associated with the dispute to rebuild the Ram temple. Nonetheless, the nationalist Bharatiya Janata Party (BJP) used the issue to engineer a surprising rise to power in the late 1990s. After a period of stunning violence and endless court hearings over ownership of the Babri Mosque property, the country had had enough. In 2003 the High Court overseeing the property dispute ordered the state-run archaeological agency to the former site of the Babri Mosque to find out what lay beneath it. What the agency claims to have uncovered, however, has led to an even uglier dispute: are archaeologists now being used to rewrite history?

Ayodhya huddles on the banks of the Sarayu River, cluttered with thousands of shrines and overrun with bad-tempered monkeys that linger in the long shadows of the Hanuman temple. According to the ancient epic *Ramayana*, Ram, the incarnation of the Hindu god Vishnu, was born in the kingdom of Ayodhya. Prince Ram eventually fell in love with the beautiful Sita, before she was kidnapped and ultimately rescued by Ram's faithful servant, the monkey Hanuman.

Several other religions have also invested their traditions in Ayodhya. Chinese visitors in the first centuries A.D. describe it as a thriving Buddhist center with several monasteries, the Buddha having spent several years there. Ayodhya is also the birthplace of the first and fourth of the twenty-four Jain *tirthankaras*, or "noble personalities," and, according to Islamic tradition, it is the burial site of Seth, the son of Adam.

Babar the Great ordered a large mosque built in Ayodhya in A.D. 1528, two years after he established the Mogul Empire. Contemporary records make no mention of a temple marking the birthplace of Ram having existed in Ayodhya, much less one being destroyed to make way for Babar's mosque, and although the town had a substantial cult to the Hindu god Shiva, it wasn't until the eighteenth century that large numbers of Ram worshipers began to settle in Ayodhya. Toward the end of the century a Jesuit priest published a description of the town that included the first association of the mosque with Ram, noting that a small platform outside the mosque was believed to be his birthplace. Subsequent accounts claimed the mosque was actually built atop a razed temple to the deity.

The origins of the dispute over the Babri Mosque go back to 1885, when a Hindu holy man filed an unsuccessful suit seeking to build a temple atop the platform outside the mosque. In 1949, as the country suffered the sectarian aftershocks of partition, Ram idols were mysteriously spirited into the Babri Mosque in the middle of the night. The building was padlocked soon after by a judge, the imam ordered out, and the site declared "disputed property" by the court. Thus began a series of civil suits by both Hindu and Muslim litigants over ownership of the property that continue to this day.

The Babri Mosque, still housing its Ram idols, was reopened to Hindu worshipers in 1986, and a foundation stone for a future Ram temple laid nearby three years later. In 1990, more than seven hundred *kar sevaks* ("volunteers") shouting slogans demanding the rebuilding of a Ram temple on the site of the mosque stormed the precinct and set upon the building with hammers and metal rods, causing some damage before being forced back by police. As a solution to the deepening crisis, some of the country's archaeologists and historians suggested that the Archaeological Survey of India (ASI), the government agency in charge of archaeology and heritage preservation, classify the 462-year-old mosque as a protected historical monument. The ASI took no action.

In that same year, as the crisis deepened, one of India's most eminent archaeologists dropped a bombshell. Former ASI director-general B. B. Lal had overseen large-scale excavations at Ayodhya between 1975 and 1980 under the umbrella of his Archaeology of the Ramayana Sites Project. Fourteen areas around the town, including the Babri Mosque precinct, were investigated for evidence associating Ayodhya with the period when events in the *Ramayana* supposedly took place (ca. 2000–1500 B.C.). Writing in the official ASI journal *Indian Archaeology: A Review* in 1977, Lal described the discoveries around the mosque precinct as "devoid of any special interest" after the first few centuries A.D.

But in 1990, Lal, now retired, revisited his excavations in the Hindu nationalist publication *Manthan*. In the article, he provided readers with a compelling detail he had left out of every previous document published on the subject. In a trench immediately to the south of the Babri Mosque, Lal wrote, were a series of brick pillar bases. Furthermore, he noted, there were a few stone pillars in the mosque, "which may have come from the preceding structure." Lal didn't need to tell his readership what "preceding structure" he was referring to. Temple campaigners finally had their hard evidence.

The Indian archaeological community was blindsided. Why had Lal waited more than a decade to make this information public? Why had such an eminent archaeologist chosen to publish his discovery not in the official ASI journal but in a Hindu nationalist publication? Lal had no comment. University archaeologists and historians asked the ASI to release Lal's excavation notes and photographs from the disputed trench for review. The ASI would not, or could not, grant the request.

Scholars opposed to the right-wing Hindu temple campaigners decried the insertion of archaeology into the Ayodhya crisis. "[The temple-rebuilding dispute] is not a question to be decided by historical or archaeological evidence," read a joint statement of historians from Jawaharlal Nehru University in the daily *Indian*

Express. "The fundamental aspect of this issue is that the destruction of the mosque and its replacement by a temple, as a means of getting even with Muslim rule, is a return to the politics of medieval times—and therefore an action which we cannot endorse, either as historians or as citizens of India."

The only photograph of Lal's controversial trench appeared in the summer of 1992, in a booklet published by a group of scholars with known nationalist associations entitled *New Archaeological Discoveries.* Detractors who examined the photograph expressed doubt that the supposed "pillar bases"—constructed of broken brick, not stone—could have sustained the weight of the heavy schist pillars that Babar allegedly had looted from the temple and used in his mosque; furthermore, the "pillar bases" were not even aligned with one another. An assessment by respected archaeologist D. Mandal (retired from the University of Allahabad) in his book *Ayodhya: Archaeology After Demolition* (1993) determined that the pillar bases were from different cultural levels, making it impossible for them to have belonged to the same building.

New Archaeological Discoveries further roused Hindu hard-liners by presenting some forty-odd stone artifacts allegedly found by "public works officials" during an unsupervised bulldozing operation next to the mosque. The booklet claimed the objects, mostly architectural fragments, were "perfectly genuine and once formed part of a Hindu temple of the twelfth century."

"Is it not ironical," a group of exasperated historians and archaeologists blasted back in a statement released to the press, "that scientifically excavated archaeological material and its primary records are being suppressed while unauthenticated, stray, and disjointed objects whose provenance cannot be verified by any means are being bandied about?"

The true archaeological prize for temple-rebuilding activists, however, was revealed during the destruction of the mosque a few months later. Carried from the rubble on the backs of *kar sevaks* was a sandstone inscription later heralded in nationalist publications as a twelfth-century account of the Ram temple's construction. Like all other discoveries of the past several years from the site, it lacked any archaeological provenience. According to archaeologist S. P. Gupta, a coauthor of *New Archaeological Discoveries,* however, the destruction of the Babri Mosque marked the end of what he called the "Battle for the Past." "From the crumbling walls of the so-called Babri [Mosque] and the old and new debris there emerged, like the proverbial phoenix, hundreds of objects which testify... to the existence of the eleventh- to twelfth-century Rama temple . . ." the archaeologist announced triumphantly in a 1993 issue of *BJP Today.*

How could an archaeologist, who makes a career of studying and understanding the past, celebrate the destruction of a historic building? Because the Babri Mosque was ultimately a victim of Hindutva, the philosophy of Hindu nationalism espoused by the Sangh Parivar, a network of organizations that includes the BJP political party and the activist Vishwa Hindu Parishad (VHP), or World Hindu Congress. Hindu nationalists view monuments of Muslim rule, which lasted in northern India from the establishment of the Delhi Sultanate in A.D. 1209 until the advent of British rule, as a bitter reminder of Hindu subjugation. If Muslim monuments on "Hindu" soil—particularly mosques allegedly built atop razed temples—are a symbol of foreign rule, Hindutva reasoning follows that the removal or neutralization of these monuments, regardless of their historical importance, will restore the "lost respect of Hindu society" and "freedom from imperial dominance." "The destruction of the structure at Ayodhya was the release of history that Indians had not fully come to terms with," explains an essay on Hindutva from the official BJP website. "Thousands of years of anger and shame . . . were released when the first piece of the so-called Babri [Mosque] was torn down." Issues of respect and self-preservation resonate in a country that had been fighting a bloody battle over Kashmir with Muslim militants backed by Pakistan throughout the 1990s, and the Ram Temple rebuilding movement is largely credited with bringing the BJP to power for the first time in 1998, displacing the more centrist Congress party after decades of rule.

But the Babri Mosque is only the first of three targets the VHP set its sights on when it began its campaign of "liberation" in 1984. There are also the Kashi and Mathura mosques, built by the seventeenth-century Mogul emperor Aurangzeb after he destroyed the grand Kashi Vishvanath temple to Shiva in the holy city of Varanasi, and Mathura's Keshava Deva temple, which marked the birthplace of Krishna. The VHP has been unwavering in its demand that the still-active Kashi and Mathura mosques, as well as the site of Ayodhya, be "handed over to Hindus," and it is this sticking point that has resulted in the breakdown of several backroom negotiations between Muslim and Hindu groups over the future of the Babri Mosque site. (The Dalai Lama recently offered to mediate the dispute, but there is skepticism about how successful his efforts could be.) If these sites are not "handed over," the VHP has threatened, Hindus would "forcibly take away as many as 30,000 mosques, which were built after demolishing temples during the medieval period." Scholars question the VHP's version of Indian history under Muslim rule, in which a Hindu population suffered as Islamic iconoclasts cut a broad swath of destruction across the religious landscape of northern India. Richard Eaton, a specialist in medieval India at the University of Arizona, has identified only eighty instances in which temples were desecrated or destroyed— primarily for political reasons and at the hands of both Muslim and Hindu leaders—but concedes the precise number will never be known.

Mustafq Ahmed Siddiqui, vice president of Babri Masjid Action Committee, a Muslim organization that has been involved in negotiations with the VHP over the Babri Mosque site, recoils at the hard-liners' demand that Muslims also turn over the Kashi and Mathura mosques. "Better to die," he says. "We cannot compromise on these terms."

During the frenzy of destruction on December 6, 1992, the idols housed in the Babri Mosque were promptly removed for safekeeping and a Ram idol reinstalled in the ruins soon afterward. Since then the shrine housing it has evolved into an elaborate, high-security complex as the deaths associated with the temple conflict continue to rise. Communal violence has been guaranteed across India on every anniversary of the Babri Mosque destruction. VHP temple-rebuilding rallies in Ayodhya have invariably led to clashes with the police. But the worst violence came in February 2002, when a train car full of Hindu pilgrims returning from Ayodhya was allegedly attacked by Muslims in the western state of Gujarat, killing fifty-eight. The retaliatory attacks left more than a thousand people, mostly Muslims, dead.

The Lucknow Bench of the Allahabad High Court is currently hearing a civil suit on ownership of the Babri Mosque site (the present suit is a combination of five previous ones from various Muslim and Hindu plaintiffs, the oldest filed more than half a century ago). Among the issues being considered is whether a temple was destroyed in order to facilitate construction of the mosque—a question declared unfair and irrelevant by the Supreme Court in 1994 when the government sought its guidance on the issue.

Alarmed by the mounting death toll, and seduced by the "archaeology" provided by bulldozers and mobs, the High Court may have felt that a solution could be sought in science. It commissioned Tojo-Vikas International, a Delhi-based remote-sensing firm with no previous archaeological experience, to survey almost an acre of the former mosque site with ground-penetrating radar (GPR). Tojo-Vikas somehow knew in advance what temple proponents wanted them to find; its report, submitted to the court in February 2003, repeatedly identifies 184 GPR anomalies as possible foundation walls, flooring—and pillars. (The report admits, however, that these anomalies may also be no more than large boulders.)

The court issued an order for excavation on March 5, declaring that "whether there was any temple/structure which was demolished and [a] mosque was constructed on the disputed site" was one of the important issues of the title suit, and that "archaeological evidence will be of importance to decide such an issue." The court's order was unnervingly vague: what exactly was the court looking for? Evidence of a temple specifically dedicated to Ram destroyed to make way for Babar's mosque? Evidence of a temple belonging to any Hindu cult directly beneath the ruins of the mosque? Or remains of any sort of "temple/structure" discovered at any depth beneath the mosque?

While the initial reaction from the Sangh Parivar was upbeat and confident, the Muslim plaintiffs and their secular supporters were more cautious. A lawyer for the Babri Masjid [Mosque] Action Committee questioned the propriety of the order. "The onus for proving that a temple was demolished to build a mosque lies on those making such a claim," he told *The Hindu* in the days following the order.

Then there were the archaeologists ordered to do the work. A high-ranking ASI official associated with the excavations (who asked not to be named in this article; the court has prohibited everyone associated with the excavation from speaking to the press) recalls that many at the ASI were against the excavation of the Babri Mosque site when the issue was first raised. "The big question was, What if we found something? What kind of Pandora's Box were we going to open?"

Excavations began a week after the order was issued. ASI archaeologists laid out ninety thirteen-square-foot trenches across the former site of the mosque and in particular areas where GPR anomalies had been detected. The remaining floor of the Babri Mosque that survived from 1992 was torn up and carted away. A fifty-square-foot area in the center of the site where the Ram idol was located, however, was left untouched by order of the court; this was curtained off, and pilgrims came daily to pray and make offerings while archaeologists dug outside.

Observers from Muslim and Hindu organizations monitored the excavations but were not allowed to talk directly to the excavators; any complaints or remarks had to be lodged with the High Court. Originally given less than a month by the court to complete the excavation and write up a report, the ASI completed its work in five months—still a hasty job by any standard.

"This is not the way an excavation is to be carried out," argues B. M. Pande, a retired archaeologist who worked with the ASI for thirty-seven years. "The archaeological process is slow and requires accuracy. These people worked under duress with [observers] breathing down their necks. This shows that you don't trust the archaeologists."

The court's policy on artifacts may have also seriously compromised the excavation. In an effort to prevent tampering or theft, all excavated material was locked away for good at the end of the day, giving researchers at best only a few hours to study, document, and conserve artifacts. Artifacts discovered at the end of the workday went straight to the storeroom without analysis.

A little less than five months after they began, the excavation was wrapped up and the ASI given two weeks to write up its findings. A 574-page, two-volume report was delivered, sealed, to the court on August 22, 2003.

So what did ASI archaeologists find beneath the Babri Mosque? Earliest evidence for human habitation at the site goes back to the first millennium B.C., and continues up to between A.D. 600–1000. The report claims a small circular "shrine" with a water chute (an opening that allows an idol to receive libations) was built at the end of the first millennium. A "short-lived" structure with a large floor made of crushed brick was laid down in the eleventh or twelfth centuries, and three successive floors of a "massive structure," some 165 by 100 feet, was later built atop it and existed until the Babri Mosque was constructed in the early sixteenth century.

It is not until the very last, breathless, somewhat bewildering sentence of the report's concluding chapter, however, that the authors reveal their position:

> Now, viewing in totality and taking into account the archaeological evidence of a massive structure just below the disputed structure and evidence of continuity in structural phases from the tenth century onwards up to the construction of the disputed structure along with the yield of stone and decorated bricks as well as mutilated sculpture of divine couple and carved architectural members including foliage patterns, amalaka [wheels displayed on temple roofs], kapotapali [cover of balcony], doorjamb with semi-circular pilaster, broken octagonal shaft of black schist pillar, lotus motif, circular shrine having pranala (waterchute) in the north, fifty pillar bases in association of the huge structure, are indicative of the remains which are distinctive features found associated with the temples of north India.

With the exception of the "pillar bases" and circular "shrine" (identified solely by its water chute; no cultic objects were found), most of these objects came from the floor level of the mosque or were surface finds and were not mentioned or described elsewhere in the report. A closer examination of previous chapters also reveals that the "shrine" has nothing to do with the "huge structure," and the "fifty pillar bases in association of the huge structure" actually are dispersed in varying numbers on the four floors uncovered by the ASI (four on floor one, six on floor three, etc.).

While authors are listed for the first nine chapters of the report, which address methodology and artifacts, the person(s) behind the report's critical yet contradictory conclusion remains anonymous. "Why does each of the ten chapters in the ASI report have authors except the conclusion?" demands Khaliq Ahmad Khan, an observer who spent five months at the excavation. "Who wrote the conclusion? Who can tell me this?" (The ASI has been unable to produce for the court any rough drafts or notes generated in the production of the final report.) When pressed on the issue of authorship, an ASI official tells *Archaeology*, "It was a collaborative effort."

Another point of contention is the treatment of the "Muslim" glazed pottery and animal bones—items not normally associated with Hindu temples—found at the site. Following complaints from observers, the court repeatedly ordered the ASI to record the bones and glazed ware found during the excavation and their context. The animal bones received one sentence in the final report's summary ("animal bones have been recovered from various levels of different periods") and the stratigraphic context of only a handful of the thousands of sherds of Muslim pottery receives mention. The summary states that the Muslim pottery does not appear until at least the thirteenth century A.D., but ASI documents later requested by the court show the pottery was recovered from levels dated by the ASI to the seventh to twelfth centuries. "The focus was on architecture," explains another ASI official.

Archaeologist D. Mandal, who was present at the excavation as an observer, claims that it was impossible for a tenth-century shrine and an eleventh- or twelfth-century temple to have existed at the site. His analysis of the stratigraphy led him to conclude that two significant floods took place during the fourth to sixth centuries A.D., resulting in abandonment of the site until the thirteenth century A.D. "It is extremely sad to observe that the remains of bones excavated at the site have not been treated even as archaeological finds," he adds, suggesting the report's vague statement on the bones may conceal the fact that they were also found in very early levels; this enables the report to sidestep the "delicate issue" that the earlier Hindu inhabitants of India were not practicing vegetarians. The archaeologist who first critiqued the "pillar bases" from a photograph in the early 1990s also finally had a chance to see them firsthand: "From their varying shapes—circular, squarish, rectangular, irregular, etc.—the credibility of their being the remains of pillar bases becomes highly doubtful," Mandal concludes. "Many of them are manipulated and could be leftover walls."

R. C. Thakran, a history professor at Delhi University, is frustrated at the discrepancy between what he witnessed as an observer at the excavation and what the ASI reported. "The way the evidence was manipulated by the ASI [in the report] forced me to speak out," he says. "During the excavation, we didn't notice a single artifact or piece of evidence that could specifically be associated with a temple."

Extensive horizontal trenching has significantly compromised the archaeological integrity of the site, and several archaeologists have questioned why the ASI decided such an approach was necessary when fewer trenches, or simply vertical trenching to locate the GPR anomalies would have been sufficient. (Of the original 184 anomalies detected, 39 were actually found.) Sending other archaeologists in to "check" the ASI's work is not an option.

Curiously, the report is silent regarding both the key assertions of the Hindutva campaign and the question posed by the High Court: there is no mention of any specific artifacts linking the alleged temple to the worship of Ram, and no evidence, such as burning or weapons, was uncovered that would have pointed to the destruction of the temple at the hands of Babar's men in 1528. Nonetheless, the report was hailed by nationalists as indisputable scientific evidence to support their efforts in building a Ram temple at Ayodhya. Most dissenting archaeologists are still reluctant to publicly speculate on what exactly the ASI has unearthed, claiming a conclusion can be arrived at only after examining the full excavation records, not the controversial final report. There is some suspicion, however, that the "massive structure" is in fact an earlier mosque.

Indian historian Irfan Habib sees the Ayodhya excavations as a product of an "increasingly untrustworthy" ASI. "Since the 1990s, the ASI has been unconcerned with scientific dating; they're eager for more and more antiquity." Habib cites a current ASI project that is attempting to locate sites along the mythological Saraswati River. "Many Western archaeologists working in India won't speak up about this because they're concerned about losing their archaeological licenses," he says.

A Western archaeologist working in the region dismisses Habib's claim. "This is not ideological. ASI archaeologists are poorly paid government employees; they do the bidding of their government. This mess won't be over until the BJP is out of power." The archaeologist, who requested anonymity, notes that most people at the ASI are "extremely unhappy" at the situation they were put in, and that those who were able to avoid working at Ayodhya did so. "The names on the report are, for the most part, not the big guns at the ASI. Are they not there because they wanted no part of it, or because the government knew they couldn't be pushed around?"

An additional source of suspicion for government involvement stems from the fact that the ASI had been ultimately overseen by Human Resources Development Minister M. M. Joshi, a pro-temple advocate. Joshi was one of three cabinet members in office during the excavation and ASI report preparation who is accused of direct involvement in the destruction of the Babri Mosque. While charges against the deputy prime minister, L. K. Advani, were controversially dismissed last fall, charges are still pending against Joshi and several other BJP members present at the mosque destruction. Joshi also replaced the director general of the ASI on the eve of the court's excavation announcement, filling the post with an officer from the government's Ministry of Culture. (The Joshi-appointed director-general has since been removed, and the position remains vacant at press time.)

Furthering suspicion that the report was pre-designed to aid the Sangh Parivar in their mission to build a Ram temple at Ayodhya, the VHP held a press conference in Delhi ten days *before* the ASI submitted its sealed report to the court. Acting as a representative of the Indian Archaeological Society, an organization that allegedly receives considerable support from the VHP, archaeologist S. P. Gupta presented the discoveries of the ASI excavation using language similar to that found in the conclusion of the report. "In light of these scientific and archaeological evidences, we now hope that the dispute will be amicable [sic] settled," the press release concluded. (Gupta initially agreed to be interviewed for this article but later refused to cooperate.)

Since the report was filed with the court, the three-judge panel has been hearing the testimony of archaeologists and historians with varying views on the ASI's evidence, as well as earlier material from the site. (The inscription allegedly discovered in the rubble of the Babri Mosque, heralded by hard-liners as proof of the temple's existence, was recently debunked in court by a top epigrapher.) In a case that has already dragged on for more than fifty years, no one is expecting a swift verdict.

The BJP recognized that the public had grown weary of the sectarian violence associated with the Ayodhya conflict, and in the run-up to the May 2004 national elections adopted a more secular platform focused on economic development. Party leaders, however, still broadcast their dedication to rebuild the Ram temple when speaking with their hard-line constituency. The dual approach failed, and the BJP was handed an unexpected defeat by India's voters at press time (a secular coalition government will be led by the Congress Party). It is too soon to say whether the defeat of the ruling Hindu nationalist political party will temper the actions and demands of India's leading Hindu nationalist activist group. Ayodhya's holy men, who support the building of a Ram temple on their own peaceful terms—not through the fiery insistence of the VHP—may still have to resign themselves to roadblocks and curfews whenever the nationalists come to rally; Muslim shopkeepers may still pull their shutters when they arrive.

One thing is certain: the ASI, a 143-year-old organization widely regarded for its archaeological work, has found itself mired in an ugly political dispute that will not go away until the contentious issue of what to build on the former site of the Babri Mosque is resolved. This greatly troubles some of the agency's archaeologists. "This was a matter of a title suit. There was no need for archaeology to settle the issue," says one top ASI official closely associated with the excavation. "The ASI is a respectable, professional organization. We've done great work. But our job is to understand the past, not to find out what was wrong in the past. I pray to god that we don't get involved in something like this again in the future."

Today, the world's most disputed archaeological excavation is a sideshow to a religious pilgrimage. Visitors entering the cordoned-off disputed area are doing so to make a *darshan* (viewing) of the Ram idol first secreted into the Babri Mosque in 1949.

The process of entering the disputed site is similar to a prison visit. There's an initial pass though a metal detector, followed by a full-body pat-down (and mouth check) to ensure no camera, cell phone, or any type of weapon or recording device is brought into the site. A military escort then leads visitors through an endless wend of anti-mob fencing, a formidable steel cage no more than two people wide and twelve feet high, designed to prevent large groups of people from rushing the Ram shrine. Following a pass through another metal detector and another pat-down, the corridor narrows to the width of a person and snakes up into a tent-covered hilltop.

Beneath the tent are the trenches dug by the ASI. Most are covered by plastic tarps and would be difficult to examine anyway as irritable armed guards hustle visitors along until they reach the hut where the idol sits, glistening black and garlanded with flowers. Worshipers quickly make prayers and offerings, then move back along out through the cage as Ayodhya's ubiquitous monkeys glower from outside the bars. The entire pilgrimage lasts no more than twenty minutes.

A few of the "pillar bases" atop the hill have been left exposed for visitors, friable stubs of coagulated brick that from their appearance seem unlikely to have ever carried the weight of heavy stone columns, much less the roof of some "massive structure." Still, rising up from their trenches they are an unsettling presence, supporting the expectations of millions of people determined to restore their notion of an injured national honor, and bearing witness to the lost lives of thousands caught up in the horror of a people trying to rewrite centuries of history.

Discussion Questions

1. What are the differences and similarities in the behavior of the scholars involved in this story and in "Faking Biblical History"?
2. Who "owns" and controls access to excavation notebooks, photographs, and other records? For how long?
3. Archaeologists, as anyone else, may have strong feelings about all kinds of political issues. How can they separate their professional assessments from their personal political sentiments, in a context such as that at Ayodhya, where they are called upon to use their professional expertise to weigh in on an essentially political argument?
4. "If Muslim monuments on 'Hindu' soil—particularly mosques allegedly built atop razed temples—are a symbol of foreign rule, Hindutva reasoning follows that the removal or neutralization of these monuments . . . will restore the 'lost respect of Hindu society.'" Apply this reasoning to Native Americans in the United States, and other minority groups living under what they perceive as the rule of conquerors or colonialist powers. Could the same argument be made for the destruction of the Bamiyan Buddhas?
5. Some archaeologists—for example, at the battlefield of the Little Big Horn—have explicitly used excavation and survey to shed new light on contentious historical events. Should archaeology be used to "prove" historical events? If so, do archaeologists on these projects have any unique professional responsibilities?
6. The crisis at Ayodhya raises some important questions about the nature of archaeological evidence, quite aside from any political biases in the

scientists involved. What is evidence and what is interpretation and how do scholars separate the two? Look at several excavation reports with these questions in mind. How well do the archaeologists make clear which is which? Do they present the basic data on which their interpretations are based, in a way that would permit another scholar to evaluate the same evidence and arrive at a different conclusion? Should this be a goal (or a requirement) for primary publication of the results of an excavation or field project?

7. Given the political context of contemporary archaeology, it is not implausible that a nation's supreme court could determine the validity of an archaeological question—or rule that an excavation must be carried out at a particular site and impose limitations on time and access to finds. What would you have done if you had been an ASI archaeologist ordered by the court to undertake excavations at the mosque site under the restrictions imposed by the court? How would you have structured the report to the court?

8. How might archaeologists handle potentially volatile situations so that they do not get to a point where courts need to intervene?

9. Discuss the comment that "Many Western archaeologists working in India won't speak up about this because they're concerned about losing their archaeological licenses." Do non-Indian archaeologists have an obligation to comment on this issue or to refrain from doing so? If you, as a non-Indian archaeologist and presumably without a stake in the outcome of the excavation, had been asked to do the work for the Indian court, what would you have done? Who determines whether a foreign archaeologist may work in a country?

Further Readings

Bernbeck, Reinhard, and Susan Pollock. 1996. Ayodhya, Archaeology, and Identity. *Current Anthropology* 37(supp):138–142.

Silberman, Neil A. 1999. From Masada to the Little Bighorn: The Role of Archaeological Site Interpretation in the Shaping of National Myths. *Conservation and Management of Archaeological Sites* 3(1/2):9–15.

Van Der Veer, Peter. 1992. Ayodhya and Somnath: Eternal Shrines, Contested Histories. *Social Research* 59(1):85–109.

Cloak and Trowel   12

DAVID PRICE

Shortly after World War I, the "father" of American anthropology, Franz Boas, wrote a letter to The Nation, denouncing archaeologists who had "prostituted science by using it as a cover for their activities as spies." Price recounts here the complicated and hidden history of professional archaeologists who were spies or engaged in espionage. Nearly a century later, Boas's words still haunt the profession, as the debate continues over archaeologists acting as spies.

IN THE FALL OF 1917, the American Mayanist Sylvanus Morley was about to photograph an old Spanish fort along the Honduran coast when soldiers emerged from it to stop him. Morley complained bitterly to the troops' commanding officer, explaining that he was an archaeologist, but the official was unimpressed. Indignant, Morely asked the mayor to intervene—to no avail. Finally, after some bureaucratic wrangling, he produced a letter of introduction by President Francisco Bertrand and was reluctantly granted permission to photograph the old fort.

There's some irony in Morley's protests. While he had indeed been touring archaeological sites scattered throughout the area, the true purpose of his trip was espionage. Morley was using his position as an archaeologist to cloak his real mission to identify possible German agents and to hunt for covert German shortwave broadcast stations and clandestine submarine bases. His archaeological credentials provided a great cover, and some historians have called Morley "arguably the best secret agent the United States produced during World War I."

The romantic image of the archaeologist as adventurer is the source of much of the speculation linking archaeology with espionage, but there is documentary evidence that the two have at times been closely linked. Some of these relationships are open secrets that have been revealed in obituaries, discussed in interviews, memoirs, and histories, but documenting others requires sleuthing. Over the past decade, I've used interviews and materials from various public archives, as well as the Freedom of Information Act (FOIA) to gain access to classified documents held by the CIA, the Department of Defense, and the FBI, to verify some of the relationships between archaeologists and intelligence agencies.

Archaeologists can move easily across borders and into the world's hinterlands. They are familiar with the attitudes and opinions of the people living where they excavate and have natural opportunities to watch troop movements, note the distribution of military hardware and bases, and even commit sabotage. Many archaeologists are trained in deciphering dead languages, a skill useful in mastering codes.

Because the connections between spies and archaeology are seldom discussed in public, they form a shadowy history that raises serious ethical questions. There are concerns that archaeologist-spies violate ethical standards established at the Nuremberg Trials that require scientists to fully disclose their agendas to research subjects. But archaeologists conducting espionage also endanger the lives and careers of their colleagues, and scholars mixing political trickery with scientific inquiry risk the legitimacy of both their science and their politics.

Western archaeologists first used fieldwork as a front for spying during the First World War. T. E. Lawrence's excavations with British archaeologist Leonard Woolley at the Syrian site of Carchemish mixed archaeology and surveillance. Lawrence's mission for British intelligence was to monitor German progress on the railroad line designed to link Berlin and Baghdad, which would allow the Germans to circumvent the Suez Canal and secure means of shipping oil and other vital supplies during the war. In 1914, Lawrence wrote his mother that these excavations were "obviously only meant as red herrings, to give an archaeological color to a political job." The Egyptian explorations of archaeologist and adventurer Gertrude Bell prior to the outbreak of World War I made her an invaluable resource to British intelligence's Arab Bureau. Her years of Near Eastern excavations provided geographic information of great importance once the war broke out. In 1916, she spied on Iraqi tribal activities around Basra.

In the New World, the war brought a heightened awareness that archaeologists could serve as intelligence conduits. Americans Alfred Kidder and Carl Guthe's excavations at Pecos Pueblo in New Mexico came under suspicion during the war after Guthe wrote Kidder (then serving in the U.S. Army) for advice on shipping hundreds of excavated human skeletons to Harvard. When Kidder cryptically telegrammed a reply to Guthe reading "SHIP 625 SKELETONS ACCORDING TO PLAN B," he was detained by military police, and Guthe was picked up for questioning in Texas as a suspected German spy—though the presence of hundreds of skeletons in shipping crates provided an explanation sufficient for his release.

During World War I, Sylvanus Morley was only one of many American archaeologists who used their profession as cover for gathering intelligence on Germany's presence in Central America. Morley traveled over 2,000 miles of Central American coastline hunting for evidence of German submarines while claiming to conduct archaeological surveys; other archaeologists carried out similar missions on smaller scales.

Some contemporaries of these archaeologist-spies viewed their duplicity as a betrayal of the principles of open science and as a threat to future research. In a 1919 letter to the editor published in *The Nation*, Franz Boas, the father of academic anthropology in America, complained that unnamed archaeologists had "prostituted science by using it as a cover for their activities as spies" in Central America. A few weeks after the publication of Boas's complaint he was censured by the American Anthropological Association (AAA) in a vote dominated by the scholars he accused of spying and their cohorts.

Whether or not one accepts Boas's ethical position that combining science and espionage is wrong, the dangers presented to fieldworkers in a world mixing archaeology and espionage cannot be easily dismissed. With time, the memory of Boas's censure faded, but the issues he raised did not go away.

During World War II, American archaeologists joined other intellectuals in the ranks of newly formed wartime intelligence agencies, such as the Office of Strategic Services (OSS), where their linguistic expertise and geographical knowledge made valuable contributions to the war effort. While most World War II–era archaeologists working for intelligence agencies did not use their credentials as fronts for spying, some did, and included in this number was Harvard archaeologist Samuel Lothrop—one of the people chastised by Boas after the previous war.

In 1940, J. Edgar Hoover wrote New York socialite Vincent Astor (a confidante of FDR who at the time was being considered to run the intelligence agency that became the OSS) that he was establishing "as comprehensive a program as is possible in utilizing the services of archaeologists" who could spy while working in Costa Rica, Guatemala, British Honduras, and Mexico. On Astor's recommendation, Lothrop was selected for this mission, which was run by Special Intelligence Service (SIS), an FBI-supervised foreign intelligence division operating in Central and South America. Lothrop received FBI training in the use of secret codes, invisible inks, mail drops, and covert contact protocols. His mission sent him to Peru, where he gathered intelligence and managed numerous local operatives—while his cover story maintained he was conducting archaeological research at Lima's National Museum.

Most of Lothrop's wartime spying involved tracking political developments in Lima, but he periodically disappeared into the countryside under the guise of field explorations to avert suspicions. He cultivated a network of informants who were separated from each other as blind, self-contained cells. Other archaeologists had their suspicions about Lothrop's work in Peru. In an interview, Harvard's Gordon Willey recalled "it was sort of widely known on the loose grapevine that Sam was carrying on some kind of espionage work, much of which seemed to be keeping his eye on German patrons of the Hotel Bolivar bar."

Willey and others working outside of the cloak-and-dagger operations viewed them with some humor: "On the lighter side, I remember seeing Sam limping around the Bolivar Hotel one day, and one of the boys, [archaeologist Marshall] Newman or [anthropologist Bernard] Mishkin probably, told me that a rival Nazi agent had stamped on his foot in the Bolivar Bar the night before. So you see there was a certain peril in what was going on."

William J. Clothier II, a tennis celebrity, was another "archaeologist-spy" operating in wartime Peru. The SIS secured letters from Harvard to establish a false archaeological cover for Clothier to facilitate his passage through the Peruvian countryside gathering intelligence during 1942 and 1943. To maintain this cover, Clothier published an article on the pottery of the Andean Recuay culture—reportedly ghostwritten by a prominent American archaeologist. Scholars have cited this article for decades, ignoring questions about how a tennis star was able to undertake such an analysis. Clothier also conducted espionage in Chile and Cuba. After the war he joined the CIA.

Interaction between archaeology and espionage during World War II did not lead to a controversy like the one sparked by Boas's letter. The intense patriotism of the time probably helped suppress objections to the use of archaeology for intelligence gathering.

The Cold War forged numerous ties between archaeologists and new intelligence services. The CIA's analytical division chief, William Langer, realized that academics could gather valuable on-the-ground intelligence. Historian Jon Weiner writes that under Langer the CIA routinely "enlisted archaeologists, art historians, and other academics to use their fieldwork for CIA intelligence-gathering purposes."

Many talented archaeologists built careers at the CIA. Most dramatically, University of Chicago–trained Assyriologist Richard Hallock helped decipher the intercepted messages—code-named VENONA—of Soviet agents operating in the United States. James Madison Andrews IV left an assistant curator position at the Harvard Peabody Museum to join the Office of Naval Intelligence during World War II; he later joined the CIA, where he served as assistant director. Waldo "Doobie" Dubberstein left a promising career in Mesopotamian archaeology to become a CIA intelligence analyst—he later committed suicide after being indicted for illegal arms sales as part of an ill-fated plot to sell weapons to Libya.

Peabody Museum archaeologist Frederick Johnson used his position as the executive secretary of the AAA to help establish covert relationships between the association and the CIA. Johnson prepared an agreement that secretly used CIA computers and personnel to compile a roster of scholars and their academic and geographical areas of expertise. The AAA was presented copies of the roster, and the CIA retained copies for their own uses—presumably to identify academics working in regions of interest to the CIA. Johnson also worked to establish a covert liaison program within the CIA that sought to link new generations of archaeologists with CIA personnel.

Some archaeologists report being asked to undertake secret missions during the Cold War. Frank Hibben claimed that while tracing paleontologist-explorer Roy Chapman Andrews's old trail in Outer Mongolia he carried out a secret mission for the U.S. government. In 1997 he told *The New Yorker*, "I was planting a device to monitor Chinese atomic tests at Lop Nor [a nuclear test site in western China]. I'm not sure this has been declassified. I hope so. My instructions were to get as close to Lop Nor as possible and leave it at a high point." The mission ended with his being chased and shot at by Chinese troops. Indirect evidence supporting Hibben's claim is found in his FBI file, where reports indicate the FBI conducted a background investigation on him for a sensitive project identified only as being "in accordance with the provisions of the Atomic Energy Act of 1946."

Other archaeologists were also asked to make observations for governmental agencies. After archaeologist Mark Papworth applied for visas to work on UNESCO's Nubian archaeological salvage operations in the early 1960s, he was approached by State Department employees and asked to record troop movements he might happen upon in the countryside outside of Khartoum. In an interview, Papworth recently recalled that, "there wasn't much to see, but I'd have reported any sort of large troop movement if I'd seen any. It would seem strange to do this sort of thing now, but it didn't seem unusual to me at the time. This was just the sort of thing one did during the Cold War. They had us jumping at our own damn shadows."

The Cold War also found CIA agents posing as archaeologists. University of Colorado, Boulder, archaeologist Payson Sheets recounts how some years ago in El Salvador he had taken a side trip to visit Ixtepeque, the famous Salvadoran obsidian source site. When he stopped to ask directions to the site, a small town's mayor told him that "two CIA agents, masquerading as archaeologists, had been discovered and killed by guerrillas the year before. One body had been fished out of the Motagua River and the other had not been found. Local people were ready to kill any other self-declared archaeologist who wandered into the area."

Gossip linking archaeologists to spying has long flowed within professional circles and in communities where archaeologists dig. But scholarly examinations of historical interactions between archaeologists and spies make some in the field uneasy. There are fears that documenting past archaeological ties to intelligence agencies could increase suspicion of contemporary archaeologists. False accusations of espionage abound. In the late 1970s, rumors circulated identifying geologist Jon Kalb, a veteran investigator of Lower and Middle Paleolithic Ethiopian sites, as a CIA agent. These accusations threatened the safety of Kalb and his family in the field and damaged his reputation—he later brought a successful lawsuit against the National Science Foundation for its role in spreading the rumors. Accusations of spying in the field can place archaeologists in real danger, but silence on the extensive relationships between espionage and archaeology does not help matters.

Professional archaeology associations should insist that archaeologists forswear connections to intelligence agencies for the safety of both themselves and their colleagues. While the ethical and professional codes of organizations like the Archaeological Institute of America and the Society for American Archaeology admonish archaeologists to obey the laws where they excavate, they don't condemn the mixing of archaeology and spying. Such statements won't stop dedicated spies from lying about their true intentions, but they can demonstrate the commitment of archaeologists to scientific rather than political goals.

As America's "war on terrorism" expands the global operations of U.S. intelligence agencies, archaeologists will likely fall under increased suspicion in the field. These suspicions will presumably be unfounded, but contemporary archaeologists should remember Boas's decades-old warning to separate themselves from any mixture of archaeology and espionage. Given the tense international political situation, his warning is as timely now as ever.

Discussion Questions

1. Do you agree with Boas's ethical position that combining archaeological science and espionage is wrong? Why or why not? Is there a difference between using one's archaeological skills and knowledge to assist one's country in wartime and using archaeology as a cover for spying (or ghostwriting an archaeological article so someone else can use archaeology as a cover)?

2. You might inquire whether any archaeologists at your institution have ever been accused of spying while in the field, or had experiences related to suspicions about archaeologists doing undercover work for their own government. Ask how these experiences affected their work, and whether they ever felt endangered by the suspicions, or felt their relations with a local community were compromised.

3. Do any archaeological codes of ethics forbid spying? Debate the pros and cons of professional organizations adding a statement to their codes of ethics about not mixing archaeology and spying.

4. Is using archaeology as a cover for spying a different kind of political involvement for an archaeologist than undertaking to support one or the other side of a political argument through archaeological interpretation? Are they all variations on a theme of misusing science—or are they valid ways to make use of professional skills?

Further Readings

Harris, Charles H., and Louis R. Sadler. 2003. *The Archaeologist Was a Spy: Sylvanus G. Morley and the Office of Naval Intelligence.* Albuquerque: University of New Mexico Press.

Price, David H. 2003. Anthropology Sub Rosa: the CIA, the AAA, and the Ethical Problems Inherent in Secret Research. In *Ethics and the Profession of Anthropology: Dialogue for Ethically Conscious Practice,* edited by Carolyn Fluehr-Lobban, pp. 29–50. Walnut Creek, CA: AltaMira Press.

Price, David H. 2004. *Threatening Anthropology: McCarthyism and the FBI's Surveillance of Activist Anthropologists.* Durham, NC: Duke University Press.

AFFECTED PEOPLES III

People without History   13

RODERICK J. MCINTOSH, SUSAN KEECH MCINTOSH, AND TÉRÉBA TOGOLA

"The nature of archaeology in the twenty-first century depends on the outcome of debates currently raging in the discipline, as 'people without history' strive to reclaim their pasts" and question traditional Western assertions about such fundamental issues as the economic basis of complex societies, or the evolution of societies from hunter-gatherers to civilization. The authors see two choices for the future: "a narrowly provincial archaeology that elaborates the current nationalistic polemic," or an archaeology that transcends polemics "to reveal the complexity of the human experience." The authors provide many examples of how the latter choice will contribute to a richer discipline and more significant contributions to the modern world.

QUICK—WHAT DO NATIVE AMERICANS, Turks, and Nigerians have in common? Answer: the finest artifacts of their most brilliant civilizations have been looted and sold to the highest Western bidders. The issue of who owns the past is an emotional one, having as much to do with the politics of the present as the conservation of the past. The fact that Nigerians, for example, must travel to the British Museum to see the finest Benin bronzes, while Britain mounts huge funding drives to prevent the sale of venerated items of its own cultural patrimony to non-Western buyers, speaks volumes about the relative wealth and power of these two countries. As archaeologists become increasingly concerned about hidden political and ideological agendas in their quest for the past, the way they recover, interpret, and conserve the past is changing. The nature of archaeology in the twenty-first century depends on the outcome of debates currently raging in the discipline, as "people without history" strive to reclaim their pasts.

People without history are those, according to Eric Wolf in his influential book *Europe and the People without History*, to whom a history has been denied by those who have claimed history as their own. As Western civilization expanded through conquest, colonization, and commerce, the primitive groups it encountered were displaced, subjugated, or exploited. And since those in power write histories and feature themselves prominently therein, it is not surprising to find non-Western peoples depicted in conventional Western histories as passive recipients of change inaugurated by Western culture-bearers. Furthermore, the historical depiction of non-Western peoples as primitive or savage has served to justify their subjugation by the West, regardless of the human misery and suffering involved. During the past two decades, there has been a great debate over the historical conventions, including categories (such as Western and non-Western), interpretive models, and research agendas, that together restrict our ability to reconstruct the past of people without history.

In recent decades, many Third World archaeologists have angrily rejected Western concepts and models that relegate their own past to inferior or peripheral status merely because it does not replicate the prehistory of Europe and the Near East. Traditional Western assertions—that complex society is always built upon an agricultural base, that social stratification is economically based, that all states are expansionist, or that societies evolve in a linear manner, in stages, from hunter-gatherers to civilization—have at times taken the form not of hypotheses to be tested but of judgmental statements about the ranking of human experience. The hidden message is that non-Western prehistories are derived, shadowlike manifestations of sequences already brilliantly experienced in the Near East or Europe. Or worse, that they represent truncated, failed, or retarded examples of human cultural evolution. Third World archaeologists understand how their national prehistories are thus demeaned; it is scarcely surprising that emotions run high, and debate degenerates into polemic. Many Third World archaeologists, among others, see clearly that the ability to name things, to create the categories of analysis through which we perceive reality, is a source of power. Pitted against each other are archaeologists who claim that archaeology's scientific authority elevates it above the cultural biases of individual practitioners and those who doubt that objectivity is possible. The outcome of the debate will determine how archaeology in these countries will develop in the future.

Global archaeology in 2050 may take one of two courses. One possibility is a narrowly provincial archaeology that elaborates the current nationalist polemic. In this scenario, individual nations would pursue their past in isolation, limiting investigation to a restricted set of questions and rejecting cross-cultural studies as irrelevant. Alternatively, archaeology may transcend the current polemics to reveal the complexity of the human experience without conferring privilege on any particular people or place. At the heart of this scenario is genuinely collaborative international research, conducted in an atmosphere of mutual respect among nations. Such an archaeology could contribute to a world order that ennobles all peoples. The debate that will lead archaeology in one of these directions or the other is in full swing, and we can expect it to continue through the final decade of this century. Let us look more closely at some of the current issues that are relevant to these two very different visions of archaeology in the future.

All nations commit to their collective memory selected episodes from the past, be they Israel's veneration of Masada or the Danes' embrace of their Viking heritage. Rather than being literal, objective accounts of past reality, national prehistories can be seen as statements to the world about how a people see themselves and would like to be seen by others. A nation's emphasis or lack of emphasis on certain aspects of its past reflects important social or political priorities. For example, in choosing a name, Zimbabwe focused on its most prominent archaeological site, Great Zimbabwe. By this one stroke, Zimbabwe not only reclaimed its heritage from the outgoing white regime (which had long insisted on the non-African origins of the site), but it also promoted unity by allowing all its multiple ethnic groups to claim a common glorious past. In the United States prior to the 1970s, the research vacuum on the archaeology of slavery reflected the near invisibility of American blacks in the national political agenda.

Clearly, nationalist archaeologies enable Third World nations to reclaim a past previously reliant on history recorded by Westerners. Mexico's National Museum of Anthropology, for example, brilliantly displays an intensely nationalistic archaeology that aggressively emphasizes pre-Hispanic cultures, as evidence of the spirit of the nation's Indian majority. There is always the danger, however, that nationalist archaeologies will devolve into provincialism. Indeed, there is currently a debate in Mexico over whether the exclusion of North American researchers, with their larger field budgets and vigorous theoretical debates, may have accelerated a provincialization of Mexican archaeology. According to Jaime King's article "Mesoamerica: Events and Processes, the Last 50 Years" (*American Antiquity*, 1985), Mexican archaeology has become the "mouthpiece of . . . demagogic politicians and generations of students trained in sloganeering."

National agendas in archaeology may be not merely provincial but downright unsavory, as when they serve to devalue certain groups within the society. Guatemala's discouragement of Maya research, for example, is part of a policy to devalue the traditions of an Indian majority that is held to be racially inferior. And what if a national agenda demands destruction of archaeological sites? Few modern instances can match the intensity of the Spanish obliteration of Aztec temples and idols during the first centuries of Conquest. But beginning in 1966 and continuing for the ten years of the Cultural Revolution, Chinese sites were considered by the Red Guard to be reactionary monuments of old thought, the last vestiges of feudal ideals to be duly obliterated. Similarly, from 1975 to 1979, the

Khmer Rouge engaged in purposeful dynamiting and defacing of Angkor Wat and other sites. Is there any place for the argument that certain sites are part of the world cultural inheritance, with international claims having priority over those based on national agendas?

We see, then, how nationalist archaeologies can liberate prehistory from Western interpretive constructs. In the process, however, the limitations imposed by Western interpretations can be replaced by those imposed by nationalist ideologies. How much progress can be claimed if all we have accomplished is the exchange of one set of limiting conditions for another? Surely an archaeological community wishing to be freed of a received canon of priorities and interpretations should actively encourage local archaeologists to feel unconstrained and unself-conscious in exploring their own.

At the moment, narrow sectional interpretations encourage hatred, as when Israeli fundamentalists in 1983 attempted to blow up Jerusalem's Dome of the Rock mosque on Haram Ash-Sharif in preparation for building the Third Temple. Archaeology's moral imperative is to demonstrate the equal claims of Israelis and Palestinians to Haram Ash-Sharif/Temple Mount. If only the combatants could see that the Holy Land is not the repository of some mystical vitalism to be jealously possessed. Rather, archaeology and history show us that it has always been a crossroads for many peoples possessing many different beliefs. It is no coincidence that the great religious systems born in the Holy Land accommodated and transcended the diverse histories of all by appealing to the universal themes of our humanity.

An archaeology tolerant of local potentialities can thrive only in an atmosphere of mutual respect among nations for the cultural priorities and beliefs of others. This will require that we lower the banner of objective science, under which archaeologists have felt justified in profaning the most cherished and sacred aspects of others' pasts. Particularly intense emotion has focused on ritual art, human burials, and the repatriation of national cultural treasures. Ritual art is frequently viewed by the society that created it as the repository for powerful spirits whose propitiation involves the observation of specific rituals. For example, the Hopi view of the world as a living spirit includes the obligation of an initiated few to provide continuous care for living spirits (Kachinas) represented by (or residing in) the well-known Kachina dolls. Without proper care of the Kachinas, the cosmological order is upset, and the world is at risk. Hopis have demanded the return of Kachinas from museums, calling them trapped friends unable to come home. By what right does the uninitiated scholar or curator disturb the Hopi cosmos by the profanity of manipulating Kachinas? It is not surprising that non-Hopi do not regard Kachinas with the same awe or emotion as Hopi. The problem, non-Westerners argue, arises when Western archaeologists or art historians invoke the authority of science and the advancement of knowledge to justify profaning what another culture considers sacred. For the Hopi, the presence of Kachinas in museums exemplifies how the world view of the powerful has triumphed over that of the powerless.

The same conflict underlies the charged issue of the repatriation of antiquities. Foreign governments view their right to control their own cultural heritage very seriously. They resent it when cherished aspects of their past are treated as commodities in Western-dominated art markets. How else could Mexico interpret the theft on Christmas Eve, 1985, of 140 of its most important pieces of pre-historic gold, jade, obsidian, and turquoise from the National Museum of Anthropology? How else should they view the wholesale destruction of entire categories of archaeological sites by plunderers whose only goal is profit? Archaeologists and art historians who authenticate, date, or appraise antiques that lack proper export papers have long been unwitting, or uncaring, accomplices in this illicit activity. The continued failure of archaeologists to address this issue can only increase the atmosphere of hostility and suspicion in which various governments, including Italy, refuse to allow any antiquities to leave the country for even temporary study. Lest we think that these issues are confined to arcane political debates among governments and scholars, consider how the entire population of Irakleon, Crete, stopped the shipment of a Minoan exhibit to England and the United States in the mid-1970s by bodily blocking its progress to the docks.

To comprehend how the fear of losing venerated aspects of one's national heritage can provoke popular uprisings, we need only imagine the groundswell of sentiment that would attend the announcement that the original copies of the Declaration of Independence and the United States Constitution would be sold to the highest bidder in order to reduce the federal deficit. If it is nearly impossible for us to imagine the sale of these objects ever taking place, it is only because of our currently strong position of world power. For many other countries, similar sales are routine and have been for some time. This, too, says much about their relative geopolitical position. Perhaps we can see why the Greeks are so tenacious and emotional about the repatriation of the Elgin Marbles from the British Museum. Once again, it is clear why the current polemic about who controls the past is firmly rooted in the politics of the present.

On other difficult issues, such as reburial of ancient human remains, significant progress has been made, giving hope that a new dialogue of respect between nations is in its formative stages. The subjects of the reburial debate are the hundreds of thousands of aboriginal skeletons from the United States and Australia that are currently stored or displayed in museums or that will be disinterred by future excavation. Aboriginal populations argue that their religious freedom is abridged when sacred burial grounds are desecrated, and their ancestors' journey through life (of which death is but a part) is interrupted by removing their bones from the ground. Archaeologists and physical anthropologists, on the other hand, assert that the scientific knowledge of adaptation and disease patterns gained from permanent museum access to skeletal material exerts prior claim over religious freedom. The outcome of this lengthy and often polemical debate has been promising. Some Native American groups and Australian Aborigines now admit the potential of archaeological studies to provide information on the cultural practices and life-style of their ancestors before contact with Europeans. Rather than the wholesale and immediate reburial they originally demanded, they will—after consideration on a case-by-case basis—accept study of new finds and of material already in storage, followed by reburial with appropriate rites. Archaeologists and physical anthropologists, in their turn, have agreed to consider ancestral remains as sacred and venerated objects, and the two sides will work together to stop looting of sites and draft ethical agreements on the treatment of artifacts and human remains. The resolution of the debate in Australia has been complicated by Aboriginal claims to land rights over sacred burial grounds, and by a legal system that permits desecration of even recent Aboriginal cemeteries while prohibiting excavation of white graves. However, the American experience is an encouraging sign that even seemingly intractable differences can lead us to new levels of tolerance and mutual respect.

We take the hopeful view that archaeology in the twenty-first century will build on a foundation of mutual respect among nations. We believe that the issues raised by the current polemics in archaeology will be seriously discussed and, ultimately, resolved. If this happens, then we likely will escape an archaeology of the future that is defined by narrow, nationalist agendas. The alternative, an international archaeology committed to pluralistic research that does not privilege any particular people or place, will embark on research paths scarcely imaginable today.

To do this, we must first attack the consequences of unequal distribution of resources. Archaeology's vitality is greatest in richer nations, where existing resources for research are not exhausted by basic inventory and salvage activities. In the future, increasingly sophisticated and inexpensive technology can lessen the disparities among nations by fulfilling various labor-intensive aspects of archaeology. Site detection, for example, today accomplished mainly by foot survey, could be revolutionized by declassification of spy satellite imagery.

Hand-recording and drawing of artifacts could be made largely obsolete by the widespread availability of an optical-scanning computer catalog system. In this system, several digitized perspective images of each object, as well as a multitude of the object's attributes, would be automatically recorded and directly fed into computerized data bases, early generations of which are already used by archaeologists. Beyond this, a proliferation of inexpensive, flexible data bases should counter the inherent threat of rigid standardization of categories. Lastly, if one can overcome some governments' distrust of open telecommunications systems, we may envision a day when archaeologists everywhere are linked in a global computer mail system. With the development of simultaneous multi-language computer translation capability, a globally interactive archaeology will become possible.

Despite all the potential offered by technology, the most significant remedies to uneven resource distribution will come from human agencies. Centralized committees such as UNESCO have led spectacular successes in the salvage and museum-conservation arena, but much more can be done to provide archaeologists from poor nations (or minorities or nonconformists from richer ones) access to expensive dating techniques, travel funds for conferences, or exchange visits to ongoing research elsewhere. Particularly important will be a greater commitment by individual archaeologists and national funding bodies to balanced international collaboration. We would like to see funding preference given to research projects with an explicitly comparative problem orientation and multinational representation among principal investigators and site supervisors. Imagine how different the past might begin to look if, for example, the members of a Senegalese-Chinese team were to spend six months in each other's countries, lending their different perspectives on tumulus burials, or if a research team of Native Americans, Kung Bushmen, and Australian Aborigines collaborated on meaning in rock art.

At a time when some assert that all cross-cultural studies are bogus and that all cultures traveled along unique and non-comparable paths, we believe that balanced international collaborative strategies are particularly important, not just to prove or disprove that claim but to transcend the limits of entrenched traditional interpretations. Archaeology has already shown that the experience of world prehistory is much more diverse than traditional models would allow. Take, for example, the expectation that past hunting and gathering societies were largely egalitarian, mobile, and small-scale. Instances are now known from Australian prehistory of nonagricultural groups living in sizable, semi-sedentary settlements, with rudimentary social hierarchies in which a small group directed the labor of others toward the expansion of settlements and redistribution networks. The complexity of hunting-gathering society appears even more developed among the Chumash of California, whose society included craft specialists serving emerging elites. More than 10,000 years ago, the Jomon period in Japan witnessed hunting-gathering societies living in dense, sedentary settlements.

Urbanism is another case in which traditional models have proven inadequate. The Western conception of early cities possessing palatial architecture with encircling walls symbolically reinforcing a despotic social structure is not useful in the study of other cultures. Early Bronze Age cities of China are clusters of hamlets—for specialists, nobles, and royalty—spread over many square kilometers. Other assaults on the idea that palatial or monumental architecture are requisites for urban life come from places as disparate as the Middle Niger of West Africa and Cahokia on the Mississippi. Traditional models of states are under siege, too. In the Near Eastern model, the state is marked by elite control of large-scale foreign trade and economic centralization. The state is also intent upon perpetual territorial expansion as a source for new wealth and subjugated labor. This model is challenged by alternative cases in which the prime concern of the state is the maintenance of cosmic order. This is most dramatically illustrated by the Aztec empire. While certainly militarist and despotic, the empire took on a form of federalism in that local chiefdoms or communities had great autonomy as long as tribute and, especially, human sacrifices required by the gods continued to flow to the center. While the state's function as a tribute-gathering machine was maintained by terror, the ultimate purpose was cosmological rather than expansionist.

We need not multiply the examples to show that no single paradigm or interpretive tradition can do justice to the real complexity of the human prehistoric experience. The archaeology of the twenty-first century must probe that complexity with new research strategies grounded in methodological and interpretive pluralism. This pluralism need not devolve into a thousand national or local prehistories, all spinning separate tales and ignorant of developments elsewhere. As the people without history reclaim their past through the polemical posturing of the current decade, it will be natural for them to ask if insights into their own prehistories have a larger lesson for developments elsewhere. If a truly collaborative dialogue among nations can be established, archaeology will enter new interpretive fields.

It would, however, be naive to think the path will be easy. Those heavily invested in traditional approaches will retrench petulantly, and on the other side of the coin, the danger of national prehistories becoming militantly isolationist is real. Neither approach will promote the liberal exchange of ideas. Particularly destructive is the radical reductionist position, taken by some Western archaeologists, that prehistory and history can never be more than stories about the *present*, written to obscure or legitimate present values, practices, and social inequities.

This argument has been used to discourage new research, by the logic that discoveries are usually made by archaeologists of wealthy nations, who then create prehistories for non-Western peoples that reflect, and thus legitimate, inequalities in the world power structure.

Such concern is noble on one level, but Third World archaeologists have been quick to label such thinking a new form of Western paternalism. With their limited resources, they depend on Western financing to excavate and document sites threatened by urban or agricultural expansion, desertification, or dam projects. They are thus wary of the extremist position that would discourage such financing, resulting in the loss of significant segments of their past forever. Further, Western proponents of this extreme view—that the past is unknowable—seem to imply that Third World people are intellectually passive and accept any externally given version of their past. If this radical view prevails and discovery is forbidden, then Third World people will forever be consigned to being people without history, with a past always derived from, and lesser than, that of nations with vigorous research traditions.

For the year 2050, balanced international collaboration and research pluralism in an atmosphere of mutual respect among nations will be the antidotes to Western paternalism in its many forms. We look forward to a vision of archaeological humanism that would actively promote mutual respect among nations and mutual intelligibility among cultures. If successful, archaeologists of the future will be in a privileged position to contribute to the enterprise of defining universal standards of human rights.

Discussion Questions

1. In writing this paper, the authors were asked, in 1989, to look ahead to what issues would face archaeology in the twenty-first century. Evaluate their predictions.
2. Explore some examples of archaeological data and interpretations that exerted power in a political context. Do you think archaeologists, when interpreting their data, should call it as they see it, and let the outcome be what it may, or should they try to anticipate the potential political and other ramifications of their work and temper their comments accordingly?
3. Is the scientific integrity of archaeology put at risk if archaeologists accept restrictions on how they may go about (re)constructing the past?
4. Does, in fact, archaeology's scientific authority elevate it above the cultural biases of individual observers? How might individual archaeologists identify and try to work through their own cultural biases?
5. Discuss whether it is possible both to respect the rights of descendant communities and claim that the cultural heritage belongs to the entire international community.
6. What are the pros and cons of "lowering the banner of objective science" to achieve a more tolerant and respectful archaeology?
7. Are all archaeologists and art historians who authenticate, date, or appraise antiquities accomplices in an illicit and destructive activity?

(Think, for example, of archaeologists in museums to whom local people bring artifacts found in their gardens and ask for identifications and information.)

8. Do scholars have a right to study and, in the openness of science, make public aspects of sacred beliefs and rituals that descendant communities consider the sacred preserve of the initiated few?

9. How is the Internet affecting the world community of archaeologists?

10. How many field projects directed and largely staffed by non-U.S. citizens are taking place in the United States? Compare this with the situation in other countries and consider the effects on the discipline and relations between archaeologists and the public.

11. Think of some particularly compelling issues in current archaeology, and design cross-cultural teams (e.g., a research team of Native Americans, Kung Bushmen, and Australian Aborigines collaborating on meaning in rock art) that might effectively and innovatively pursue those issues.

Further Readings

Layton, Robert (editor). 1989. *Conflict in the Archaeology of Living Tradition.* London: Routledge.

Schmidt, Peter R., and Thomas C. Patterson (editors). 1995. *Making Alternative Histories: The Practice of Archaeology and History in Non-Western Settings.* Santa Fe: School of American Research Press.

Wilk, Richard R. 1985. The Ancient Maya and the Political Present. *Journal of Anthropological Research* 41(3):307–326.

Wolf, Eric. 1982. *Europe and the People without History.* Berkeley: University of California Press.

When Artifacts Are Commodities 14

JULIE HOLLOWELL

Hollowell provides a history of archaeological investigations of prehistoric Inuit settlements and their ivory carvings on St. Lawrence Island in the Bering Sea, and how the early work of archaeologists contributed to the exploitation today of these resources by the native Yupik population. St. Lawrence, where the digging and the ensuing sales are, unusually, entirely legal, otherwise shares the discovery of isolated communities elsewhere that digging in their ancestral sites provides them with a viable way to participate in the modern cash economy.

> *"Our ancestors used ivory to make the tools they needed for survival. We have a different use for ivory today, but it is no less important for our survival."*
>
> —GAMBELL RESIDENT, quoted in *Archaeological Survey and Site Condition Assessment of St. Lawrence Island, Alaska* (1984)

A TREELESS, ROADLESS TUNDRA, slightly bigger than Rhode Island and shaped like a piece of clay formed in a clenched hand, St. Lawrence Island sits at the southern approach to the Bering Strait, closer to Russia than to its home state of Alaska, which lies 150 miles to the east across the cold and unpredictable Bering Sea. On rare days without fog, the bluffs of Russia's Chukotkan peninsula loom in the distance, less than forty miles from the village of Sivuqaq, or Gambell, perched at the island's northwestern tip. Rocky cliffs of black basalt line the island's perimeter, teeming in the summer with rookeries of cormorants, auklets, and murres. The few beaches have served as haulouts for herds of Pacific walrus for millennia. Twelve thousand years ago, this land, with its interior peaks, must have made a striking landmark along the wide bridge that spanned the continents.

Today St. Lawrence Island is home to close to 1,500 Yupik people living in the two villages of Gambell and Savoonga. Not long ago, before stores and schools and epidemics, more than a dozen villages dotted the coast, some of them large and ancient enough to have left expansive mounds and deep middens. The cape at Gambell has been continuously inhabited for around 2,000 years. Excavations here by the Smithsonian's Henry Collins in the 1930s distinguished Gambell as the "type site" for the distinctive Old Bering Sea, Okvik, and Punuk artifact styles across this northern maritime region. Savoonga, established as a reindeer camp in the early 1900s, lies just a few kilometers from the major ancestral sites of Kukulik to the east and Ivetok to the west.

The island's relative isolation and extreme environment have contributed to the strength and persistence of local cultural traditions, but also make life extremely hard. There are no cars, but frequent accidents involving four-wheelers, snowmobiles, small planes, guns, and ice cut lives short. Everything here costs more and is more difficult to maintain. People depend on seal, walrus, and bowhead whale for the majority of their food, and the costs of subsistence hunting are high. One way some villagers make ends meet is by mining former dwelling sites to recover marketable artifacts and raw materials of walrus ivory and walrus and whale bone. Digging for old ivory and artifacts has been a common summer "subsistence" activity on St. Lawrence Island for generations, and also takes place, though on a less industrious scale, in many other coastal villages along the Bering Strait, wherever ivory is found.

In most countries, archaeological materials found on private property are owned by the nation-state. In the United States, archaeological protection laws apply only to public (state and federally owned) lands or to acts performed on private lands without the permission of the landowner. Archaeological materials found on private property are the property of the landowner. In 1971, the two St. Lawrence Island Native Corporations that formed as a result of the passage of the Alaska Native Claims Settlement Act (which extinguished all claims to aboriginal title and replaced it with corporate status) refused the option of a larger monetary settlement and chose instead to secure fee simple title to their entire island under a special provision of the act. As a result, the island is owned privately and jointly by the two Native Corporations for their approximately 850 indigenous shareholders. In the absence of other regulations and as long as the corporations allow, it is legal to dig and sell artifacts. The St. Lawrence Island artifact trade is probably the most lucrative *legal* market in archaeological artifacts in the world today.

The market in these archaeological materials operates on several levels. On the island itself, old ivory, aged bone, and artifacts are gathered, traded, and utilized locally by Native artisans as raw materials to make carvings and crafts for the tourist market. Mineralized (often mistakenly called "fossil") ivory is often used as a color contrast to new, white ivory and black baleen.

A regional and global market for raw archaeological materials also thrives. Dealers come to the island and purchase raw materials and artifacts that they then sell, either wholesale or retail—often by the pound—to non-native artisans to carve into jewelry and sculpture. Old walrus and whalebone sell for $1.50 to $14 a pound, while pieces of old ivory sell for anywhere from $40 a pound up to $200 a pound for a whole tusk. "It's getting scarce," one man told me. "It's hard to find whole pieces; it's just the scraps, chunks. These are non-renewable resources so they don't grow like crops or other things that replace year after year. They are there just one time. And once you find it, there's no more left."

Because of the high price and size limitations of ivory as a carving medium, the market in raw materials recently expanded to include bulk quantities of whale and walrus bone. In the early 1970s, the Canadian government subsidized the use of whalebone by Inuit art cooperatives until a study by archaeologist Allen Mc-Cartney—published in 1979 as *Archaeological Whalebone: A Northern Resource*—showed that archaeological sites were being destroyed in gathering the material. Now that the popularity of whalebone sculpture has exploded on the Alaskan tourist market, the process is being repeated on St. Lawrence Island.

Some of the old ivory and bone purchased in Native villages gets exported by dealers to Bali. There, it is carved by workshops into goods for the tourist market that are brought back to sell in Alaska. One Seattle-based artist I met in Skagway, a popular stop for cruise ships in Alaska's Southeast, had designed a series of ivory sculptures made from ancient walrus tusk, supplied the raw material to carvers in Indonesia, and was selling the results of this "remarkable collaboration" in a Skagway gallery.

In addition to the market for raw materials is the market for a wide variety of old tools and worked pieces of ivory, sold as individual artifacts. Small worked pieces may be sold as souvenir fragments pasted on index cards, others as framed groupings marketed as "St. Lawrence Island artifact boards." The ubiquitous presence of cases full of "St. Lawrence Island" artifacts and objects fashioned from archaeological ivory and bone in gift shops all across Alaska gives tourists the idea that buying and selling artifacts is not just acceptable, it's part of the Alaskan tourist experience. Advertised romantically as "expressions from long lost millennia found in the frozen earth of ancient villages," their age, patina, and the overt association with remote, "authentic" Eskimo culture create the sense that one is purchasing a piece of a prehistoric past *and* at the same time supporting animal rights since "no animals were killed to make this piece."

At the high end are artifacts that have entered the domain of art objects or antiquities. These include decorated Old Bering Sea, Okvik, and Punuk animal and anthropomorphic figurines that fetch high prices in galleries, at auction houses and from art collectors the world over. The highest price paid so far at public auction for one of these was $122,000 for an Okvik figurine at Christie's in 1995, but private collectors will pay even more to a dealer to have "first pick" of newly excavated ("virgin") pieces, which have not yet been "seen" or "walked around" in public at an auction. Dealers at this level create demand by advertising in special interest magazines, placing artifacts in galleries, exhibits and auctions, grooming wealthy collectors, and extolling the unique or "shamanic" qualities of their products—their elegance, mystique, and possible connections with the spirit world; their combination of ancient and modern aesthetics. "The price of these pieces is as much as someone is willing to pay," one art dealer admitted.

Back on the island, local diggers set their own prices, and dealers, who travel to the island during the late summer digging season, are free to accept or reject them. Prices of raw ivory, bone and small objects are fairly standardized, but the prices diggers ask for the finer artifacts are over-inflated, well beyond what any collector or dealer is likely to pay. In some cases, negotiations over a piece continue for years. It's estimated that sales of archaeological materials on St. Lawrence Island amount to over a million dollars annually.

Besides the obvious economic impact, it's critical to understand the historical, social, and political contexts of this unique and controversial market if archaeology is to have a future on St. Lawrence Island. People first came to St. Lawrence Island, long known in Siberia as "the land of plenty," to take advantage of the tremendous migrations of marine mammals that funnel through the strait. We know from the archaeological record that hunting, gathering, recycling, and reuse of any available resources—from the wood, bone and hides used in house construction to the re-working of broken tools—were, and continue to be, important facets of daily life. The Bering Strait was a highway for intercontinental trade long before recorded history. The importance of trade in developing and maintaining relationships with "outsiders" is still significant today.

Early accounts of European explorers and whalers in the Bering Strait indicate they traded extensively with local residents for basic needs such as food and clothing. Many collected "rare and curious specimens" of Native life, or surreptitiously took skulls from graves for "scientific" study in Europe's burgeoning museums or out of curiosity and adventurism. Traders in search of walrus ivory, whale baleen, and oil soon followed the whalers, and with them came diseases, alcohol, and firearms. Long-buried un-worked ivory, usually found cached in former dwelling sites, always commanded a higher price than new, white tusks and, because of this, it came with a "caveat emptor." Stories exist of Natives burying or urinating on white ivory to make it look old. One trader recounted how, on a trip to Siberia, he had purchased a stunning "black" walrus tusk at the request of a Nome curio dealer, only to find the sellers had buried a new white tusk in the bottom of a lake until minerals blackened the ivory. The color lasted only a few days on exposure to the air.

Cutlery handles made from old ivory were manufactured in San Francisco by the 1870s. Much of the early trade in curios, which flourished during the Gold Rush, focused on ethnographic objects or things made from new, white ivory, such as cribbage boards, engraved pipes, ivory carvings, and jewelry specifically for the souvenir market. But by 1889, whalers, traders, and field collectors were rifling burials for "relics" during their voyages along the Siberian and Alaskan coasts. And the minute someone was willing to pay or trade for these items, there were local people willing to dig them up. Daniel Neuman, a doctor in Nome during the Gold Rush, amassed one of the largest private collections from the region. The following story comes from a collection of oral histories in Orma Long's 1978 book, *Eskimo Legends and Other Stories of Alaska*:

> Dr. Neuman knew that there were Eskimo and Indian villages buried in the Arc-
> tic, so he went up to see if he could find them. An old Eskimo woman who had
> sore eyes told him if he cured her eyes she'd tell him where they were buried. He
> said that he never worked harder on any case, and he effected a cure. He dug up
> the villages and found a wealth of treasures.

In the early twentieth century, museum-sponsored field collectors turned to gathering antiquities, both because there were by now so few "pure" household ob-jects to be had and because there was growing interest in these "scientific specimens" as windows to the puzzle of human origins. The global market for baleen (used in hoop skirts and buggy whips) had just crashed, leaving Bering Strait villagers in need of a different local resource they could use as a commodity to acquire store goods. In 1912, Vilhjalmur Stefansson sledded into Barrow and offered to buy whatever ar-chaeological specimens local diggers could find for the American Museum of Nat-ural History, paying them $0.10 to $1.00 in the form of credit at the local trading post. Stefansson left at the end of the summer with 20,000 specimens, but—as trader Charles Brower noted in his 1994 autobiography *Fifty Years Below Zero*—his en-thusiasm lingered, inciting digging in many of the old sites around Barrow. Over the next few years as the number of field collectors wanting to buy excavated materials increased, so did the digging. When William Van Valin started collecting for the University of Pennsylvania in northwestern Alaska in 1916, the competition was fierce, as he wrote in the 1944 book *Eskimoland Speaks*: "It looked as though I would have to dig my own antiquities because my rivals had already engaged all the natives available for that kind of work. But as I felt that there would always be antiquities to be found, if I put forth the effort, I was not greatly discouraged."

Archaeological interest in Bering Strait prehistory really took off when, in 1926, Diamond Jenness acquired several highly decorated artifacts during his field research on Little Diomede Island. That same summer Aleš Hrdlička bought several specimens from local diggers during stops on St. Lawrence Island, Little Diomede, and at Point Hope while he was traveling aboard a Coast Guard cutter. After Hrdlička returned to the Smithsonian, *Science Newsletter* published an article in January 1930 sensationalizing the discovery of an "Ivory Age" in the Bering Strait, contemporaneous with the great Mayan civilizations of South America. The St. Lawrence Island artifacts were called mysterious wonders, evidence of an ancient civilization, a "high fossil ivory culture" in the Far North, "one of the richest and finest stone age cultures yet discovered in the world." The following year institutionally sponsored archaeological excavations commenced on St. Lawrence Island.

Memories of how these early digs were conducted and how people were treated by archaeologists are still vivid among local people. At the time it was common practice for archaeologists to buy artifacts without much concern for context. Otto Geist, who excavated on the island over a ten-year period, told people in Gambell that he would "buy all the perfect specimens they unearthed," but soon realized that this made it impossible to keep track of what was coming out of the ground. From his first year of excavation in 1927, Geist sent around three tons of materials back to the Alaska College in Fairbanks, including over 7,000 archaeological specimens. Very few local men were willing to work with archaeologists if human remains were involved, and those that did demanded higher and higher prices for their time and the artifacts they found.

In 1937, after passage of the Indian Arts and Craft Act (1935), the Bureau of Indian Affairs created the Alaska Native Arts and Crafts Clearinghouse (ANAC) and required teachers in each village to act as their dealers for Native-made crafts ranging from jewelry and buttons to animal figurines and office supplies. This government program also encouraged the mining of old ivory to use as a carving material. In 1939, when archaeologist Froelich Rainey arrived on St. Lawrence Island with plans to excavate on the Punuk Islands off the southeastern coast, the source of the rare Okvik-style materials, he found that local diggers had decided to save him the trouble and had already "taken care" of most of the site. They were eager to sell him artifacts, at least whatever they hadn't already sold to the Coast Guard.

For several years beginning in 1941, ANAC actually promoted sales of artifacts, featuring objects excavated at Point Hope in their catalogs. With the onset of World War II, ANAC lost its monopoly to military personnel stationed in the Arctic who were willing to pay higher prices for crafts and artifacts. Digging for artifacts was also a favorite pastime on military outposts throughout Alaska. For villagers, during and after the war, it was a way to obtain ivory, for carving when other supplies ran out, or artifacts that could be traded for food, hunting supplies, and other necessities.

Until the early 1970s, teachers, construction workers, and government officials were the main patrons of local diggers, and prices remained stable. Locals remember stories of large Okvik "dolls" being sawed up and made into ashtrays,
then sold to Japanese fishermen. But things changed radically in the early 1970s,
soon after St. Lawrence Island became private land. Meanwhile, the praises of archaeologists had secured a place in the history of world art for Bering Strait
ivories, and examples began to show up in the collections of a few "primitive" art
connoisseurs. In 1973, the National Gallery of Art held an exhibition, "The Far
North," and Bering Strait ivories suddenly became valued as fine art objects, examples of the primitivism that inspired modern masters like Brancusi, Modigliani,
and Henry Moore. The catalogue called Alaska "one of the major world centers
of primitive art" and granted Okvik- and Old Bering Sea-style ivories a primor-
dial role in the history of North American art. One art dealer explained to me
how, from his perspective, such art value is created:

> Once people had a chance to visually see prehistoric ivory material in "The Far
> North" exhibit in 1973, it really stimulated a taste among fine art collectors for
> this kind of archaeological material. Before that people didn't really even know
> this great stuff existed. . . . The groundwork first has to be laid by seeing these
> things at auctions and in [trade] shows or ads, then once there's an emerging in-
> terest, museums will bring their artifacts out of the basement and show them to
> people.

As the desirability and art value of the artifacts increased, so did their prices.
A digger who would have sold a figurine for $10 in the 1950s might approach a
museum asking $250 for the same object in the early 1970s. By the end of that
decade, a digger might see $50,000 for the object from a dealer coming to the is-
land to buy for clients in over 21 countries, primarily galleries and collectors with
interests in African, Oceanic, or other "tribal" arts.

The rise in the economic and artistic valuing of Bering Strait artifacts paral-
lels the rise in concern among archaeologists over the connections between commercialization of antiquities and site destruction, not just in North America, but
all over the world. Except in connection with the monitoring of water and sewer
projects, no systematic archaeological excavations have occurred on St. Lawrence
Island since Hans-Georg Bandi's work in the mid-1970s. In 1984, Aron Crowell
conducted a survey of sites and site destruction on St. Lawrence Island, as a joint
project of the Smithsonian and the Sivuqaq Native Corporation, with the aim of
identifying sites that still had archaeological significance and integrity that could
perhaps be made off limits to commercial digging. No such actions were taken after the survey, and locals sometimes refer to the report as the "digger's guide." In
1986, when the American Federation of Art opened its exhibit, "Ancient Eskimo

Ivories of the Bering Strait," unlike a decade earlier, it met with criticism from the archaeological community. By 1987, the Anchorage Museum of History and Art stopped purchasing artifacts "off the street" from diggers, and today even the donation of an old ivory piece requires special consideration by the museum's board before it can be accepted.

A number of political positions and government policies help sustain the market for St. Lawrence Island antiquities. The fact that under current U.S. law, the market is a legal enterprise, is a rarity in the antiquities market. Unless an importing country regulates the walrus ivory or marine mammal bone under the aegis of an endangered species (e.g., under the Convention on International Trade in Endangered Species [CITES]), there are no restrictions on trade in artifacts from St. Lawrence Island. The Marine Mammal Protection Act (MMPA), in aiming to protect our marine mammal population, has inadvertently increased the demand for ancient ivories. The act allows only Alaska Natives to make arts and crafts using ivory or other marine mammal products harvested since its passage in 1972, but materials older than that can be sold to and worked by non-Natives. The MMPA has thus contributed to a steady demand for the *older* raw materials, found in archaeological sites. Market pressures have also increased due to the global ban on elephant ivory, as makers of musical instruments, knives, and other custom crafts and inlays turn to "St. Lawrence Island fossil walrus" as one of the few remaining legal sources of this exotic substance.

As landowners, the Native Corporations have the power to make policies concerning land use. Some Native corporations have successfully restricted digging at specific archaeological sites, but the policies and positions of the two Native corporations on St. Lawrence Island currently support commercial digging. Digging is restricted to stockholders, and some say that the right to dig for artifacts replaces the dividends that the two Native corporations can't afford to distribute. Although the results of digging are in essence a common property resource, the current policy is one of "finder's keepers."

St. Lawrence Islanders are known as staunchly independent-minded, even among the larger Alaska Native community. All offers from outside entities to lease, mine, or develop natural resources on the island have been rejected, an indication of the strong determination to retain local control over land and resources. The right to dig and sell artifacts is, in a very real sense, an expression of Native sovereignty.

Today, "subsistence digging" is an integral part of the local economy and can even be considered part of the heritage of St. Lawrence Islanders. Artifact sales often help individuals and households meet basic subsistence needs—paying bills, buying boats, guns, four wheelers, ammunition, gas, and clothing—or sometimes a luxury like a computer or a washing machine in a remote community where un-

employment and basic living expenses are extremely high and few other local resources are so readily converted to cash. In a village where massive dependency on
government subsidies and grants for goods and services is viewed as distressing but
necessary and federal agencies attempt to regulate hunting and fishing, the artifact
market is one arena neither controlled by nor dependent on anything other than
individual enterprise and market demand. Digging for artifacts is also an ingrained
part of the social fabric on St. Lawrence Island. Older diggers are regarded as
knowledgeable professionals and community historians. Finding and selling a
valuable artifact confers status and prestige. Young people are anxious to make
their first important sale. Families think of digging as a recreational or seasonal
subsistence activity, much like berry picking. Teenagers in the village, watching the
world from 58 channels of satellite TV in Air Jordan sneakers and Raiders jack-
ets, find it hard to believe that people on the "outside" know or care much about
them on their remote island, but they are aware that buyers want their artifacts.
Third grade primers depict children going out to dig; obituaries remark how "She
loved to dig for artifacts." When asked about digging, villagers often reply that
"our ancestors left us these things so we could survive in a cash economy."

Yet concern over the loss of this nonrenewable cultural property is far from
absent. Local residents hold a range of sometimes conflicting opinions about digging and selling artifacts. Once a young woman brought a newly-found artifact to
show me, an ivory animal worth thousands of dollars on the market. "I know I
shouldn't sell this, Julie," she said, "but it will help pay for my college education."
Another day in Gambell a female elder waved at my window. "You see all those
diggings out there? That's what made all the problems in our village, when people
started doing that for money." There is a sense of remorse that ancestral objects
end up far away in unknown places and hands. "We have lost so much already. The
people are gone who remember these things."

In 1989, the National Historic Landmark status of the five old village sites in
Gambell was removed by the Park Service's enforcement archaeologist. No one
seemed to care much, especially since Historic Landmark status was interfering
with plans to locate the new school. However, a lot of press about local digging
practices ensued, and St. Lawrence Islanders became known as the people who were
"cannibalizing their own heritage." But selling artifacts does not necessarily equate
to selling one's heritage. Could it be that the Euro-American notion that venerates
objects of material culture, kept under glass or in a museum as "heritage," is somewhat inappropriate for people whose heritage is performed and experienced in daily
practices like speaking their own language, whaling, eating Native foods, and
drum-dancing *sans* tourists, and whose elders are the real cultural treasures? This
may be changing in the wake of Native American Graves Protection and Repatriation Act (NAGPRA) repatriations and the new forms of symbolic power this

process accords to objects of material culture. Several institutions have returned human remains and artifacts to the St. Lawrence Islanders under the NAGPRA. The human remains have been reburied on the island, and though many people would like to see a safe place in the community where the artifacts could come home, these are, for now, prudently kept in a museum on the mainland. The two council members I was told to talk to about plans for a community museum were both "out digging" when I called.

A few years ago, the Village Council of Gambell, with the help of Susie Silook, a gifted ivory carver and writer whose grandfather worked beside the archaeologists Geist and Collins, received grants to study the feasibility of starting a business to handle archaeological materials that would provide more local control over how these goods left St. Lawrence Island. I was asked to share my research findings and knowledge of the market with the business consultants hired to conduct the studies. This presented what was, for me, an ethical dilemma, knowing that information I provided would likely be used to improve artifact sales. In the end, I relied on my belief that the more information community members had, the better decisions they would be able to make about the future of the gifts their ancestors had left them.

In August, 1999, the final proposal was presented to the shareholders of the two Native Corporations, who committed their support and monetary resources to the plan. The business now distributes and markets old ivory and bone (but, so far, not artifacts), purchasing from local residents and selling directly to artisans and collectors. The goal is to eliminate the middlemen, stabilize prices, and run a successful, profitable business. "Okvik," as the business is called, plans to provide certificates of authenticity, sell materials on the Internet, and possibly manufacture replicas. Long-term goals include training local people in archaeological methods and techniques, scientific study and preservation of sites, and development of a world-class museum. This solution addresses present local concerns and has the potential to benefit the archaeological record in the long run. It remains to be seen, however, whether such a business can return as much to local diggers as they have received through direct sales to dealers, and whether "Okvik" can develop strategies that successfully circumvent dealers to reach their buyers.

Current ethics in archaeology oppose any activities that stimulate undocumented excavation or commercialization of archaeological materials. In the process of subsistence digging, most of the archaeological value of artifacts and sites is disregarded and destroyed. Many archaeologists think the subsistence digging constitutes an irretrievable loss of knowledge about a very important area of the world, and have been, understandably, opposed to the activity. But if local people are forced to make a choice between allowing artifacts to be sold and doing scientific archaeology, there is no question that the former will prevail.

The question becomes how to balance and integrate longstanding and vital economic interests with emerging cultural heritage interests. Studies in conservation and development have found that if resource conservation efforts are to succeed, indigenous communities must develop viable economic alternatives and practices that also meet demands of the cash economy. And archaeologists the world over are learning the importance of community-based development and local decision-making for archaeological site protection. Several positive examples of alternative forms of collaboration exist in the Bering Strait region today. A project directed by Roger Harritt (University of Alaska-Anchorage) has spent five seasons excavating sites in the Native Village of Wales, situated on the Alaskan mainland at the narrowest point of the Bering Strait. Here, scientific excavation cautiously coexists with commercial digging within guidelines set by the Wales Native Corporation and negotiated by the project director. Another project, initiated after a NAGPRA repatriation stimulated community interest in archaeology, has been directed not by archaeologists, but by the Chignik Native Corporation of Golovin, Alaska, about 100 miles east of Nome. The Corporation hired the archaeologists and staff it wanted for the job and with them designed and implemented project goals and objectives, which included summer employment for local youth, and now plans to develop an exchange program with Russian youth.

As for the prospect of doing archaeology on St. Lawrence Island, it can either wait for the artifact market to collapse—surely a *long* wait—or archaeologists will need to compromise and work with local authorities to negotiate terms of stewardship and research that benefit both the community and the archaeological record.

Discussion Questions

1. Hollowell documents that it was a particular set of museum special exhibits of Arctic art, and their catalogues, that suddenly created a demand for Arctic artifacts among collectors of fine art and spurred on the local diggers. Explore whether other exhibits have had a similar effect for other categories of ancient art. Are there any special exhibits going on now that could have a similar effect? Do museums have a responsibility to consider such effects of their exhibits?

2. Collectors and legal scholars—such as John Henry Merryman—have long argued that establishing a legal basis for the international trade in antiquities would stop the destruction of sites to meet the demands of an illicit market (see Merryman 2000). The market for St. Lawrence Island artifacts is currently one of the few, perhaps the only, entirely legal

market in antiquities in the world. What does it teach us about the arguments in favor of legalizing the trade elsewhere?

3. The author notes that the report of an archaeological survey aimed at identifying and preserving sites on St. Lawrence is now known locally as "the digger's guide." The 1954 Hague Convention calls for an inventory of monuments that should be granted special protection during wartime in each participating country; critics have suggested that, like the St. Lawrence report, such inventories would merely serve as handy guides for enemies bent on destroying cultural monuments in, e.g., a campaign of ethnic cleansing. Can archaeologists control the ways in which their publications are used? Should some archaeological information be kept out of the public domain?

4. Do you agree with the author's decision to share her research and knowledge about the art market with Islanders who were considering how and whether to start up their own business to market their artifacts?

5. Artifacts from the Arctic have been portrayed as "timeless," imbued with a sense of mystery that attracts collectors thrilled by owning an object "never seen before." Discuss how this portrayal removes any sense of context, history, and indigenous meanings from these objects. Do museums and dealers have a responsibility to portray objects as they were valued and perceived by their makers and original owners?

6. Imagine (if you can) yourself in the shoes of the young St. Lawrence Islander who found a lovely animal figure and told Julie, "I know I shouldn't sell this, but it will help pay for my college education." How would you reach and defend your decision?

7. Discuss whether or not the suggestion that, if archaeologists ever want to dig on St. Lawrence Island again, they will have to negotiate terms with the Native people, threatens the integrity of the scientific process.

8. If the Native Corporation on St. Lawrence Island decides to set aside a place for scientific excavation, should archaeologists walk away or work with local authorities to negotiate terms of stewardship and research that benefit the community, scholars, and the archaeological record?

Note

This research was funded by the National Science Foundation's Office of Polar Programs Arctic Social Sciences Program, the David C. Skomp Fund of Indiana University's Department of Anthropology, the Arctic Institute of North America, and the Phillips Fund for Native American Research of the American Philosophical Society.

Further Readings

Hollowell-Zimmer, Julie. 2003. Digging in the Dirt—Ethics and "Low-End Looting." In *Ethical Issues in Archaeology*, edited by Larry J. Zimmerman, Karen D. Vitelli, and Julie Hollowell-Zimmer, pp. 45–56. Walnut Creek, CA: AltaMira Press.

Merryman, John Henry. 2000. A Licit International Trade in Cultural Objects. In *Thinking about the Elgin Marbles: Critical Essays on Cultural Property, Art and Law*, edited by John Henry Merryman, pp. 176–226. Cambridge: Kluwer Law International.

Scott, Stuart. 1994. St. Lawrence: Archaeology of a Bering Sea Island. *Archaeology* 37(1): 1, 46–52.

Staley, David P. 1993. St. Lawrence Island's Subsistence Diggers: A New Perspective on Human Effects on Archaeological Sites. *Journal of Field Archaeology* 20(3):347–355.

The Rape of Mali

15

MICHEL BRENT

In this case study, Brent covers the wide range of issues related to looting and the antiquities market. The pillaging of Mali's past by peasant looters serving local dealers, and ultimately wealthy European collectors, is seemingly out of control. Among the world's poorest countries, Mali has few means to enforce antiquities laws. Dealers organize teams of farmers that work as much as 24 hours a day, digging for antiquities. In return, the ex-farmers receive food and the chance to earn up to 20 times their annual pay as farmers with a single find, while their fields remain unfarmed and the agricultural economy suffers. Dealers, museum curators and trustees, conservators, forgers, graduate students, analytical laboratories, and others, are implicated in the massive destruction of one of Africa's great archaeological cultures.

EUROPEAN DEALERS AND COLLECTORS HAVE SYSTEMATICALLY plundered the heritage of one of the world's poorest countries. "You absolutely must take this message to our friends in Europe and America: If we catch them in the act, we will make sacrifices and offerings with the blood of those who still come to steal our fetishes. And even if the officials in Bamako come to question us, I assure you that they will find no proof, not the least trace, and they will have to return to Bamako empty-handed." Sitting in a hut in the company of two other patriarchs, Barassor Mariko, the guardian of a sanctuary in the village of Denie Koro, spoke again and again of the disaster that had befallen his Bambara people. Four of the most important fetishes had been stolen from his village in less than ten years and the life of the village had been severely disrupted. Townspeople had become lazy, births had declined, and the harvests had been poor. To make matters worse, religious sacrifices could no longer be performed. "Do you realize," said the old man, "that by stealing our fetishes those impious ones have stolen our very gods? These fetishes have been at Denie Koro since the very beginning of the village several hundred years ago. When you tell me that the gods they stole from us are probably in the house of a man who does not even know our religion, I am deeply hurt. To us, this is a crime."

The government of Mali also considers it a crime, but can do little about it. The pillaging of the country's past by peasant looters serving local dealers, and ultimately wealthy European collectors, is today out of control. Not since the wholesale rape of Egypt's archaeological treasures in the first half of the nineteenth century has a country been so methodically stripped of its national heritage. Unlike most African countries, Mali is a source of both finely crafted ethnographic objects such as masks and fetishes, and artifacts such as bronze sculptures and terra-cotta statues. The latter are believed to represent the spirits of people who flourished here for some 2,000 years. Prized by collectors the world over, they have sold at auction for as much as $275,000. Hundreds of known archaeological sites on Mali's Inland Niger Delta have been looted. Work parties organized by Malian antiquities dealers comb the earth for marketable items. Meanwhile, European dealers crisscross the Malian outback in Land Rovers, their trunks filled with bundles of French francs for the purchase of newly found antiquities.

Mali is one of the world's five poorest countries. Life expectancy here is only 44 years, caloric intake is 30 percent below the minimal requirement, and only ten percent of the population is literate. It is a large country (744,000 square miles), and its borders go largely unpatrolled. Laws prohibiting the export of antiquities were passed in 1985 and 1986, but there is little means to enforce them. Furthermore, only five major art-importing nations—Italy, Argentina, the United States, Canada, and Australia—have implemented the 1970 UNESCO Convention on cultural property, a treaty that sets guidelines for the return of illegally exported artifacts.

How Malian antiquities have been looted and spirited out of the country is a story of the skewed relationship between First and Third World countries and how poverty, bribery, and unbridled acquisitiveness have decimated the archaeological record of one of Africa's great civilizations before even a fraction of it has been studied scientifically.

Fueled by the public's interest in the primitivism of Braque and Picasso, art dealers earlier in this century began encouraging European colonials in Africa to collect tribal art. By the 1970s, trafficking in Malian antiquities had become an extremely lucrative business. One of the world's finest private collections was assembled by the Belgian Count Baudouin de Grunne. Mayor of Wezembeek-Oppem, a suburb of Brussels, de Grunne was introduced to Malian ceramics by a collector friend in the 1960s. The friend traded a few Malian terra-cotta heads for a Batcham mask from Cameroon that the Count had in his collection. De Grunne fell in love with the terra cottas and soon began to acquire similar pieces from

Mali with the help of antiquities dealer friends—Philippe Guimiot and Emile Deletaille in Brussels and Alain de Monbrison in Paris. One Malian antiquities dealer, Boubou Diarra, eventually named one of his sons "Emile" in honor of his profitable business dealings with Deletaille.

Terra-cotta statuettes were dug from the Niger Delta by farmers working in teams, sometimes 24 hours a day. Hired by local antiquities dealers who gave them food and caffeine-laden kola nuts, these peasants raked the earth with *dabas* (hoes), hoping to find a fine piece that would net them a sum equal to ten or 20 times their annual pay as farmers. In the beginning, such clandestine digs were poorly organized. As market demand grew, more and more peasants were diverted from traditional farming, thus destabilizing the local economy. Even modest local dealers began forming their own crews. More than a thousand peasants were soon engaged in looting year-round within a 100-mile radius of Mopti, a town at the confluence of the Niger and Bani rivers.

What left Mali was rarely intact. Broken pieces had to be reassembled by craftsmen in Brussels and Paris. Restorers had to guess which head went with which torso, which foreleg belonged to which horse, which arm would best fit a shoulder. When missing pieces could not be found, restorers simply created them by grinding up stray fragments to make a mortar that would stick to any form— and fool any expert. De Grunne and his dealer friends were so single-minded in their quest, and so refined in their taste, that even today de Grunne's collection of Malian terra cottas is considered the finest in the world.

The venerable appearance of Belgium's Tervuren Museum, which houses a 450,000-piece collection of African art, is belied by its links with the illicit artifact trade. In the 1970s the museum decided to improve its collection of West African art. Its curators had two options—they could buy from antiquities dealers or they could organize scientific excavations in West Africa and collect in the field. Their decision to buy from dealers was prompted by the presence of antiquities dealers like the "Friends of the Museum" committee. Like many European museums, the Tervuren is influenced by organizations like Friends of the Museum, a nonprofit group whose board of directors consists of art collectors, influential people from the world of politics or business, as well as antiquities dealers. Friends of the Museum runs a small gift shop within the Tervuren. In exchange for the right to run the shop, the group is expected to make donations to the museum. A dealer in a position to choose what is to be given to the museum picks an item that is part of a group or series of objects. The rest of the series, for sale in his or her gallery, can then be valued much higher. The fact that one object from the group is on display at a prestigious museum is proof of its high quality. This cozy arrangement has worked for 20-odd years, with the full complicity of the Tervuren's ethnography department. And in a similar arrangement, the department has ensured that the museum takes on loan a number of items belonging to merchant friends, which raises the value of their other pieces.

Museums shouldn't necessarily be lumped with private dealers and collectors. What goes into a museum becomes accessible to the public and is available for research; objects in private collections are often inaccessible. But museums have contributed to the expansion of the trade in illicit artifacts. During my research, I called Sylvia Williams, director of the National Museum of African Art at the Smithsonian Institution. I wanted to check on the museum's 1983 purchase of several African objects from Emile Deletaille. The museum reportedly paid $1.5 million for the objects. Williams was at first extremely guarded, and asked repeatedly why I needed to have this information. Eventually, she admitted that the Smithsonian had bought a "few" items from Deletaille. There is little doubt that the objects purchased by the Smithsonian were exported illegally.

Meanwhile, the looting in Mali goes on, unabated. "Whether it is around the region of Jenne, or the valley of Tilemsi near Gao, at Timbuktu, or in the cliffs of the Bandiagara, to the south in the region of Bougouni, or in the region of Mema," says Téréba Togola, an archaeologist from the Institute of Human Sciences in Bamako, "we hear reports of pillaging from everywhere." Between 1989 and 1991, a team of scientists directed by the Dutch archaeologist Diderik van der Waals surveyed a 125-square-mile area between the Bandiagara plateau and the city of Diafarabé, inventorying plundered sites. Out of 834 catalogued sites, 45 percent had been looted. "On several occasions, we even encountered the looters at work," says van der Waals. "They were either isolated individuals or well organized groups who worked for their own account or were employed by a local merchant." If one of these diggers had not perished, buried in a tunnel that collapsed in February 1990, the authorities in Bamako may never have known about the looting of a site about an hour by foot from the village of Thial. "I tried to count the pillage holes," says Mamadi Dembélé, the chief archaeologist on a government team sent to investigate the site three months later, "but I had to rapidly abandon that because there were so many. These holes were spread out over many acres. It was a real carnage! The state of the site suggested that these digs had begun at least two months before the accident happened, and that many ceramic objects had been removed. Of course, the digs had stopped. But to see the remains of the campfires on these sites, one could only conclude that, among the 200 looters who had been digging there, many had probably been permanently camping on the site." Instead of being transported to the storage rooms of the National Museum in Bamako, many statuettes found during the investigation at Thial were stored in Mopti, then sold by corrupt officials to an art gallery in Paris three months later.

It is not only ceramics and other archaeological pieces that leave Mali clandestinely. Ethnographic objects such as fetishes, sculptures, the canes of ancestors, amulets, and ritual jewelry have for years been the prey of antiquities dealers. And they are still being smuggled out of the country, despite the fact that, according to specialists in ethnographic art, "good pieces" are becoming increasingly rare. In the Dogon region along the Niger River the thefts have reached such proportions that exasperated village people have even mutilated or destroyed their own sculptures to discourage thieves from sacking the villages. "Where we live, we are always on the alert. In many villages, such as Kerigamana, Tireli, Dono Sogu, or Komboro Pei, to name only a few, the people have destroyed their Toguna bas-reliefs," says Apomi Saye, a Dogon who lives in the village of Tireli. Toguna are carved wood pillars, much appreciated by collectors, that support the straw roofs of meeting halls used by the men. "They are sick of the youths who come to steal them to sell in Mopti where they find antique dealers who receive stolen goods and will give them two or three hundred dollars for our works of art," he says. "There are also the famous Dogon doors that everyone in the West knows of. These no longer, alas, decorate the houses of our villages for the good and simple reason that they have all been sold, stolen, or taken away by the dealers. Do you ever ask the question, you who live in the West, if the important collection of Dogon objects at The Metropolitan Museum in New York, for example, has all its export licenses in good order?"

No government money is currently earmarked for the fight against looting. The paltry salaries of ministers contribute to corruption, which exists at every level of authority. In 1992, Eric Huysecom, an archaeologist at the University of Geneva, was on a mission to Mali accompanied by a Malian colleague from the Institute of Human Sciences at Bamako. In a stopover at Sofara, a town 35 miles southwest of Mopti, they found illegally excavated ceramics for sale in the local market. "After we notified the director of the Institute," said Huysecom, "we decided to ask the authorities in Mopti, the Regional Department of Youth, Sports, Art, and Culture that also administers Sofara, to intervene. We wanted to wait until the following Tuesday, the day of the weekly market, to do so. One week later, not one ceramic was for sale in the market of Sofara, and an employee of the Regional Department who was supposed to have joined us, arrived at our rendezvous six hours late on a motor scooter. Who had warned the local merchants?"

Important merchants like Bonbon Diarra of Sevaré, or Youssouf Cissé of Mopti have for years exported authentic pieces in great quantities without the least trouble. They have accomplished this with the complicity of various public and private organizations in Bamako. Gifts have been showered on the directors of airline companies and local customs officials, many of whom are unable to differentiate between tourist curios and genuine artifacts. Furthermore, Malian antiquities dealers have a very articulate spokesman and advocate in Mamadou Kaba Diane, a man of great learning and one of many highly sophisticated "facilitators" who know how to defend the profession and use political influence to maintain the status quo.

Once artifacts leave Mali, it is hard to get them back. On November 27, 1991, a cargo of art objects from Bamako was seized by American customs authorities in New Orleans. Examination of the cargo by a specialist revealed that it consisted of eighteenth-century artifacts of great value, and that the shipment violated Mali's 1985 law forbidding the exportation of antiquities. The personalities in this transaction were well known. The exporter was Samba Kamissoko, a Malian antiquities dealer from Bamako who had been imprisoned for a year for illegal trafficking in art objects. The shipment was addressed to Charles Davis, the owner of the Davis Gallery of New Orleans, an important commercial gallery selling ethnographic art in the United States. I obtained documents detailing the pieces in the cargo and their price tags. The shipment (by air freight) contained 22 door locks valued at $85 each, five canes at $680 each, three Bambara doors at $1,300 each, a Dogon door valued at $5,000, a puppet valued at $40,000, two masks at $2,500 each, and a Bambara figure in iron valued at $8,300. The invoice totaled $67,000. Two months after the objects were seized, Clark W. Settles, the customs officer assigned to the case, notified Malian ambassador Mohammed Alhousseyni Toure that the pieces could not remain under seizure much longer and that, if measures were not taken rapidly by Mali to recoup these objects, they would be handed over to the Davis Gallery. Settles pointed out that no crime had been committed under American law. The ambassador appealed to Malian authorities to expedite the return, but nothing happened. Since legal action was too costly, no effort was made to reclaim the cargo. A few weeks later, Charles Davis took possession of the shipment. In September 1993 the United States enacted an emergency import ban on Malian antiquities. The action, requested by Mali, was taken under the terms of the UNESCO Convention. Since then, direct shipments to the United States have ceased. More circuitous routes through Europe are now being utilized.

European antiquities dealers have various sources of supply. Some still buy directly from African dealers, but this practice seems to be less widespread now than it was ten or 15 years ago. I was told by dealers in Germany, France, and Belgium that 20 percent of their purchases are through public auctions, 20 percent in the countries of origin, 10 percent from private African citizens who bring objects to Europe, 10 percent from fellow dealers, and 40 percent from former colonials. Diplomatic pouches are also suspected of being used to transport objects. An archaeologist, who asked to remain nameless, told me: "You only need walk around the more affluent neighborhoods of African cities to perceive the extent of the traffic that goes on."

A recent trend in Europe resulting from the illicit trade involves students, and is giving archaeologists serious cause for concern. Antiquities dealers know very well that most students of art history and archaeology want to work in the field. They also know that there are few scholarships and that most parents are hard pressed to finance a stay of a few months in the bush. Traders have therefore taken on the guise of patrons, sometimes through pseudo-cultural foundations created to finance fieldwork. But the grants come with strings attached: the donor either asks to be rewarded in objects, or with photographs and information about sites where it still is possible to find objects. When I asked a few such students if they didn't fear the possibility of being corrupted, they told me, matter-of-factly, that the illegal aspect of the trade was not their problem.

Another trend involves traders who behave as if they were scholars of art. They write articles and publish magazines and books about ethnic groups or about a given aspect of African art. If a spate of books or articles suddenly appears about, say, the art of Tanzania, it is sometimes because traders have just found a new source of objects in that country, and publication is the best way of advertising their wares and inflating their value.

In the antiquities business, dated and authenticated pieces are worth considerably more than those without pedigrees. Until a few years ago, the Oxford University Research Laboratory for Archaeology and the History of Art performed thermoluminescence tests on ceramics from Mali, dating and authenticating them. While making a film in 1990, dealing with the traffic of ceramics between Mali and Europe, the Dutch anthropologist Wouter Van Beek asked Michael Tite, director of the lab, why he was authenticating Malian artifacts in view of the country's looting problem. Tite replied that the authenticating business paid for scholarly work, and that if the Oxford lab did not do the work, someone else would. Since then, Tite has said he never had the slightest suspicion that the objects were being smuggled out of Africa and has ceased dating objects originating from West Africa. He also categorically refuses to be interviewed.

The Oxford lab authenticated the majority of pieces in the de Grunne collection, which was recently sold to the Dapper Foundation in Paris for some $10 million. The Foundation, actually the private collection of French millionaire businessman Michel Leveau, has in recent years spent some $25 million for African art, including the de Grunne collection. De Grunne paid between $15,000 and $150,000 for each of the 50 pieces in his collection. It is estimated that he realized at least $4 million in profit from the sale. On July 12, 1990, before the pieces left Brussels, Mali's Minister of Culture, Bakary Traore, sent a letter to de Grunne informing him that Mali was interested in bidding for its purchase and requesting a catalog. Since negotiations were already under way with the Foundation, de Grunne's secretary politely turned down the Malians, writing that the Count was on vacation in another country and that he would answer them on his return. De Grunne never responded, and the Foundation purchased the objects. It has asked scholars such as Samuel Sidibe, director of Mali's National Museum, to assist in assembling an exhibition of Malian ceramics, all of which were most likely illegally exported from his own country. Sidibe, needless to say, has refused to cooperate. In the meantime, the collection appears to be off-limits to scholars, despite the Foundation's statements to the contrary. Jacqueline Evrard, who in 1977 was the first art historian to study de Grunne's ceramics, wrote to the Foundation requesting to view the collection again in the company of a few interested friends. She never received a response. And an ethnology student at the University of Sapienza in Rome was categorically refused permission to view the collection.

The European community must address several questions concerning the trade in African art. Why, for instance, of the 78 countries that signed the UNESCO Convention, have only the poorest European countries or those experiencing the most looting—Italy, Greece, Spain, and Portugal—ratified it? The exportation of works of art may be forbidden in Africa, but their importation into Europe is not. In Belgium, for example, possession of a stolen object can be redressed by law only if a complaint is lodged within three years of the date of the theft. As a result, my country has become a hub of the illicit trade not only in African objects, but in antiquities from around the world. Legislation would perhaps not halt the traffic, but would no doubt do much toward diminishing it.

Blame for the current state of affairs is difficult to assign; not all of the players in the illicit trade fit easily into "white hat-black hat" categories. After all, is there a strong ethical reason for preventing an African family, or ethnic group, from selling things that are their own property if they wish to do so? Should we feel indignant that museums go on buying objects without proper export authorizations, or should we be thankful that these objects do not end up hidden away in private collections or bank vaults? How should we define a cultural heritage, a patrimony, and to what extent? Should it include every small object from the past?

One thing is certain: Rich and powerful Europeans have focused their attention on African art and intend to possess it. They are buying the history of Mali.

Discussion Questions

1. Interest in the "primitivism" of modern art is said to have fueled the illicit traffic in African tribal art. Compare the situation with that described by Hollowell in Chapter 14. Are there new trends in art fashion that could have a similar effect on archaeological sites and materials?

2. What repercussions on the local economy and social organization follow from local participation in the illicit antiquities market? Do these suggest

ways that efforts to combat looting and save the heritage might be redirected and made more effective?

3. What are the chances of detecting fakes made from ground-up stray fragments of original materials? What difference does it make whether such fakes are detected or not?

4. To what extent do (or should) dealers play an advisory role for museum acquisition committees? (Ask your local museum.)

5. What is the nature of the relationship between museums and dealers? How do museums learn about what is on the market and where it has come from?

6. The Metropolitan Museum in New York City and the Smithsonian's National Museum of African Art are cited as among the museums in the United States that include illegally exported materials from Mali in their collections. Would anything be gained by calling for a return of those materials to Mali? Does the fact that no U.S. law was broken (since the acquisitions predate invocation of the UNESCO emergency clause)[1] in acquiring the pieces mean there is no obligation to do anything about their presence in U.S. museums?

7. How do museums contribute to increasing the value of objects on the market and in private collections? Is it in their own best interest for museums to do this?

8. Whose responsibility is it to determine whether ethnographic objects, offered for sale, are significant religious items needed for current practices?

9. If U.S. Customs officers do not recognize Malian antiquities unless they are coming directly from Mali, and diplomatic pouches (exempt from Customs inspections) are used by government officials to remove art works illegally, it would seem that U.S. government personnel are poorly educated on the values of cultural property. What training in this area do U.S. government officials and representatives receive? Are there opportunities here for archaeologists?

10. How would you respond if you discovered that a grant you received (and badly needed) for field research was funded by a dealer-patron who expected, in exchange, information about sites and available art works?

11. Have you seen any "scholarly" articles written by dealers? If legitimate archaeological publications can stimulate, unwittingly, market demand for antiquities, are archaeologists in a position to criticize dealers for doing the smae thing, if intentionally?

12. If you could have radiocarbon dating and other analytical work on materials from your field projects done free of charge by your university research labs because they make money by charging dealers for authentication work, would you support the lab's policy?[2] (Think of other comparable arrangements that affect archaeological work.)

13. Should African families, or members of any ethnic group, be forbidden to sell their own heritage if they choose to? How is the Malian case different from that of the St. Lawrence Islanders described by Hollowell in Chapter 14?

Notes

1. For a discussion of the imposition of an emergency ban on Malian imports under the Cultural Property Implementation Act, see Katherine Biers, "Mali Import Restrictions," *Archaeology* (January/February 1994): 20.

2. For the new policy on authenticating unprovenienced materials of the Oxford University Research Laboratory for Archaeology and Art History, see R. R. Inskeep, "Making an Honest Man of Oxford: Good News for Mali," *Antiquity* 66 (1992):114.

Further Readings

A good film to view is *The African King* (1990) distributed by Pilgrim Pictures, Ltd., London.

Biers, Katherine. 1994. Mali Import Restrictions. *Archaeology* 47(1):20.

Inskeep, R. R. 1992. Making an Honest Man of Oxford: Good News for Mali. *Antiquity* 66:114.

Lekson, Stephen. 1997. Museums and the Market: Exploring Santa Fe. *Nonrenewable Resources* 6(2):99–109.

McIntosh, Roderick J., Boubacar Hama Diaby, and Téréba Togola. 1997. Mali's Many Shields of Its Past. *Nonrenewable Resources* 6(2):111–129.

Schmidt, P. R. and Roderick J. McIntosh, editors. 1996. *Plundering Africa's Past*. Bloomington, Indiana: Indiana University Press.

Udvardy, Monica, Linda L. Giles, and John B. Mitsanze. 2003. The Transatlantic Trade in African Ancestors: Mijikenda Memorial Statues (Vigango) and the Ethics of Collecting and Curating Non-Western Cultural Property. *American Anthropologist* 105(3):566–580.

Archaeotourism

16

MICHAEL BAWAYA

Archaeologists and government officials have recently become more engaged in actively developing sites to encourage international tourism. In this chapter, Bawaya presents an example of development for "archaeotourism" in Belize, a small country in Central America with a rich Mayan past. Tourism is a complicated business, and Bawaya explores the role of archaeologists in caring for the well-being of sites, altering local social structures, and seeking to improve national economies.

IT's A LONG, SLOW DRIVE TO CARACOL. A badly rutted, punishing dirt road takes visitors to this place deep in the lush jungle of southwestern Belize. As she has done many times, Sherry Gibbs patiently wends her way along this road that is more than a match for the sturdiest four-wheel-drive vehicles.

For three weeks at a time a single-room pole-and-thatch hut serves as her office and home. A mosquito net covers her bed. Hers is one of a number of such austere huts that form a small village inhabited by a handful of archaeologists and dozens of other workers. These huts are adjacent to several far larger and grander structures—the awesome handiwork of the ancient Maya.

Caracol is the largest site in Belize and one of the largest in the Maya area. According to one estimate, it covers approximately 100 square miles and includes thousands of structures of varying sizes. For centuries it was the jungle's secret. In 1937 it was discovered by a logger who reported the finding to A. H. Anderson, the first archaeological commissioner of Belize. Anderson investigated the site that year, finding eight carved stone monuments, some architectural remains, and numerous mounds. More work was done in the 1950s, and in 1985 archaeologists Arlen and Diane Chase of the University of Central Florida embarked on a major investigation of the site that is still ongoing.

It's believed that Caracol once yielded considerable political, economic, and military power. The site was first inhabited some time around 600 B.C., and it reached its zenith during the Maya Classic Period (A.D. 250-900). Many of its numerous structures were built during this period. The Chases believe that the population of urban Caracol could have grown to roughly 140,000 people, which is more than twice that of Belize City, the largest city in the country today. Its inhabitants excelled at city planning and agriculture; the latter is all the more remarkable since the site is far from any source of water. Caracol warred with, and defeated, Tikal, an extremely powerful Maya city in nearby Guatemala, in A.D. 562, and then Naranjo, also in Guatemala, in the early A.D. 600s. Roughly 400 years later this great city was abandoned.

Jaime Awe, laden with 15 chickens, has returned from town. Before setting out for Caracol, he performed one of his many obligations: making sure his crew would have dinner. Working in the jungle can be very difficult, but he boasts that his workers eat well. Awe, the director of Belize's Institute of Archaeology, supervises a huge project devoted to excavating and stabilizing structures at Caracol. Gibbs, who sports a Maya glyph tattoo just below her left ear, is his crew chief. The work is done under the auspices of the government of Belize, and its purpose is twofold: to contribute to the country's archaeological record and to increase tourism to its Maya sites, thereby bolstering its economy.

The project began in the fall of 2000, when Awe and his crew of about 25 set to work building their own village of huts, complete with a community dining room, basketball court, and a soccer field of sorts. These pole and thatch huts mirror the Maya dwellings of centuries ago; and like those ancient residents, Awe's crew, some of whom are Maya, can build these huts without use of a single nail.

There are but two native Ph.D. archaeologists in all of Belize, and Awe, who has done research in the country for 20 years, is one of them. With that distinction comes significant responsibility. The work at Caracol is part of the Tourism Development Project, a grand effort that also includes archaeological work at four other sites in Belize: Altun Ha, Lamanai, Cahal Pech, and Xunantunich. Awe also directs the work at these sites, and therefore he's often in motion, going from one place to the next. "It means that I would love to be cloned," he says.

Awe is of medium build and has dark, wavy hair. He is plain-spoken, and frequently jokes with his crew. He tries to spend at least two days a week at Caracol. Upon returning here he gathers a few members of the crew and begins "the walk." Gibbs informs him of the good and the bad that's occurred in his absence as they tour the excavation areas, assessing the various situations. "I'm making decisions as I go," Awe says. "I don't have the luxury of being every day, every minute at these sites." Due to the lack of highly trained archaeologists and the lesser-credentialed archaeologists being "swamped," Awe states that he "can't call upon a host of other Belizian archaeologists to come and assist us." This personnel shortage is addressed by foreign archaeologists." We have very good relationships with our foreign colleagues," Awe observes.

"We have a hundred people up here," he says. "At one time we had 150." They work throughout the year. Given the size of their task, they need every worker and every day. Over the decades archaeologists have exposed and stabilized, either partly or completely, the tiniest fraction of Caracol's structures. The rest are buried under a layer of jungle, appearing as mounds that stud the site. Compared to many other archaeological projects, Awe has vast resources at his disposal; nonetheless, he has nowhere near sufficient time, money, and manpower to recover all of these structures.

The crew is working in the center of Caracol in sections known as the A and B groups and the South Acropolis. The A and B groups feature plazas surrounded by large structures. It's thought that the A group plaza was used for ritual activity. There are a number of large stones lying on the ground and the archaeologists believe they are fragments of stelae and altars. Several of the A Group's structures were temple pyramids and there was also an observatory from which the Maya tracked the movements of the celestial bodies.

The B Group features the huge pyramid named Caana (or "Sky Place") which, at approximately 136 feet, remains the tallest building in Belize. Various ritual, administrative, and commercial activities probably took place here. It was probably home to Caracol's rulers. The South Acropolis was a place where the elite resided. "We know that because of the size and quality of a masonry structure," Gibbs notes. "The everyday farmer or common person wasn't living in structures like this." They have also found jade and tombs with grave goods that also suggest it was an upper-class residence.

The weather is hot and sticky and there's no lack of bugs. Though it's the rainy season, the sun is relentless. The incessant din of the jungle's wildlife reaches every corner of the site. When first heard, the roar of the howler monkeys is alarming. The crew is accustomed to these conditions. Their work is painstaking and orderly. The excavators, under the supervision of the archaeologists, peel off the foliage and collapsed stone covering a structure to expose its architecture. That done, "we have a drafts crew that goes in, they map, draw, photograph, illustrate, do profiles, elevation, plan views," Gibbs explains. "Then the masons move in and stabilize." It took about 18 months to expose and consolidate the front half of Caana. The back half, from which sprouts a number of trees, is still firmly in the jungle's grasp.

Across the plaza from Caana is a temple pyramid called B5. There are roughly 10 men working on this structure, the upper portion of which is covered by vegetation. They are working on B5 because, "when you climb Caana and turn around you look at this thing," Gibbs states. "We really had to do something about it."

Two masks (human, animal, or god-like effigies), roughly nine feet tall and eight feet wide, have been discovered here. "When we found them it was like opening Pandora's Box," she says. They were faced with the sort of decision they have to make from time to time: Should they leave the original exposed? Or should they make a replica that would be used to cover the original in order to preserve it? The decision is determined by the condition of the mask. In this case, they decided to cover the originals with precise replicas made of fiberglass.

When they discover masks that are extremely fragile, extra care is required to make the replicas. They map, photograph, and draw the original, using this information to create an exact clay copy. The map details "every single stone," says Gibbs, as well as informing the craftsmen how deep to draw crevices. Any cracks or other evidence of deterioration in the original will be reflected in the replica. "They mess up the clay a little bit in spots," she says, to give it a stone-like texture.

Needless to say, it requires skilled hands to craft these clay models, though some of their tools are surprisingly simple. Two craftsmen sit under a sheet of corrugated metal held up by poles at the foot of B5 fashioning a clay replica. The metal shields them from the sun. A map and an illustration of the mask they're recreating are next to the clay mold they carefully sculpt with spokes from a bicycle wheel that have been customized for this task. They employ several triangular and oval tools made from spokes. One of them says that he learned of these tools and how to use them from "a guy in Guatemala." One of their craftsmen is scheduled to receive more formal training by attending a class in replica making in Taiwan.

The challenges inherent in keeping an operation the size of Caracol's going from one day to the next extend far beyond archaeology. Awe says it costs about $50,000 a week to field his crew, and they work year-round. "When you're doing a big research project like this, it's all about logistics," he observes. Logistics "takes up easily 50 percent of your time." They run short of supplies, their equipment breaks down. They have about six vehicles to get the crew to and from Caracol, but they could use twice that. The site is so remote that two-way radio provides their only communication with the outside world. Sustaining the operation requires a variety of skills. The workers range from archaeologists to mechanics to cooks to artists. As it was for the Maya, water is a concern for Awe's crew. They estimate their daily usage at roughly 3,000 gallons. The Macal River, their nearest source of water, is 12 miles away.

There are also the occasional acts of nature to contend with. The road to Caracol crosses the Macal, and come the rainy season the river may flood. "Last year we were stuck back here for a week," says Awe. "We could not get out." The river, by his estimation, rose 10 to 12 feet over the bridge. Consequently, keeping sufficient food on hand to last for 10 days is a priority. "We might be eating beans and rice and canned goods," he says," but at lease we won't starve."

Hurricane Iris hit Belize in October of 2001. Having gotten more rain than wind at Caracol, the crew thought the site had escaped serious damage. "Then I went up to the top of Caana. We lost the whole back side of the western pyramid," Gibbs recalls, referring to one of the small pyramids at the top of the structure. "It was gone."

The wall forming the back of the pyramid had collapsed and its stones had tumbled down the length of Caana. "It was a big, big mess," she says. Nor did their budget allow for such a problem. The fallen stones had to be recovered and the wall rebuilt, an emergency that required nearly three-quarters of the crew to work nonstop. "We had to beg and plead our case" to get the money to pay the crew overtime. A number of the workers arranged themselves in a "stone line" running from the base to the summit of Caana. The hurricane's swift fury was methodically remedied as the many stones, conveyed from hand to hand, were eventually returned to the summit to rebuild the wall.

Breakfast is over and the dining room, which had been full of workers, is nearly empty. The cooks are planning lunch, the highlight of which will be pigs' tails, a delicacy, in many a worker's estimation, that ranks with cows' feet soup. Awe sits at a picnic table and explains the demise of the people who long preceded him here. Some scholars think warfare took a heavy toll on the Maya, but he considers it a factor rather than the primary cause, which in his mind is environmental degradation.

"We think people first came here because the soils were very good and there was available water to support a certain level of population," he explains. Whereas the Chases estimate that Caracol's population grew to some 140,000, Awe believes it was somewhere in the range of 60,000 to 100,000.

The Maya consumed natural resources such as water and wood while paying little heed to sustainability. By about A.D. 600 "we have millions of people living in the central Maya zone," he continues. "Belize alone may have had close to a million people." Agriculture was their main means of sustenance, requiring the clearing of large tracts of land. They also needed wood to construct their homes. "We're talking thousands of homes," adds Awe. The Maya used wood to cook their meals and fire their pottery. The mortar holding their remarkable pyramids together was made of lime. They produced lime by heating limestone to approximately 900 degrees centigrade, an extreme temperature that necessitated a lot of firewood. "They were doing major deforestation," he concludes.

Citing the construction of skyscrapers as an example, Awe states that humans try "to develop technologies that will increase the carrying capacity" of their environments. The Maya's technical prowess was evidenced in the reservoirs they built to increase their water supply as well as the terraces they constructed to prevent erosion and increase the moisture in, and thereby the fertility of, the soil. The Maya adapted to a degree but, he states, "ultimately they failed because they abandoned this area."

Caracol's environmental decline had political consequences. Unable to maintain their lifestyles, the people refused to support the ruling families who, though once thought to be omnipotent, had seemingly lost the power to provide for their subjects.

Caracol is a major archaeological site but hardly a major tourist attraction. A mere handful of tourists wander the plaza between Caana and B5. Of the Tourism Development Project's five sites, Altun Ha gets the most tourists—approximately 800 to 1,000 a day—and Caracol the least. Altun Ha benefits from its proximity to Belize City, getting traffic from the cruise ships that dock there. Caracol suffers for its remoteness. Awe and the Belize government (the Institute of Archaeology is part of the Ministry of Tourism) would be happy to lure 1,000 tourists a day to Caracol which now, during high season, gets perhaps 100. "We hope to eventually make this our anchor site," he explains, "just like Tikal is the anchor site for Guatemala.

The main problem is the condition of the road, "I've destroyed I don't know how many vehicles on that road," laments Arlen Chase, who's been driving it for nearly two decades. There are plans to improve the road and an airstrip located about 30 minutes from the site. Then tourism could flourish. But could a swarm of visitors overtax Caracol as the Maya once did? "A lot of people say, 'Oh my god, would you want that many people at the site?'" Awe says, mimicking the concern in their voices. His answer, of course, is yes. Because of its size, Caracol has a large "carrying capacity." He adds that the limestone used to build the structures here is more durable than that used at some other Maya sites.

He admits it's possible to be too successful, and that he wouldn't want it to draw the huge crowds that Chichén Itzá, in southern Mexico, does. Despite the few tourists Caracol gets, they have caused problems now and again. A tourist climbed a mask and damaged it. Another visitor, having made her way to the top of a structure, froze in fear. Members of Awe's crew were dispatched to escort her down. Other tourists have ignored flagging tape and entered restricted areas that were being stabilized.

But Awe is optimistic. One of the advantages of Belize's archaeology department being subsumed by the tourism department is that the archaeologists are in regular contact with, and can influence the decisions of, tourism officials. "What we want is sustained tourism," he states. "And if we want to sustain tourism in Belize into the distant future, we've got to manage appropriately and properly."

Discussion Questions

1. Developing a site for tourism is often suggested as a way to bring economic benefits to the local community and to engage the locals in

protecting, rather than looting, sites in their vicinity. Discuss this idea in light of the information in this chapter.

2. What additional work, not mentioned in the chapter, needs to be done to make Caracol an effective destination for tourists?

3. How can those involved in developing a site for tourism avoid being "too successful"? What, in addition to the minor mishaps noted here, does "too successful" imply?

4. What aspects of tourism in Belize, external to the Caracol site itself, contribute to the probability of success for developing archaeotourism at Caracol? Think about attempting to do something similar in other places: what considerations would be paramount in making a decision to go ahead with such a project?

5. At archaeological sites developed for tourism, where do the benefits go? Who pays the price for tourism and who profits from it? Should archaeologists try to balance local needs with the economic needs of the nation?

Further Readings

Adams, Kathleen M. 2003. Cultural Displays and Tourism in Africa and the Americas. *Ethnohistory* 50(3):567–573.

Clifford, James. 1997. *Routes: Travel and Translation in the Late Twentieth Century.* Cambridge: Harvard University Press.

Hoffmann, Teresa L., Mary Kwas, and Helaine Silverman. 2002. Heritage Tourism and Public Anthropology. *SAA Archaeological Record* 2(2):30–32, 44.

Mortensen, Lena. 2005. The Local Meanings of International Heritage at Copán, Honduras. *SAA Archaeological Record* 5(2):28–30, 44.

Silverman, Helaine. 2002. Touring Ancient Times: The Present and Presented Past in Contemporary Peru. *American Anthropologist* 104(3):881–902.

REBURIAL, REPATRIATION, AND REPRESENTATION

IV

Burying American Archaeology

17

CLEMENT W. MEIGHAN

Sharing Control of the Past

LARRY J. ZIMMERMAN

*On November 16, 1990, Congress passed the Native American Graves Protection and Repatria-
tion Act (NAGPRA). One controversial provision of the act requires the return, on request, of skeletal remains and burial goods to Native Americans who can prove cultural affiliation with the
materials. Meighan presents a negative response to the legislation; Zimmerman defends it.*

Burying American Archaeology by Clement W. Meighan

IN 1991 THE WEST VIRGINIA DEPARTMENT OF TRANSPORTATION and a committee of Indians and non-Indians claiming to represent Native American
viewpoints signed an agreement whereby everything unearthed in advance of
road construction near the 2,000-year-old Adena mound was to be given up for
reburial within a year. "Everything" included not only cremated bones but artifacts
such as chipping waste, food refuse, pollen samples, and soil samples. The $1.8
million rescue excavation was federally funded in the interest of science. Yet nothing of tangible archaeological evidence was to be preserved. In addition, Indian activists were paid by the state to monitor the excavation and to censor
"objectionable" photographs or data appearing in the final report. The activists
also insisted that, following an alleged ancient custom, human remains be covered
with red flannel until reburial and that no remains, including artifacts, be touched
by menstruating women.

American Indians, Australian aborigines, and ultra orthodox Jews in Israel have
all attacked archaeology in recent years and continue to seek restrictions on archaeological study. In North America, the argument has been put forward that the
archaeological study of ancient Native American people is a violation of the religious freedom of living Indians. Some Indian spokesmen have claimed their right,
on religious grounds, to control archaeological study and specimens regardless of

the age of the remains, the area from which they come, or the degree of claimed Indian ancestry.

whoa!
B is a
assumption!

In my view, archaeologists have a responsibility to the people they study. They are defining the culture of an extinct group and in presenting their research they are writing a chapter of human history that cannot be written except from archaeological investigation. If the archaeology is not done, the ancient people remain without a history.

A number of confusions have led to the present conflict over archaeological study of Native American remains. One is the assumption of direct genetic and cultural continuity between living persons and those long deceased. Who knows whether the Indians of 2,000 years ago believed that a corpse must be covered with red flannel and not touched by menstruating women? As if to emphasize their contempt for real ancestral relationships, the activists who demanded reburial of the remains from the Adena mound included Indians from tribes as far away as northwestern Washington, as well as non-Indians. Meanwhile, the views of a local West Virginia tribe that favored preservation of the remains were ignored.

A year before, the government passed the Native American Graves Protection and Repatriation Act. According to preliminary interpretations of this law, some sort of relationship must be shown between claimants and the materials claimed. However, no line has been drawn at remains over a certain age, despite the obvious impossibility of establishing a familial relationship spanning 20 or more generations of unrecorded history. Millions of dollars have now been spent to inventory collections, including those containing items thousands of years old, and to add a corps of bureaucrats to interpret and administer the legislation. An enormous amount of scientists' time is also being diverted from research that might otherwise be done on those bones and artifacts soon to be lost to repatriation.

One wonders why museum directors are so eager to relinquish the holdings for which they are responsible. Museums house a great variety of collections and their directors are rarely trained in any of the natural sciences or have any special interest in physical anthropology. Being, for the most part, public institutions, they are dependent on good public relations, which can be undermined by activists. Like politicians, museum directors seem all too willing to satisfy activists by dissatisfying scientists. Meanwhile, in university departments of anthropology, physical anthropologists are normally outnumbered by cultural anthropologists. The latter have little interest in osteological collections; more important to them is maintaining good relations with the living tribes with whom they work. As a group, cultural anthropologists include a considerable number of politicized academics. Many of them welcome an opportunity to demonstrate their solidarity with an allegedly oppressed minority, especially when it means insisting that the latter's native religion be respected. Since their own research will not be adversely affected, they have nothing to lose. Political correctness has rarely been so all-around satisfying.

It is questionable whether Indian activists and politicized professors and curators could succeed in influencing politicians and administrators if the latter found their claims to be utterly implausible. Even the most cynical and opportunistic lawmakers would not want to be observed supporting self-evidently absurd demands. Yet the multiple laws inhibiting archaeological research, physical anthropology, and museum studies have all been instigated and justified in the name of Indian religious beliefs. This is remarkable for a number of reasons. First, no other religious group in the United States has been given the same protection. Second, most Indians no longer hold these beliefs. Third, Indian knowledge of the traditions of their ancestors is derived in large part from the collections and scholarship that the activists among them are now seeking to destroy.

That measures hostile to science have gained so much ground in this nation's legislative bodies, universities, and museums—and on so flimsy a basis—suggests that there has been a sea change in the opinions and sentiments that have hitherto guided the public in support of scientific endeavor. The New Age disposition to invoke or invent beliefs no one really holds, and to maintain that they are of a value at least equal to, if not supremely greater than, those that account for the triumph of Western civilization, is given concrete expression in the repatriation movement. Conversely, the success of this movement will further reinforce these newly fashionable doubts about the value of Western science in particular and rational thought in general.

Reasonable doubts have been raised about whether the large quantity of bones tucked away in museum drawers and cabinets are really of scientific value. In fact, these are frequently studied by physical anthropologists and their students. The techniques of statistical research require as large a sample as possible so that generalizations can be well-formulated. In addition, bones that have already been examined may be needed again when new analytic techniques are developed. Only recently has it been possible to extract antibodies and genetic material from ancient bones, making it possible to trace the evolution of specific human diseases. Future laboratory advances in dating bones and in determining the source of artifact materials will also require these objects to be available for study. Finally, the bones belonging to particular tribes are precisely those that are most valuable to historical studies of those tribes.

But even if it were true that the bones, once examined, need never be studied again, the demand that they be reburied conflicts with the scholarly requirement to preserve data. If research data are destroyed, there can be no basis on which to challenge honest but possibly erroneous conclusions. Reburying bones and artifacts is the equivalent of the historian burning documents after he has studied them. Thus, repatriation is not merely an inconvenience but makes it impossible for scientists to carry out a genuinely scientific study of American Indian prehistory. Furthermore, it negates scientific work that has already been done, since the evidence on which that work was based is now to be buried.

Repatriation also raises other issues. It is a violation of a museum's public trust to give away materials that it has held legally and at public expense. A similar violation is involved when a museum has received these materials from a private donor or at a private donor's expense. In particular, such action ignores many Indians who donated or sold materials on the understanding that these items would go into a permanent repository for the benefit of future generations of Indians.

An entire field of academic study may be put out of business. It has become impossible for a field archaeologist to conduct a large-scale excavation in the United States without violating some law or statute. The result is that archaeology students are now steered away from digs where they might actually find some American Indian remains. American archaeology is an expiring subject of study—one in which new students no longer choose to specialize. Instead, they specialize in the archaeology of other countries, where they will be allowed to conduct their research and have some assurance that their collections will be preserved.

Scientific disciplines are not immune to change, but the scientific ideal is that these changes are the consequence of new discoveries and theories driven by developments internal to science, and not imposed from without. It may therefore be questioned whether the repatriation movement is not a massive invasion of the freedom of scholarly and scientific disciplines to define their own goals and chart their own course.

What the activists know about the Indians' past depends almost entirely on the records of European explorers, missionaries, and settlers, and on the studies of past and present historians, ethnographers, anthropologists, and archaeologists. These scholars and scientists often thought of themselves as helping the American Indian to preserve his heritage. A great many Indians, past and present, shared or share that conviction. It would be interesting to know whether a majority of living persons of Indian descent actually favor reburial or the continued preservation, display, and study of Indian remains and artifacts.

Sharing Control of the Past by Larry J. Zimmerman

Scholars have been slow to realize that the scientific archaeology that sprang from Euroamerican rationalist and empiricist roots may not be the only valid archaeology. Part of the rift between archaeologists and Native Americans stems from a fundamentally different conception of the past. To archaeologists, the past can be known because it has already happened and left markers—artifacts—

that give clues about it. To know the past requires that it be discovered through written sources and archaeological exploration and interpretation. To Native Americans, the idea that discovery is the only way to know the past is absurd. For the Indian interested in traditional practice and belief, the past lives in the present. Indians know the past because it is spiritually and ritually a part of daily existence and is relevant only as it exists in the present. In fact, Indians object to heavy reliance on artifacts, preferring instead to focus on people and how they experienced their lives.

Archaeologists often claim to speak for past peoples, however remote. Implicit in this claim is the notion that they, as practitioners of a science, are the only ones capable of doing so. Native Americans do not accept this and challenge the very authority of archaeological knowledge. Cecil Antone of the Gila River Indian Tribes said at a conference on reburial, "My ancestors, relatives, grandmother so on down the line, they tell you about the history of our people and it's passed on . . . basically, what I'm trying to say, I guess, is that archaeology don't mean nothing." When archaeologists say that the Native American past is gone, extinct, or lost unless archaeology can find it, they send a strong message that Native Americans themselves are extinct. University of Arizona anthropologist J. Jefferson Reid believes that Native Americans see archaeological accounts of their past as a threat to traditional, Indian accounts of that same past. They fear that the archaeological version eventually will replace the traditionally constructed past and their culture, once again, will be eroded. Indians told Reid, during a recent archaeological conference, that the archaeology of the Southwest had no relevance for southwestern Indians; in their view ". . . archaeology was only relevant to other archaeologists."

Archaeology has been slow to recognize that epistemological shifts must be made if archaeology is to have any relevance to any group other than archaeologists. We can begin by broadening archaeological ideas about the past to include an interest in how others know the past and by rejecting the view that archaeologists are somehow the only capable stewards of it. Southern Illinois University anthropologist Jonathan D. Hill has challenged the belief that historical interpretations based on written documents are necessarily more objective, reliable, or accurate than those embodied in oral tradition. In his introduction to a volume analyzing Native South American perspectives on the past, he notes that "Although oral and non-verbal formulations cannot be literally read as direct accounts of historical processes, they can show how indigenous societies have experienced history and the on-going means by which they struggle to make sense out of complex, contradictory historical processes." He concludes that history is not ever reducible to "what really happened." This suggests that the past—the very medium in which archaeologists work—is fluid; objectivity itself changes. Accepting this notion is critical if archaeology is to accommodate Native American accounts of their history.

Nowhere have these conflicting viewpoints been more visible than in the re-burial issue. Some archaeologists maintain that the past is lost with reburial. Of course information from the remains is lost, but only to the archaeologist. Those who believe that American Indians or other groups are getting preferential treatment do not understand that many of these groups have been subjected to the "preferred" views of the Western world, which includes the science of archaeology.

The idea that anyone can "save" the past is a false notion. Preservation itself reveals that permanence is an illusion. As University College-London geographer David Lowenthal has written, "Saviors of the past change it no less than iconoclasts bent on its destruction." The past is always interpreted from the perspective of the present. For archaeologists, interpretations reflect changes in theoretical viewpoints, analytical techniques, and the politics of contemporary society. New interpretations replace the old; that is, they "destroy" the past. Archaeologists construct the past, they do not reconstruct it.

Many archaeologists view the past as everyone's heritage. This implies that archaeologists, because of their special skills, are the most capable of preserving and interpreting it. Many indigenous peoples don't agree. At the 1982 meeting of the Australian Archaeological Association, Rosalind Langford, an Australian aboriginal, commented, "You . . . say that as scientists you have the right to obtain and study information of our culture. You . . . say that because you are Australians you have a right to study and explore our heritage because it is a heritage to be shared by all Australians . . . We say that it is our past, our culture and heritage, and forms part of our present life. As such it is ours to control and it is ours to share on our terms."

What steps should archaeologists who study native peoples take to insure an amicable working relationship? We should be activists in consulting groups that might be affected by our work. And we shouldn't be doing it just because it is required by law or is politically correct. Rather, we should consult Native Americans because we recognize their valid interests in the past. Working with them, they will provide us with insights into their past.

In so doing, archaeologists can share the past, rather than impose their own version of it. There are examples of archaeologists and indigenous peoples who have good working relationships. In Australia, Colin Pardoe, an osteologist studying aboriginal remains, does no excavation or analysis without intensive community involvement. He seeks permission to work on remains even if he suspects that they are not related to groups now occupying the area in which bones are found. He asks people their opinion of the research problems he is addressing. He tells them why he needs to do certain tests, and if they involve destructive techniques, he asks permission to use them. Pardoe's community reports are instructive in that they provide a mechanism for community involvement in his construction of the past. He usually has little difficulty conducting his research and he learns a great deal more in the process by sharing his study with aborigines.

Consider a recent reburial in Nebraska. The Pawnee Indians successfully collaborated with archaeologists to summarize the archaeological record of their tribe for a court case involving repatriation of human remains. At the same time Pawnee tribal historian Roger Echo-Hawk gathered previously recorded oral history and other materials pertaining to Pawnee origins and history. Since the case, archaeologist Steve Holen has worked with Echo-Hawk, to compare the archaeological record and the oral history to see what concordance there might be. Echo-Hawk and Holen are learning from each other. Many Pawnee narratives are reflected in the archaeological record. Others are not. Disagreements are put aside pending further consultation.

Involvement of non-archaeologists puts some control into their hands, and most archaeologists will be reluctant to relinquish control over their research. Who is willing to do this? The World Archaeological Congress (WAC) in its ethics code has taken steps to share control with indigenous peoples. The WAC code even puts the development of research into indigenous hands. For example, WAC has eight indigenous representatives on its executive committee. Its ethics code demands that WAC members seek representation for indigenous peoples in agencies funding or authorizing research to be certain that their views are considered in setting research standards, questions, priorities, and goals. Archaeologists do not stop developing research questions—the difference is they share them with indigenous peoples, who then become more familiar with archaeological thinking.

Collaborative efforts unquestionably will limit our cherished academic freedom. Accountability to Native Americans will create a very different discipline, one that will not be scientific according to our current standards. At the same time, this new science can and will open many investigative possibilities for us, especially in areas where we wish to understand the meaning of prehistoric events or materials. We will certainly develop a better understanding of what people's lives meant to them. We may be allowed better access to areas now closed to us, particularly in the realm of the sacred. We may better learn about a commonality of human experience that is analogous to and as valuable as any we have generated using scientific theory.

Native American peoples have been extraordinarily patient with archaeologists. They recognize that some archaeology is useful to them if applied using their rules. What archaeologists must understand is that their view of the past is peculiar to their discipline and has an impact on those they study. To communicate effectively with Native American people, archaeologists will need to learn how to share control of the past.

Groups like WAC and the Society for American Archaeology have begun serious examination of what constitutes ethical practice. What is exciting about this new direction is that it does allow us the chance to become something quite different. If we don't take steps that are bold and creative in reinventing our profession, we will continue to lose access to the artifacts, sites, and people we wish to study.

Discussion Questions

1. How can a people whose historical memory does not rely on written records and Western science convey the essence and import of that history to a dominant community that puts primary value on written records and Western science?
2. What are some of the "different views" of Native Americans on reburial and repatriation?
3. How widespread among the Native American community are the concerns about the "scientific study" of the Native American past?
4. Without archaeological study, how can anyone know to whom skeletal materials may be related or what religious beliefs were held 2,000 or more years ago?
5. What institutions in your area are involved in NAGPRA-related repatriation claims? How much time and money is involved? Are scientific benefits resulting from the repatriation work?
6. What role do museum directors and curators and cultural anthropologists play in this whole debate? What role should they play?
7. Do other religious or ethnic groups in the United States have the same kind of protection?
8. Do most American Indians still hold traditional beliefs? Does it matter, for purposes of the present argument, whether they do or not?
9. How has the work of archaeology made a positive contribution to the lives of present-day Native Americans?
10. Historically, what have been the attitudes of various cultures about digging up graves and making some use of human skeletal remains?
11. How might the scientific needs of physical anthropologists and archaeologists be made more compelling to Native American groups? And the reverse?
12. Is repatriation a violation of a museum's public trust? What is a museum's "public trust"? What happens to Native American sacred objects and human remains that may be in non-U.S. museums?

13. If objects now in a museum collection were acquired some time ago by purchase from an informed and consenting Native American owner, do descendants of that Native American have any right to request repatriation of the objects? (Consider also the example of the St. Lawrence Islanders, Chapter 14.)

14. How healthy is the discipline of archaeology in the United States? In other countries? What changes can you detect in the last decade or two?

15. Are American Indians' fears that the archaeological version of the past will replace their traditional accounts justified?

16. What are some potentially positive outcomes of accepting others as legitimate stewards of the past? What are some of the potential and actual problems and difficulties?

Further Readings

For current information on NAGPRA and extensive bibliography go to www.nagpra.org.

Deloria, Vine, Jr. 1992. Indians, Archaeologists, and the Future. *American Antiquity* 57(4):595–598.

Echo-Hawk, Roger C., and Walter R. Echo-Hawk. 1994. *Battlefields and Burial Grounds: The Indian Struggle to Protect Ancestral Graves in the United States.* Minneapolis: Lerner Publications.

Goldstein, Lynne, and Keith Kintigh. 1990. Ethics and the Reburial Controversy. *American Antiquity* 55(3):585–591.

Klesert, Anthony L., and Shirley Powell. 1993. A Perspective on Ethics and the Reburial Controversy. *American Antiquity* 58(2):348–354.

Mihesuah, Devon A. (editor). 2000. *Repatriation Reader: Who Owns American Indian Remains?* Lincoln: University of Nebraska Press.

Mulvaney, D. J. 1991. Past Regained, Future Lost: The Kow Swamp Pleistocene Burials. *Antiquity* 65:12–21.

Ubelaker, Douglas, and Lauryn Guttenplan Grant. 1989. Human Skeletal Remains: Preservation or Reburial? *Yearbook of Physical Anthropology* 32:249–287.

Ravesloot, John C. 1990. On the Treatment and Reburial of Human Remains: The San Xavier Bridge Project, Tucson, Arizona. *American Indian Quarterly* 14(1):35–50.

Thomas, David Hurst. 2000. *Skull Wars: Kennewick Man, Archaeology, and the Battle for Native American Identity.* New York: Basic Books.

Swidler, Nina, Kurt E. Dongoske, Roger Anyon, and Alan S. Downer (editors). 1997. *Native Americans and Archaeologists: Stepping Stones to Common Ground.* Walnut Creek, CA: AltaMira Press.

Richman, Jennifer R., and Marion P. Forsyth. 2004. *Legal Perspectives on Cultural Resources.* Walnut Creek, CA: AltaMira Press. (Especially Part III.)

Banned Books

18

MARK MICHEL

In recent years, the bookstores at Mesa Verde National Park and Petroglyph National Monument have not sold books that identify the ancient peoples of the Southwest as "Anasazi," a Navajo term that many contemporary Pueblo people find offensive. In this brief article, Michel discusses the conflicts between the values of intellectual freedom and respect for Native American viewpoints.

T HE PECOS CONFERENCE, the major group of Southwestern archaeologists, has condemned the exclusion of selected books from National Park Service bookstores. At the annual meeting in Bluff, Utah, on August 14, 2005, scholars complained about the exclusion of books from Mesa Verde National Park and Petroglyph National Monument. "This form of censorship is detrimental to the dissemination of knowledge and adversely impacts both (archaeological) professionals and the interested public," states the Conference's resolution. "Interested readers are prohibited from reading examples of the best professional research."

Most of the criticism was directed at Mesa Verde National Park, which has perhaps the busiest American archaeology bookstore in the country. Mesa Verde bans books that identify the ancient inhabitants of Mesa Verde as "Anasazi," including such popular works as *The Anasazi of Mesa Verde and the Four Corners* by William M. Ferguson and *Understanding the Anasazi of Mesa Verde and Hovenweep* by David Grant Noble. According to reliable sources at the park, Superintendent Larry T. Weise ordered the books banned because of concerns expressed by some Pueblo people. Weise did not respond to numerous requests for comment.

The use of the word "Anasazi" to describe the ancient Puebloan people of the Four Corners has become controversial in recent years because of its Navajo origins, and Mesa Verde and other parks are replacing it with "Ancestral Puebloan." Both Navajos and Puebloans have claimed to be descendants of the Anasazi in order to control human remains from Mesa Verde and influence the archaeological work on related sites, many of which are on Navajo lands. According to Mary A. Willie, a linguist at the University of Arizona and a Navajo, Anasazi is "a conglomerate of two separate words meaning 'non-Navajo' and 'ancestor.'" A reasonable translation of Anasazi would thus be "Puebloan ancestors," ironically confirming the Puebloans' claim.

At Petroglyph National Monument in Albuquerque, park officials have barred books that contain photographs of petroglyphs to which Pueblo people object, including human figures, masks, and four-pointed stars. They also object to the term "rock art," because "it connotes leisure time activity," according to Dian Souder, supervisory park ranger. Books that interpret the meaning of specific rock art symbols are also unwanted at the park bookstore. "It's a terrible infringement on intellectual freedom," according to Polly Schaafsma, whose classic rock art studies *Rock Art in New Mexico* and *Warrior, Shield, and Star* are among the scholarly tomes banned from the park.

Because of the economic power of the park bookstores, publishers in the Southwest are struggling to conform, but their efforts are hampered by ambivalent policies. A spokesman for one of the biggest publishers in the region said, "I'm not quite sure what the park superintendents are trying to achieve, but I know I had better not send them a book with 'Anasazi' on the cover."

Discussion Questions

1. What do you think about the Park superintendent's decision: a good faith effort to respect Puebloan viewpoints or a form of censorship?
2. How important is a name? Think about different ethnic labels in the United States, such as African-American and Hispanic. What are the differences between "White," "Anglo," "Caucasian," and "honkey"?
3. Does respecting the concerns of Native Americans (or any other minority group) become, at some point, an infringement of intellectual freedom? Explain your position.
4. Other scholars translate Anasazi as "ancient enemy" instead of "Puebloan ancestors" and point out that this is still a Navajo term to describe ancient Pueblo peoples. What terms should be used to describe archaeological cultures? How does power relate to these discussions about who gets to define what terms?
5. Can you suggest a viable alternative for banning the books at these shops? If you were in charge, how would you go about reaching a decision?

Further Reading

Brown, Michael F. 2003. *Who Owns Native Culture?* Cambridge: Harvard University Press.

Out of Heaviness, Enlightenment   19

ROBERT W. PREUCEL, LUCY F. WILLIAMS, STACEY O. ESPENLAUB, AND
JANET MONGE

NAGPRA has presented many challenges to archaeologists, but also many opportunities. In this article, the curators and keepers of collections at the University of Pennsylvania Museum of Archaeology and Anthropology explain how and why NAGPRA works. The authors argue that archaeologists must confront their legacy of colonialism and collaborate in true partnership with Native peoples to create viable museums for the new millennium.

On September 29, 2000, John Johnson of the Chugach Alaska Corporation arrived in Philadelphia to take formal possession of ancestral Eskimo human remains and grave goods from Prince William Sound and Kachemak Bay in the collections of the University of Pennsylvania Museum of Archaeology and Anthropology. This was a profoundly significant experience for him since he was finally fulfilling one of the central wishes of his elders. They had entrusted him with the weighty responsibility of locating their ancestors in museums throughout the world and returning them home. After the transfer of ownership, he escorted the remains back to Yukon Island, Alaska where they were baptized under the Greek Orthodox Church and buried in an unmarked, mass grave. This ceremony was the denouement of a lengthy ten-year process, initiated in 1990, just prior to the passage of the Native American Graves Protection and Repatriation Act (NAGPRA).

These human remains and grave goods were originally excavated by Dr. Frederica de Laguna in 1931 and 1932, as part of a University Museum-sponsored research project, focusing on the prehistory of the Chugach Eskimo people. This research was crucial in defining the Kachemak Bay Eskimo Tradition (1880 B.C. – A.D. 1100).

The collections contain over 6,600 artifacts including hunting, fishing, and manufacturing tools; household objects; and items of personal adornment. In the 1930s, it was common practice for anthropologists to excavate "abandoned" village sites. Cemeteries were especially valued since burial practices were regarded as important indicators of cultural identity. De Laguna's research was conducted under a Federal permit, and with the assistance of Native workers, and thus was entirely consistent with the best anthropological practices of her times.

Today, there is a new appreciation of the legal rights and religious values of Native peoples, due in part to the Civil Rights Act (1964), the American Indian Movement (founded in 1968), the Indian Civil Rights Act (1968), the American Indian Religious Freedom Act (1978), and now NAGPRA (1990). Since the 1960s, Indian activists have patiently asserted their rights and interests in the proper and respectful treatment of Indian human remains. As a result, it is now broadly accepted that the intentional excavation of Indian burials and inadvertent discovery of burials during commercial development projects must involve consultation with appropriate descendant communities. In addition, it is increasingly accepted that Indian peoples have a legitimate interest in the disposition of ancestral Indian remains in museum collections. NAGPRA is thus broadening American anthropology by requiring the profession to confront its colonialist past as a means of envisioning a new and more inclusive future.

What is NAGPRA?

NAGPRA is the popular acronym for the Native American Graves Protection and Repatriation Act (PL 101-601), passed into law on November 16, 1990. Basically, the law provides a legal mechanism for federally recognized Indian tribes, native Alaskan corporations, and Native Hawaiian organizations, to make claims for human remains and certain categories of objects held by museums and other institutions that receive Federal funding. Four categories of objects are identified in the law: associated funerary objects, unassociated funerary objects, objects of cultural patrimony, and sacred objects.

Prior to NAGPRA's passage, many museums and professional archaeological organizations actively opposed the legislation. They argued that tribes would empty museums of their collections, making it impossible to mount exhibitions and conduct anthropological research. There is, to this day, a vocal contingent of scholars who find NAGPRA to be misguided and would like to see it repealed. But despite dire predictions, NAGPRA has not meant the end of anthropology or museum studies. It simply requires that anthropologists develop their research projects in ways that acknowledge the rights and interests of Native American descendant communities. Significantly, it offers new opportunities for establishing mutually beneficial relationships between museums and tribes.

The popular characterization of NAGPRA as representing an intractable opposition between science and religion fails to acknowledge the historical and political context of Indian peoples in the United States. NAGPRA must be understood as part of a unique body of legislation known as Federal Indian law. In the context, NAGPRA finally recognizes tribal rights of self-determination in regard to the control of human remains, sacred objects, and objects of cultural patrimony. With regard to other much larger issues, however, American Indians live today under competing doctrines of legislation that give them only partial sovereignty within the United States. Similarly, repatriation and reburial have long been topics of concern outside the United States, particularly among indigenous peoples in colonial contexts such as Australia, New Zealand, South America, and Africa. New national and state laws in these countries, based upon the NAGPRA precedent, may well emerge.

Implementation of NAGPRA

The Museum is working assiduously to implement NAGPRA and has established a Repatriation Office and a Repatriation Committee to assist in the compliance process. All claims are submitted in writing to the director who forwards them to the Repatriation Office where they are evaluated for completeness. Viable claims are then brought forward to the Repatriation Committee that makes recommendations to the director. In the case of human remains and associated/unassociated funerary objects, the director is authorized by the Trustees of the University of Pennsylvania to make repatriation decisions. However, in the case of objects of cultural patrimony and sacred objects, the Trustees retain the right to review each case and render a judgment.

The Museum has also mailed over 500 letters to federally recognized tribes, informing them of our holdings and extending invitations to consult with us on these collections. As of 2002, 30 formal repatriation claims, seeking the return of human remains and/or objects defined by the law, have been received and 21 repatriations have been completed. However, because there is no time limit on NAGPRA and because tribes are entitled to make multiple claims, we expect this number to increase, as tribes become more familiar with the law and reprioritize their needs.

The Museum has also established a state-of-the-art website, with a link to our NAGPRA program, to communicate our repatriation efforts to the public and to tribes (see www.museum.upenn.edu).

Ancestral Human Remains and Associated and Unassociated Funerary Objects

From the Museum's experience and as seen nationally, it is clear that the majority of tribes are concentrating their efforts on the repatriation of human remains.

They are seeking to "bring their ancestors home." For John Johnson, the reburial of his Chugach ancestors at their traditional cemeteries is crucial so that his "elders will once again have peace of mind in knowing that these significant historical places will be made whole again." For Edward Ayau, of Hui Malama I Na Kupuna O Hawai'I Nei, the reburial of Native Hawaiian ancestors is part of a process of healing the devastating toll that colonization has wrought upon Native Hawaiian cultural identity.

The Museum has repatriated approximately 207 sets of human remains to 12 tribes. The largest repatriation has been to the Chugach Alaska Corporation of approximately 120 human remains removed from Prince William Sound and Kachemak Bay. Approximately 85 remains were repatriated in 1994, and an additional 35 human remains were repatriated in 2000. The second largest set of 73 remains was repatriated to Hui Malama I Na Kupuna O Hawai'I Nei over a period of eight years. The first repatriation was of an infant mummy, collected in 1893 from a cave in Hanapeepee Valley in Kauai, in August of 1991. In November of 1996, an additional 62 Hawaiian remains were repatriated. Eight more remains were returned in October of 1997, and a final two remains were repatriated in September of 1999. All of these remains were part of the famous Samuel G. Morton Collection that was officially transferred to the Museum from the Academy of Natural Sciences in 1997.

In addition to the human remains, the Museum has repatriated 750 associated funerary objects and 14 unassociated funerary objects. The majority of the associated funerary objects were glass beads repatriated to the Chugach Alaska Corporation. One of the unassociated funerary objects was an 8-foot-long burial canoe.

Sacred Objects and Objects of Cultural Patrimony

Many tribes are also actively working to repatriate sacred objects and objects of cultural patrimony as a means of revitalizing their cultures. Significantly, this is not an attempt to recapture idealized pre-contact lifestyles, but rather is part of a larger process of instructing their youth in tribal values and a means of "bringing the world into balance."

The Museum was involved with two prominent repatriation cases prior to the passage of NAGPRA, both of which involved objects that subsequently became written into the law as examples of "objects of cultural patrimony." The first of these is the case of the Iroquois Confederacy Wampum belts once owned by George Gustav Heye, a trustee of the Museum. These belts are charters for the existence of the League of the Haudenosaunee and its political relations with other tribes and groups. In 1899, eleven Confederacy belts held by an Onondaga chief were secretly sold under uncertain circumstances. In 1910, Heye purchased them and temporarily placed them on exhibition at the Museum. University of Pennsylvania anthropology professor Frank Speck immediately recognized them as the missing Six Nations belts and notified his former Penn colleague Edward Sapir, the chief ethnologist of the Anthropological Division within the Geological Survey of Canada. Sapir, in turn, contacted Cameron Scott, the deputy superintendent general of Indian affairs in Ottawa, to press the issue. Speck's actions insured that the Onondaga people knew the location of the "lost" belts, and they were eventually repatriated to the Iroquois on May 8, 1988, by the Museum of the American Indian-Heye Foundation in New York City.

The second case is that of the Zuni War Gods, known collectively as *Ahayu:da*. Each year, the religious leaders of Zuni Pueblo create wooden images of the twin war gods *Uyuyemi* and *Maia'sewi* and place them in shrines to protect the village. During the twentieth century, anthropologists, collectors, and government agents illegally removed the communally owned figures from their designated shrines and sold them on the antiquities market or donated them to museums. The Zuni elders regard the violation of their shrines as sacrilege, and they determined that the return of the figures was necessary to restore harmony and to protect the Zuni community. In April 1978, they began their first repatriation discussions with representatives from the Denver Art Museum. On November 12, 1990, the Museum repatriated one war god to Zuni. As of 1992, the Zuni had successfully repatriated 69 *Ahayu:da* from 37 different sources.

Since passage of NAGPRA, the Museum has received three claims for three sacred objects, five claims for 1,300 objects of cultural patrimony, and three claims for 103 objects claimed as both. Of these, the Museum has approved three claims, and denied two claims, with four claims pending and two withdrawn.

In 1996, the Mohegan Tribe of Uncasville, Connecticut, claimed a wooden mask made by Harold Tantaquidgeon as a "sacred object." The Museum enjoys a special relationship to the Mohegan people through Frank Speck, who grew up on the reservation, and sponsored the education of their revered medicine woman, Gladys Tantaquidgeon, at the University of Pennsylvania. After considerable discussion, the Repatriation Committee denied this claim, on the grounds that it did not meet the legal NAGPRA definition of "sacred object" and offered it to the Mohegan Tribe as a long-term loan. The Mohegan initially declined our invitation, but in 1999, under a new tribal administration, the Tribe contacted the Museum to inquire if the offer of a loan was still standing. A five-year, renewable loan contract was drafted, and on August 30, 2000, Lucy Williams personally conveyed the mask to the tribe.

On February 17, 2000, the White Mountain Apache Tribe submitted a claim for one Mountain Spirit (*Gaan*) headdress as a "sacred object" and an "object of cultural patrimony." The headdress was on display in the Museum's "Living in Balance" exhibition curated by Dorothy Washburn, in consultation with Edgar Perry of the White Mountain Apache Heritage Center. According to the tribe's NAG-PRA representative Ramon Riley, the headdress is "a unique sacred object hand-crafted to support the transformation of an individual Apache (*Ndee*) girl into womanhood" and "once such a headdress has been used by the *Gaan* spirits it is put away—retired forever as a means for the perpetuation of the healing and har-monizing derived from the ceremony." Further, Mr. Riley explained that "the headdress should never have been removed from its resting place, and its repatria-tion will contribute to the reestablishment of harmony, health, and good will." The Museum determined that the headdress was an object of central importance to the White Mountain Apache Tribe and that it qualified as an "object of cul-tural patrimony." The headdress was repatriated to the tribe on January 10, 2002.

In 1993, Henry Deacon, Chief of the Native Village of Grayling, requested information regarding the Museum's holdings from Central Alaska. This was fol-lowed by a claim from Denakkanaaga Inc., working on behalf of the village, for 19 wooden masks as "objects of cultural patrimony" on May 25, 2000. The masks had been collected by Frederica de Laguna in 1935 from a refuse pit be-hind a collapsed ceremonial house at Holikachaket, an ancestral village of Grayling. According to De Laguna, the masks were once used in the Mask Dance or the Feast of the Mask. The purpose of this ceremony was to insure a contin-ued supply of fish and game, by thanking the spirits of the animals. After careful analysis, the Museum found that the masks were "objects of central importance" to the Native Village of Grayling and could not have been alienated by any one individual. The masks were repatriated on October 26, 2002.

Ongoing Challenges

NAGPRA poses a number of difficult challenges for museums and tribes alike. The most obvious of these is funding. NAGPRA has often been characterized as an unfunded mandate, since there were originally no monies appropriated by Con-gress for its implementation. The funds that have now been made available are in-adequate. In 2000, the National Park Service (NPS) received 112 applications from 76 Indian tribes, Alaska Native villages and corporations, and Native Hawaiian organizations, and 27 museums, for a total request of approximately $6 million. A total of 45 grants, worth $2.25 million dollars, were funded by the NPS, of which only 12 were for repatriation. Most large museums, including this museum, have had to supplement grants with funds from their parent institutions or other sources.

One of the most difficult problems in implementing NAGPRA is grappling with the language of the law. Its enigmatic definitions and the legal discourse it entails are foreign to most tribal members and museum employees. This is one of the reasons that some tribes have turned to specialized organizations, such as the Native American Rights Fund, to press their cases. Similarly, many museums have had to seek in-house legal counsel or outside attorneys. Terms like "cultural affiliation," "alienation," and "right of possession" pose significant interpretive questions. For example, the process of determining cultural affiliation requires tribes and museums to consider multiple lines of evidence, including geographical, kinship, biological, archaeological, linguistic, folklore, oral tradition, historical or other information, or expert opinion. And yet there is often disagreement over how to weigh these different lines of evidence.

Another issue is identity politics. NAGPRA requires that tribes represent themselves through a relationship of shared group identity that links them to past groups and geographical regions from whom and where remains and objects were collected. However, Indian tribal groups are not static; indeed, like all communities, most have changed over time, sometimes quite dramatically, due to a host of social and political factors, and these changes mean that traditional connections are sometimes tenuous or difficult to establish. This is a particular problem with human remains that are extremely old, as in the case of Kennewick Man, as well as in those cases where there may be multiple tribal descendants of a specific archaeological culture.

An unresolved issue is the final disposition of "culturally unidentifiable human remains." Although the NAGPRA Review Committee was tasked by law to address this issue, it has yet to devise a solution. The current draft legislation is clear, however, in its intent to repatriate all Indian human remains, regardless of their age. For the scientific community, this raises questions and concerns about the future possibility of learning more about important topics such as the peopling of the New World.

On a practical level both tribes and museums are concerned with the treatment of human remains and objects with consolidants and pesticides. At the turn of the century, it was common museum practice to treat objects made of organic materials, especially feathers and fur, with arsenic as a preservative. Baskets, for example, were sometimes dipped in mercury. Today, we know that many of these treatments are toxic, and they are no longer used. Unfortunately, early record-keeping was less than adequate, so it is difficult to know, without expensive testing, which objects were given which treatments. This is a special concern for Indian peoples who may want to reintegrate sacred objects and objects of cultural patrimony into their ceremonies. Some tribes, such as the Hupa of California, are taking the lead in devising decontamination procedures.

Re-Representing Native Americans

The Museum is committed to understanding and documenting the diversity of Native American peoples in the twenty-first century. This requires not only that we comply with NAGPRA, but that we also represent the character and vitality of Indian cultures to the public in new ways. We are doing this through permanent and traveling exhibitions, publications, new acquisitions, internships, and visiting artists programs.

The Museum currently displays two permanent exhibitions devoted to Native America. In 1986, Susan A. Kaplan and Kristen J. Barsness curated "Raven's Journey," which provides an introduction to the worldview and lifeways of the Tlingit, Inuit, and Athabascan peoples of Alaska. In 1995, Dorothy Washburn curated "Living in Balance," which gives an overview of the Hopi, Zuni, Navajo, and Apache peoples of the American Southwest.

This later exhibition was prepared with Native consultation and included a children's component involving an exchange of photographs between Philadelphia-area and Pueblo and Navajo grade schools. In addition, the Museum has an active traveling exhibitions program. In 1998, Sally McLendon and Judith Berman curated "Pomo Indian Basket Weavers, Their Baskets and the Art Market," which opened at the Grace Hudson Museum, Ukiah, California, and traveled to the National Museum of the American Indian in New York and the Mashantucket Pequot Museum in Connecticut, before being displayed in Philadelphia.

Although funds for new acquisitions are limited, the American Section has made several recent purchases of contemporary Native American art. Some acquisitions have been made as the result of NAGPRA consultations. Raymond Dutchman's modern carvings, for example, were inspired by 100-year-old masks in the collection that reminded him of events and masking traditions no longer practiced in his own Native Alaskan community of Anvik.

The Museum is an active participant in the National Museum of the American Indian's Artist-in-Residence Program. Many Native people have a strong adherence to and respect for tradition, innovation, and craftsmanship, and museums that house old collections are uniquely positioned to offer keys to understanding those traditions in support of modern goals. Choctaw visiting artist Jerry Ingram studied the Museum's collection to gain insight into the style and construction techniques of Southeastern shoulder bags. The information gathered has influenced his work.

Conclusions

Edward Ayau and Ty Tengan have likened the repatriation efforts of Native Hawaiians to the seafaring legacy of their ancestors. Just as their ancestors made long journeys which involved hardships and challenges, so too do their people to-day make long journeys and confront seemingly insurmountable obstacles, as they work to repatriate their ancestors' remains. Extending this metaphor, we suggest that museums are also embarking upon a long journey to confront their own challenge. This challenge is to redress their history of representing Indian cultures as "primitive," "static," and "dying." We must devise new ways of representing indigenous peoples that acknowledge their vitality, resilience, and ongoing struggles to gain political standing. Because this history is part of a shared American history, we cannot make this journey alone; rather, we must make it in partnership with indigenous peoples. As the Native Hawaiians have so eloquently expressed, out of "heaviness" (*kaumaha*) must come "enlightenment" (*aokanaka*).

Discussion Questions

1. Is there an inherent contradiction in repatriating Native American human remains out of respect for Native American beliefs, and then having the Native Americans baptize the remains prior to reburial, under the Greek Orthodox Church?
2. Explore the ways in which NAGPRA has forced anthropology to confront its colonialist past.
3. What impact has NAGPRA had on your local institutions? Have they repatriated any materials? How has it changed the way the archaeologists and physical anthropologists in your institution teach and do research?
4. Explore the issues of repatriation and reburial as they are playing out in countries other than the United States.
5. Why does the University Museum have slightly different procedures for responding to claims for human remains and for objects of cultural patrimony and sacred objects?
6. If the intent of NAGPRA is to repatriate all human remains, what does this mean for the scientific community for learning more about such questions as the peopling of the New World? What other areas of archaeological concern are likely to be most seriously impacted? What options do scientists have to pursue these topics?
7. Explore possibilities for new ways for museums to represent indigenous peoples. In the process, consider what was/is inappropriate and misleading about the older styles of exhibits.
8. For most of the twentieth century in the United States, when Native American burials were discovered they were studied and stored in museums, while marked burials of Euro-Americans were immediately

reburied. Consequently, some observers call NAGPRA "hun
legislation. Agree or disagree and defend your position.

Further Readings

Bray, Tamara L. (editor). 2001. *The Future of the Past: Archaeologists, Native Americans, and Repatriation*. New York: Garland Publishing.

Dongoske, Kurt E., Mark Aldenderfer, and Karen Doehner (editors). 2000. *Working Together: Native Americans and Archaeologists*. Washington, D.C.: Society for American Archaeology.

Fine-Dare, Kathleen S. 2002. *Grave Injustice: The American Indian Repatriation Movement and NAGPRA*. Lincoln: University of Nebraska Press.

Merrill, William L., Edmund J. Ladd, and T. J. Ferguson. 1993. The Return of the Ahayu:da: Lessons for Repatriation from Zuni Pueblo and the Smithsonian Institution. *Current Anthropology* 34(5):523–567.

Rose, Jerome C., Thomas J. Green, and Victoria D. Green. 1996. NAGPRA Is Forever: Osteology and the Repatriation of Skeletons. *Annual Review of Anthropology* 25:81–103.

Zimmerman, Lawrence J. 1998. When Data Become People: Archaeological Ethics, Reburial, and the Past as Public Heritage. *International Journal of Cultural Property* 7(1):69–86.

Remembering Chełmno

20

JULIET GOLDEN

The Chełmno Extermination Camp in Poland was a place where as many as 300,000 adults and children, mostly Polish Jews, were executed and cremated as part of the Nazi "final solution." While the Nazis systematically destroyed evidence of the camp's existence, archaeology, carried out since the late 1980s, has provided one means to give a "voice" to those who died there. This research touches on important themes of representation, respect, and reburial.

I FIRST CAME TO CHEŁMNO ON CORPUS CHRISTI DAY, a spring religious holiday when Poles flock to the streets and join long processions in cities and villages across the country. The thick fragrance of rose petals strewn across the ground mingled in the air with homilies broadcast from the village church, beckoning parishioners who knelt in prayer on the asphalt-covered main thoroughfare. From a small knoll near the church, I admired the timeless village scene, framed by the lush Ner River Valley and an agricultural landscape that has changed little over the centuries. A Russian general, obviously taken with the view, built his country estate here in the nineteenth century.

Today, only a scatter of cobblestones and a granary remain from the estate, together with a few trenches dug by archaeologists and surrounded with blue memorial candles from Israel, marking the center of the Chełmno Extermination Camp.

The first camp where mass executions were carried out using gas, Chełmno was a testing ground for the Nazis looking to develop increasingly efficient methods to carry out their "final solution." Between 1941 and 1945, as many as 300,000 adults and children, mostly Polish Jews, were executed and cremated here. Before the Nazis retreated in early 1945, they destroyed or buried much of the evidence of the camp's existence. Little remained—on the surface at least—to attest the mass exterminations.

Since the late 1980s, however, excavations by Lucja Nowak, director of the Konin Regional Museum, have uncovered traces of the camp facilities and large quantities of personal effects belonging to its victims. Her findings have led to a more complete version of the camp's history than the existing handful of eyewitness accounts provide; they also give a voice to those who died here.

"When you say that 200,000 or 300,000 people were killed here, that doesn't really say much," says Nowak, a spritely, determined woman with thick, wavy black hair and dark piercing eyes. "For me, when we find a small toy or a shoe, that represents a living person. Through these small things we re-create the history of people who had dreams and life plans."

Unlike Auschwitz, Birkenau, or Dachau, Chełmno was not a concentration camp, encircled with barbed wire and lined with barracks where prisoners lived and worked. Rather, it operated exclusively as an extermination center—in two separate phases and at two sites roughly two miles apart. In phase one (December 1941 to April 1943), victims were transported to the estate, commonly referred to in Polish as a palace, where they were told that they were to shower before being transported to work camps. Inside the palace, victims undressed then were led to the basement, where they were forced into trucks and suffocated by redirected engine exhaust. The trucks were then driven to the forest outside the village, where the bodies were dumped in mass graves. Concerned about a typhus outbreak, the Nazis exhumed the bodies in 1942 and incinerated them in two crematories built in the forest. The Nazis razed the palace and later covered the ruins with a thick layer of soil when killings at Chełmno were temporarily halted, for unknown reasons, in the spring of 1943. In phase two (June 1944 to January 1945), victims spent the night in the village church, then were brought to barracks in the forest where they were collected and forced onto trucks to be gassed. In the second phase all the victims were cremated.

The Polish government erected a memorial to Chełmno's victims at the forest site in 1964. The land, however, was managed by the state forest service, while the palace grounds served as an agricultural cooperative. In the 1980s, Nowak and her husband, also an archaeologist and former regional museum director, wanted the two sites incorporated under the aegis of the museum.

Archaeology would provide the opportunity to do so. "People said that the Germans had liquidated all traces of the camp and that nothing was left," recalls Nowak. Work began at the forest site in 1986; it was incorporated into the museum the following year. Nowak and her team, made up of members of the museum's archaeology department and local volunteers, located the barracks and three crematories and uncovered pits where the victims' personal effects were burned. In one section of the crematory wall, excavators found metal parts of a baby carriage, used to reinforce the concrete structure.

During the Nazi occupation, most of the villagers were evacuated from Chełmno, with the exception of families near the river, away from the center of town. Older villagers agreed to talk with Nowak's team; they also provided photos carried by Chełmno's victims that were found on the grounds of the palace after the war.

Zofia Szalek was 11 when the Nazis established the camp. During the occupation, she pastured cows and goats in the ravine near the church. A small, nervous woman, Szalek recalls people being murdered in the palace. She remembers the screaming. While she supports Nowak's efforts, Szalek fears that in excavating at Chełmno, the dead will come back to haunt the living. Nonetheless, she has volunteered during the recent excavations of the palace grounds, sifting through dirt in search of minute personal effects.

The former village priest played a key role in the positive approach to the work at the site. "Father Idzi helped us a lot," says Nowak. "I spoke to the priest, and he said that while they were cleaning around the church they found strange things—scissors, spoons." These finds inspired Nowak to excavate near the church where the Germans had also burned looted goods.

The priest's decision to permit archaeologists onto church grounds paved the way for work later carried out at the palace, which at the time was owned by the agricultural cooperative. Father Idzi left the village in 2001, however, and the new priest has not taken an active role in support of the excavations. Moreover, he has not continued Father Idzi's tradition of organizing Masses in which he talked about the history of the Chełmno camp.

In 1997, Nowak and her team were permitted to make a limited excavation on palace grounds. Using architectural drawings of the estate, excavators made a small three-foot-deep probe. "We hit the bull's eye," says Nowak. "We had found the small hallway where the people were actually led from the basement into the trucks." Up to then the only source of information on the role that the palace played in the extermination process were testimonies of survivors and camp staff.

Vast amounts of property plundered by the Nazis have been uncovered. "It's a little strange, but with every movement of the shovel you unearth dozens of objects," says Przymyslaw Gaj, a 26-year-old archaeology student. "You find as many things here in one day as you would normally find in an entire season in the usual dig." The meticulous segregation of goods adds to the surreal nature of the excavation. In one place archaeologists uncovered a thick layer of medicine bottles, followed by a layer of eating utensils. Another pit was filled with combs. Archaeologists have also dug up thousands of dental bridges and false teeth picked over to recover precious metals used in dental work.

There is obviously an emotional dimension to the work at Chełmno that is seldom encountered in archaeology. Small fragments of bone catch the sunlight at the forest site where the crematories once stood. "It's one thing to hear about the crematory, it's another to stand inside an enormous pit that is filled with human bones," says Krzysztof Gorczyca, an archaeologist who directed last summer's excavation. "Only then did it occur to me just how many people were murdered here."

Many of the recovered objects speak volumes about how victims lived in the weeks and months before they arrived at Chełmno. In a pit of goods looted from victims brought in from the Lodz ghetto, two brooches, crudely fashioned from wire, bear the names of Bela and Irka. Other relics give names of victims or their hometowns and reveal their hobbies or passions. Hundreds of medicine bottles found in a single pit originated in Germany, Luxembourg, and Czechoslovakia. A charm bearing the image of a tombstone gives a family name and the burial location in a Jewish cemetery in what was once the German city of Breslau, now Wroclaw. Jozef Jakubowski carried a cigarette case he won in a 1936 edition of the "Gordon-Bennet" motorcycle race.

The most valuable artifacts, such as fragments of paper and items that can be tied to specific people or locations, are photographed immediately and sent to the Konin Museum for conservation. Because of the sheer number of objects found daily, archaeologists have to perform a sort of triage. Preliminary probes showed that one pit, for example, was full of metal cooking pots. The team decided not to excavate it.

Among the most wrenching finds for Nowak were the remains of a three-month-old baby buried on the palace grounds with a knife engraved with the words "Keep the Sabbath." Eyewitness testimonies revealed that a brothel operated inside the palace. Nowak suspects Jewish women were forced to work in it. "Somehow that child must have been kept alive," Nowak says.

Chełmno is considered holy ground by Jews, and as such is subject to Jewish laws and traditions. Jewish leaders have praised Nowak's scrupulous approach to her work. "The research at Chełmno is carried out with the absolute agreement and cooperation of the Jewish community," says Simcha Keller, head of the Jewish community in Lodz. "Dr. Nowak is a guarantor that the work is done with complete respect." Human remains found during the excavations are interred in a Jewish cemetery established in the forest. The burial ceremonies are attended by Jews from around the world.

The government agency that supervises wartime cemeteries and monuments in Poland also finances the excavations at Chełmno, which cost about $17,500 a year. The country faces a large budget deficit, however, and additional funds that would allow Nowak to realize her plans of opening a museum, visitors' center, and learning center on the palace grounds are in short supply. For now, some of the objects found at Chełmno are on display in an austere, one-room makeshift museum on the site. Articles from the Polish press and pictures from Chełmno before and during the war cover the walls. The building is not well secured and Nowak is afraid of displaying valuable items, so she has had duplicates made of some of them, such as the cigarette case from the motorcycle race. Other objects found at Chełmno are on permanent loan to Yad Vashem, the Holocaust memorial and museum in Jerusalem, and the British War Museum. Part of the crematory foundations were sent to the Holocaust Museum in Washington, D.C.

Nowak's effort to piece together the history of Chełmno is only one element of a much larger mission: she wants young Poles to understand how generations of Jews contributed to the history and culture of the region. "I am an enemy of doing lectures focused solely on the Holocaust," she says.

In the forest near the main Chełmno memorial, Nowak has reconstructed a traditional Jewish cemetery from gravestones that once stood in the nearby town of Turek. Leveled by the Nazis in 1941, the cemetery was rediscovered by Nowak in 1990, after a vigilant factory worker informed her that stones "with strange writing on them" were being dug up on the grounds of a local dairy. Nowak learned Hebrew in order to read the stones and document the history of those buried there. For Nowak, the retelling of their lives and traditions is critical in ensuring that the Holocaust is not removed from the larger historical and cultural context.

"For young people in Poland, a Jew is an unknown quantity," she says. "They don't know about the contribution Jews made to Polish culture and history. If they understand that, then they will look at the Holocaust differently."

Discussion Questions

1. Many native peoples consider the invasion and colonization of North America by Europeans a genocide—a holocaust. With this in mind, compare the approach of this excavation on Jewish holy ground with archaeological work done in Native American burial grounds and sacred places. Why are the remains of Jewish holocaust victims ceremonially reburied in cemeteries, when Native American human remains have for so long been stored in museums? Why are the excavations at Chełmno "carried out with the absolute agreement and cooperation of the Jewish community" while most Native American sites in the United States are excavated without consent, consultation, or collaboration?

2. A number of chapters have mentioned the use of replicas in museum and other exhibits, usually noting that they are used for security reasons. What do you think about this practice? Might replicas be an option for

scholars who want to retain access to certain remains (human and otherwise) for future study but that are scheduled for reburial under NAGPRA? What about electronic replicas?

3. Discuss the similarities and differences between Nowak's concerns to educate a younger generation in Poland about the contributions made by Jews to Polish culture and history and the efforts by the University Museum (Chapter 19) and others to tell a story about Native Americans that is fuller than that once told in exhibits.

Further Readings

Koff, Clea. 2004. *The Bone Woman: A Forensic Anthropologist's Search for Truth in the Graves of Rwanda, Bosnia, Croatia, and Kosovo.* New York: Random House.

McGuire, Randall H. 2004. Letter from Ludlow: Colorado Coalfield Massacre. *Archaeology* 57(6):62–70.

Nash, Steve. 2004. Battles over Battlefields. *Archaeology* 57(5):24–29.

Silberman, Neil Asher. 2004. In Flanders Fields. *Archaeology* 57(3):24–29.

Zerubavel, Yael. 1994. The Death of Memory and the Memory of Death: Masada and the Holocaust as Historical Metaphors. *Representations* 45:72–100.

The New Acropolis Museum   21

JARRETT LOBELL

The construction of a new Acropolis Museum in Athens, Greece, has been controversial in numerous ways—from its location on top of rich archaeological remains to its unabashedly modern architecture and its goal of housing the Elgin (or Parthenon) Marbles, which the Greeks say should now be repatriated from the British Museum in London.

G REECE'S HIGHEST CIVIL COURT HAS thrown out a lawsuit that had threatened to permanently halt construction of Athens's new Acropolis Museum, the disputed future home of the hotly contested Parthenon Marbles. Although the museum was not ready for the August 2004 Olympics as officials originally hoped, this decision has enabled contractors to restart work on the building. The museum was originally envisioned fourteen years ago to replace its decaying nineteenth-century predecessor, which holds archaeological materials from the Acropolis, including works from the Parthenon.

The lawsuit was brought early this year by the International Council on Museums and Sites (ICOMOS) and residents of the neighborhood where the museum is being built. Both contend that archaeological remains on the building site—including a late Roman and three Early Christian baths, a seventh-century bathhouse, and sculpture and pottery dating from the Classical to Byzantine periods—would be damaged by construction. "For the purists, it is better to have no excavations, not to touch anything," says Dimitrios Pandermalis, archaeologist and president of the Committee for a New Acropolis Museum. "For us, the realists, it is better to excavate and then to protect. We have to cover this fragile excavation, so why not cover it with a museum? We're not building a hotel." Cynics point out that no one complained when similar excavations were done during the construction of the Acropolis metro station, only a few hundred yards from the site of the new museum. They suspect that some of the recent lawsuits were a result of local residents' desire to attract attention to the destruction, not of the archaeological site, but of their own houses, hoping to wrest more money from museum developers. More than one-third of the entire budget for the museum project has already been spent buying up property at the site.

The new Acropolis Museum, a three-story glass structure mounted on pillars, is intended not only as an upgrade but also as an enticement. While elements of the Parthenon now sit in ten museums in eight countries, the majority of those not in Athens, known as the Parthenon (Elgin) Marbles, are in the British Museum in London. These include sculptures that have been traditionally interpreted as depicting the procession to the religious festival of the Panathenaia in the goddess Athena's honor. While the majority of the British public and even government officials support the return of the Marbles to Greece, according to a recent BBC survey, the British Museum has consistently refused, citing many factors including Greece's inability to care for and display them properly. The new Acropolis Museum, with its state-of-the-art display areas, will go a long way toward answering this charge.

Although some have attacked the museum's design as too contemporary, Bernard Tschumi, former dean of Columbia Graduate School of Architecture and the architect of the museum, told *Archaeology*, "Some people have said it is disrespectful to the Parthenon not to have Doric columns [on the new museum], but I am not interested in imitating the Parthenon. I am interested in [achieving] that level of perfection in my buildings, and for early twenty-first-century architecture to match it in its own way." Pandermalis says both natural and artificial light will be used to "show every detail of the sculpted surfaces, to demonstrate how artists in the fifth century B.C. were interested in the smallest details." Studies are currently being conducted by the museum on whether light or dark backgrounds are better for displaying sculpture, and on how to protect the newly restored sculptures from the city's heat. The results of these studies will be incorporated into the building when it finally rises from its foundations, the only part that has so far been completed.

Visitors to the new museum will walk to the top floor on a ramp that mirrors the ascent up the Acropolis. Once there, they will see the Parthenon's architectural sculpture, including portions of the frieze as they appeared on the building, but with gaps where the missing British Museum pieces would be. "The way we will display the Marbles will be a permanent protest for their return," says Pandermalis. "People believe that these works of art [on the Acropolis] are important, but they don't know why. Most people know about their artistic quality, and we will show that through the use of light. But the frieze is also important for its subject matter. This was the first time the people of the world's first democracy put themselves into their art. These are not mythical gods and creatures, but real people, from Athens, who are participating in the process of democracy."

Both Tschumi and Pandermalis are eager to get back to work. "When the museum gets built, the marbles will come back. There is no question about it," the architect insists.

Discussion Questions

1. Should the Greek court have ruled against ICOMOS and the residents of the neighborhood? Do you side with the "purists," the "realists," or the "cynics" in this debate? Where else have there recently been controversies about building site museums and tourist shops on land that is known to hold ancient remains? What are the issues involved? Compare this controversy with the development for archaeotourism at Caracol in Belize (see Chapter 16).

2. Do you think that, with a new state-of-the-art museum on the slopes of the Acropolis that provides a view to the standing remains of the Parthenon soon ready for their exhibit, the British Museum should now return the Elgin Marbles to Greece? Do you think they will be returned?

3. Should a site museum be designed to interfere as little as possible with the existing monuments whose former contents it holds? Should it reflect the style of architecture of the ancient site? What specifications would you make to the architect hired to design a new site museum for your site?

4. What are the arguments for and against creating new museums to house the finds from a particular excavation on (or very near) the site itself, even if in a poorly developed rural area, rather than sending the objects for conservation and exhibit to an existing large museum, usually in a major urban center where more people are concentrated and likely to see the exhibits?

5. Collectors and dealers often argue that having the artifacts from one culture on exhibit in another contributes to greater appreciation of cultural diversity. Discuss this in relation to collecting generally, and specifically in relation to the Parthenon Marbles staying in the British Museum. International traveling exhibits are sometimes touted as the better approach to appreciating the diversity of world culture. Discuss the costs and benefits of such international exhibits.

Further Readings

Hamilakis, Yannis. 1999. Stories from Exile: Fragments from the Cultural Biography of the Parthenon (or 'Elgin') Marbles. *World Archaeology* 31(2):303–320.

Hitchens, Christopher, and Graham Binns. 1998. *The Elgin Marbles: Should They Be Returned to Greece?* London: Verso.

Lobell, Jarrett A. 2004. Does Greece Need the Olympics? *Archaeology* 57(4):21–27.

Merryman, John Henry. 2000. Thinking about the Elgin Marbles. In *Thinking about the Elgin Marbles: Critical Essays on Cultural Property, Art and Law,* edited by John Henry Merryman, pp. 21-63. Cambridge: Kluwer Law International.

St. Clair, William. 1999. The Elgin Marbles: Questions of Stewardship and Accountability. *International Journal of Cultural Property* 8(2):391–521.

Silverman, Helaine (editor). Forthcoming. *Archaeological Site Museums in Latin America.* Gainesville: University of Florida Press.

Stavrakakis, Yannis N. 2000. Subway to the Past. *Archaeology* 53(2):36–41.

THE PROFESSIONAL ARCHAEOLOGIST V

Archaeology's Dirty Secret

22

BRIAN FAGAN

The author was taught that publishing one's research before new field projects are undertaken is a sa-cred principle of archaeology. He finds it ironic that, in an academic culture in which publication is deemed the most noble of activities, "most archaeologists prefer to keep on digging." Preliminary re-ports and short articles, often derived from conference papers, and often published repeatedly in only slightly differing versions, have, too often, replaced definitive reports on sites, artifacts, and survey work. Non-archaeological pressures may receive some of the blame, but ultimately it is up to archae-ologists to meet their fundamental responsibility for publishing their research.

SOME YEARS AGO, I attended a retirement party for a distinguished colleague at a prominent Midwestern university. Several generations of former stu-dents were on hand to praise his many seasons of fieldwork at home and abroad. But they were tactful not to mention one problem with their beloved men-tor's career: only one of his excavations had ever been published in full. Alas, the professor has now passed on, leaving behind nothing but sketchy field notes and a museum storeroom full of inadequately labeled artifacts. Even in retirement he could not find the time to publish his fieldwork. In fact he was still digging right up to the end. The loss to science is incalculable.

I was brought up to believe that publishing one's research was a sacred princi-ple of archaeology, a task to be completed before new excavations were begun. The great British Egyptologist Flinders Petrie was an early advocate of prompt and full publication. His reports are verbose and far from complete by modern standards, but at least they provide a body of basic information with which to work. Mor-timer Wheeler was also careful to publish his excavations in full. My mentors did not always practice what they preached, but they taught us that prompt and full publication was a fundamental responsibility for any archaeologist who ventures into the field. The archaeological world has changed since Wheeler's day. A generation ago most site reports were the work of a single scholar. Today even a modest dig can involve a team of specialists and a quantity of data that may take years to study and write up. Ironically, in an academic culture that considers publication the most desirable of all scholarly activities, most archaeologists prefer to keep on digging.

The common forum for presenting field data is the academic conference, where 20-minute papers summarize new work. In recent years, publishers have printed volume after volume of such papers, often grouped under a general title, with little editorial coherence. Invariably, conference papers give a nod to current theoretical debates, present some limited original data, and end with a brief synthesis noting how the new work advances research in a particular subject area. Often, the same paper appears in several places, recast slightly to reflect a different audience or academic emphasis. In an academic world where jobs are scarce and publication of any kind is seen as the road to employment, such bibliography-padding has become commonplace, if not endemic. In one's later career the pressure to publish such papers to obtain tenure and regular promotions continues unabated. Too often definitive reports on sites, artifacts, or survey work never appear.

I know of numerous preliminary reports published a generation ago that are still the only source of basic information on excavations of first-rate importance. There are major Lower Paleolithic sites in sub-Saharan Africa excavated in the 1950s and 1960s that are still accessible only from such reports. The same can be said for many important North American and Mesoamerican excavations of the 1970s. Much of the evidence for early agriculture in Europe and the Near East is only available in the periodical literature. Kathleen Kenyon's famous excavations at Jericho are still incompletely published. Some classical excavations have been underway for decades, with no sign that digging will stop and long-term publication begin. Some guilty parties argue that laboratory work must come first and that the whole process takes longer than it did a generation ago. But if you look closely you will find the same people hard at work in the field each year, digging up yet another site.

Clearly an overwhelming case can be made for less excavation and more analysis of previous work. Unfortunately, our scholarly culture rewards people for new and original research, sometimes defined in the narrowest terms as participation in an active fieldwork program. Grant-giving agencies contribute to the problem by funding field research while rarely giving monies for laboratory analysis or publication. Neither is a terribly sexy pursuit in a world in which museums and universities thrive on headline-catching discoveries, and, to quote a recent University of California staff document, "productive faculty publishing in refereed journals."

The problem is further compounded by the exigencies of cultural resource management or salvage archaeology, whose requirements for prompt reporting result for the most part in factual accounts with limited, if not restricted, distribution. A researcher can spend days, sometimes months, tracking down what is technically published information. Meanwhile, definitive archaeological monographs, such as those on the Maya city of Tikal that appear at regular intervals, are becoming a rarity. Few outlets remain for such valuable studies. Economic realities make it ever harder for even the best endowed academic presses to produce such monographs.

Surprisingly, there is little, if any, academic discussion of these issues. Perusing the programs of several major conferences, I see no panel sessions on this issue, nor on alternative means of disseminating archaeological data. Hershel Shanks, editor of *Biblical Archaeology Review,* calls the crisis "archaeology's dirty secret." In a recent editorial, he recommended the creation of a new profession: archaeology editor/writer, "specialists who know how to publish reports."

The obligation to publish basic research is a fundamental part of archaeological ethics; some would say it is the most fundamental. It is enshrined in the Archaeological Institute of America's recently adopted Code of Professional Standards: "Archaeologists should make public the results of their research in a timely fashion, making evidence available to others if publication is not accomplished within a reasonable time. All research projects should contain specific plans for conservation, preservation, and publication from the very outset, and funds should be secured for such purposes."

Desktop publishing, CD-ROMs, and other electronic media offer fascinating opportunities for publication, and for distribution of research results and data over the Internet and other such channels. Electronics offer staggering possibilities for wide distribution of highly specialized, peer-reviewed monographs and reports. Soon, researchers will have interactive access to their colleagues' and predecessors' artifact data bases. Such access will make new demands on archaeologists to curate and analyze their data promptly. The demands of the electronic forum will make it harder to duck the responsibility of preparing one's data for scholarly use and scrutiny. In many cases, "publication" will consist of meticulously organized data bases, including graphics. The compiling of such data bases raises fascinating implications for future financing of archaeological projects. Grant-giving agencies will have to bow to the new reality and finance such far-from-spectacular activities, while cutting back on funding for more excavations.

Archaeologists have a clear obligation to publish their research promptly, and in full. After all, ours is the only science that "murders its informants," as American archaeologist Kent Flannery once put it. If we were to devote as much time to publishing as we do to excavating, we would not be accused, with some justification, of being a self-serving, special interest group that keeps its finds to itself. Some of those who make such accusations are now picking up on the publishing problem and arguing that by not producing final reports we are effectively looters ourselves. Writing final reports and monographs is far from glamorous work. But as Mortimer Wheeler and others pointed out many years ago, only the archaeologist who did the work and led the research team can write the final and definitive report that records exactly what was found and what it means. We are witnessing a sea change in the way archaeologists go about business.

I do not agree with Hershel Shanks that the solution lies in specialist report writers. It lies in archaeologists living up to their fundamental responsibilities. Fortunately, creative solutions await those bold enough to seize them.

Discussion Questions

1. What happens to the records and finds from a field project when the director retires or dies without publishing them?
2. Most universities want to hire an archaeologist with an active field project. Why? What impact does this hiring preference have on individual archaeologists and on the discipline? How can we define other ways to demonstrate new and original research and make non-archaeologists understand that archaeology is not all about digging?
3. What are the different publishing practices and expectations for archaeologists working in different parts of the world? Are site reports a standard form of publication in the area of the world you are interested in? How regularly do you read or use data from site reports in your research? If you work in, or are planning to work in a country where the primary language is other than your own, do you expect to publish in that language as well as in your own? Does the language you publish in matter?
4. What is wrong with publishing slight variations on the same paper in different places? What encourages the practice?
5. Why does it take so long to produce final reports on field projects? What could be done to improve the speed of such publications?
6. Explore some of the new forms of electronic publication and other technological developments that are affecting archaeological publishing.
7. What are the expenses of publication, and who pays for the actual costs of publishing field reports? Who buys field reports?
8. What are the different costs and issues of Cultural Resources Management and academic publishing?

9. Would the creation of a new category of professional, the report writer suggested by Shanks, be a useful addition? Who would pay for the services of such professionals?

10. Given the already limited funding available for archaeological research, would you advocate that funding agencies direct more funds to publication and less to fieldwork? Defend your position.

11. What effect on the public perception of archaeology does lack of attention to publishing fieldwork have?

12. What are the problems faced, by the individuals directly involved and by the discipline as a whole, when people not originally part of a field project undertake publication of materials from an older excavation? What do you think of the suggestion that unpublished materials from old excavations should be assigned as Ph.D. dissertation topics?

Further Readings

Doelle, William H. 2002. Publication and Preservation: Two Imperatives in Heritage Conservation. In *Archaeological Research and Heritage Preservation in the Americas*, edited by Robert D. Drennan and Santiago Mora, pp. 26–37. Washington, D.C.: Society for American Archaeology.

Fagan, Brian, and Mark Rose. 2003. Ethics and the Media. In *Ethical Issues in Archaeology*, edited by Larry J. Zimmerman, Karen D. Vitelli and Julie Hollowell-Zimmer, pp. 163–176. Walnut Creek, CA: AltaMira Press.

Shanks, Hershel. 1994. Archaeology's Dirty Secret. *Biblical Archaeology Review* 20(5):63–64, 79.

Intellectual Property Issues in Archaeology? 23

GEORGE NICHOLAS AND JULIE HOLLOWELL

In recent years, questions about archaeological ethics have focused primarily on the stewardship of archaeological objects—the physical remains of the past. Nicholas and Hollowell argue here that new and vital issues in the domain of intellectual property rights, or IPR, will soon demand equal or greater attention from archaeologists. From rock art images to information gained from DNA studies, the results of archaeological work are being claimed as the intellectual property of particular groups, who can therefore determine what, if any, use can be made of the information or ideas. The authors suggest ways for archaeologists to negotiate this new terrain.

IN RECENT DECADES, new interpretations of cultural property rights have prompted a paradigm shift in the policies and practices of archaeologists, biological anthropologists, Indigenous groups, governments, and museums everywhere as we face the complex politics, policies, and ethics surrounding the question, "Who owns the past?" These discussions have focused largely on issues of material or physical property—repatriation, curation practices, the artifact market, heritage site management—but a topic of even greater challenge in coming years is likely to be that of intellectual property rights (IPR).

Worldwide, archaeology has met growing involvement on the part of Indigenous peoples, local communities, for-profit companies, and host governments in everything from permitting excavations to claims exerted over artifacts and research data. Researchers may well find themselves increasingly limited in the freedom to use scientific knowledge or indigenous sources of knowledge. At the same time, descendant communities have legitimate concerns about the procurement, dissemination, and exploitation of "traditional knowledge," which they consider their intellectual property. As commercial use of aspects of the cultural pasts continues to expand, questions about sharing the benefits of research and concerns about unauthorized or commercial uses of knowledge, images, stories, and designs will persist and fuel debate and, potentially, lawsuits.

We can only benefit from proactively addressing these concerns about intellectual property rights and their implications for archaeological practice, for the archaeological record, and for our relationships with stakeholders. Indeed, as Larry Zimmerman has noted, not to do so opens the door to uninformed decision-making and an uncertain future for the discipline.

Where IPR Issues Emerge

In archaeology, intellectual property issues have surfaced in relation to information and ideas derived from past knowledge systems (often referred to as traditional or indigenous knowledge); to images, designs, artifacts and sites created in the past; and to ethical and proprietary claims to the design, results, and interpretations of archaeological research.

A few examples will illustrate the provocative and complicated questions intellectual property issues raise for archaeology. All of them underscore the unavoidable entanglements of archaeology with economics, nationalism, and cultural politics, and the increasing complexities of managing information in a global world.

Rock art and other archaeological images have been widely used in business logos, t-shirt designs, and even on refrigerator magnets, but seldom with permission of their traditional owners or caretakers, who are beginning to raise objections. In 2000, the Snuneymuxw Nation of British Columbia successfully registered with the Canadian Intellectual Property Office ten petroglyphs within their traditional territory as "official marks" to prevent them from being reproduced or commercially exploited. In the Deaf Adder Creek case in Australia, an Aboriginal clan pursued legal action against a company that reproduced rock art images on t-shirts. The case established that Australian rock art is not freely available for copying and imitation with impunity. And in New Zealand, producer of *The Lord of the Rings*, Peter Jackson, negotiated with local Maori elders to establish conditions for including footage of Mount Ruapehu, a sacred mountain, in the film. The Maori consider it offensive and dangerous to draw, photograph, or even to look at the top of a sacred mountain—lest such acts drain it of its *mana* (spiritual strength). Jackson was given permission to include the mountain if he altered the actual image with digital enhancements.

Concerns exist even when commercialization is not at issue. Some Native American groups, for example, believe that making certain kinds of information available to uninitiated people will bring harm to their community. Museums that want to provide wider access to images and materials in their collections are finding that they need to accommodate specific intellectual property concerns of descendant communities. Other intellectual property disputes reflect the political salience of archaeological symbols—as when heated controversy erupted a decade ago over the choice to place an ancient motif from excavations in Greek Macedonia on the new flag of the Former Yugoslav Republic of Macedonia.

Archaeological studies occasionally produce findings with patentable commercial or social applications. These situations can raise questions about the equitable sharing of economic benefits, similar to those faced in ethnobotany today. For example, archaeozoologist Jane Wheeler's research on Inca textiles from archaeological sites in Peru has established a DNA bank to restore a genetic line of alpaca that was bred centuries ago for its exceptionally fine wool, far superior to what local weavers use today. Wheeler is not alone in thinking about potential economic applications for her work.

In a yet more sensitive arena, data derived from DNA studies of human remains could play a role in future medical treatments for contemporary diseases. For example, recent tests permitted by the people of Brevig Mission, Alaska, on the remains of villagers who died in the influenza epidemic of 1918 may well help to develop a new vaccine to protect us from similar influenzas in the future. Even older genetic material has been recovered from other glacial, desert and wetland settings. How should a descendant group be recognized and compensated for its contributions to such a broadly significant development? The collection and use of data without the acknowledgement or permission of host communities constitutes scientific colonialism and is a clear breach of trust with Native peoples. One example of this occurred in British Columbia following research on rheumatic diseases based on blood samples obtained from Nuu-chah-nulth communities. The blood samples were later used in mitochondrial DNA studies. Not only were the Nuu-chah-nulth unaware of the mtDNA research, they were never informed of the results of the original study.

Archaeotourism is fast emerging as a global industry that employs and exploits commercially intellectual aspects of the past. It comes in many packages—everything from remote eco-tours to living history museums and archaeological theme parks. Archaeotourism raises questions about what versions of the past are being promoted and who has the right to benefit from the commercial development of archaeological knowledge.

Increasingly, communities are drawing on intellectual property rights and archaeology to protect or develop significant sites and landscapes. In North America, prehistoric medicine wheel sites still in use by Native Americans are also being used by New Age groups, which, in some locations, have built their own, or actually rebuilt the original. The irony here is that New Agers are not only appropriating, but actually threatening both the intellectual and cultural heritage of those whose values they seek to emulate. In Australia and elsewhere, Aboriginal knowledge holders have faced dilemmas such as having to divulge knowledge that should be kept secret to protect significant sites from development. And in many places, it is recognized that community-based archaeology provides a powerful bridge between past and present, one that has the potential to generate cultural, economic and intellectual benefits.

Dealing with IPR

Archaeologists may find two specific recommendations helpful in contending with the new IPR concerns that require new approaches, policies, and research paradigms. The first is to recognize how intellectual property and intellectual property rights are being used and defined in particular situations, both by archaeologists and by other stakeholders. How do people employ these concepts to lay claim to the past? This approach underscores the need to articulate the unique intellectual contributions that archaeology makes to our understanding of the human past. It also demands thoughtful scrutiny of the assumptions about intellectual property rights that underlie our notions of archaeological stewardship, significance, and privilege. At the same time, these issues require an astute awareness of the historical, economic, and political contexts in which various stakeholders make claims about intellectual property and what those claims imply for the archaeological record, for research, and for society-at-large.

The second recommendation is to consider archaeology as a "negotiated practice" among parties with varied, and sometimes conflicting, interests and responsibilities. Doing so may well entail crafting new terms of engagement and compromise (including, at times, agreeing to disagree) that seek to protect and respect both indigenous knowledge and the archaeological record. Rather than surrendering standards of good archaeology to censorship or prevailing world-views, this approach promotes archaeology as one particular way to appropriate and interpret the past. Valuable precedents and examples, both positive and negative, can help us learn how to negotiate IPR in archaeological research. One example is the protocol that Claire Smith has developed in her work with Barunga people of Australia. Barunga people have the right to censor harmful or offensive aspects of her research, but Claire designs the terms and parameters in consultation with them to minimize the need for them to invoke this right. The researcher retains ownership over intellectual property that results from the research process itself.

Sharing Research Benefits

In many ways, paying attention to intellectual property rights is a continuation of the critique that has made archaeology a richer, more accountable field over the past two decades. Significant changes have also occurred in the process of doing archaeology, as members of descendant communities are now more frequently involved directly in the study of their own cultural legacy. Nevertheless, real inequalities remain as to who benefits from this information. Much of the knowledge produced by archaeology still contributes to a relatively select group, without benefits returning to source communities.

Attention to intellectual property rights in archaeology makes us more accountable, more aware of, and prepared to navigate the complex terrain in which the discipline finds itself today, a terrain that in many ways is the legacy of its colonialist origins. We suggest that archaeology and other disciplines cannot truly claim to be "postcolonial" until they deal with issues of intellectual property rights and the equitable sharing of benefits and knowledge produced by research.

Discussion Questions

1. You and other members of your excavation team have been talking with local community leaders about how they might realize some economic benefits from the excavations in their area. A shopkeeper says he thinks he could sell a lot of T-shirts with a picture of some of your most interesting artifacts, the name of your project, and the name of the town, and asks if you would design such a t-shirt for him; he'll take care of the rest (including claiming any profits from sales). Explore the intellectual property rights involved in such an arrangement, which means considering where your excavation is located, whether relevant local law exists, who the shopkeeper is, and the like. If present in the community, how might the descendants of the site's original occupants feel about this?

2. What are the problems and limitations of couching these issues in terms of "intellectual property"?

3. Discuss the question of appropriate compensation for the example cited here of Alaskan villagers who permitted excavation of their ancestors for testing if those tests, indeed, contribute to a new and widely used vaccine. Find similar examples in other disciplines.

4. Compile a list of images derived from archaeological work that are in use as business logos, archaeological journal covers, designs on clothing, household objects, games, and other goods, and discuss the potential intellectual property rights infringements they represent. What are the pros and cons of having these images in the public domain?

5. You are an archaeologist who worked on an excavation years ago and have spent the years since—basically, your professional life—analyzing and publishing your interpretations of the very substantial ceramic assemblage from that excavation. You and your colleagues have come to think of those potsherds as, in some sense, "yours," even though they are permanently curated in a government-run museum. In fact, what part of those years of work constitutes your own personal intellectual property, and what part is someone else's? Could you use a photograph of your favorite pot as your logo on stationery for a new consulting business you're thinking of starting without infringing on anyone's IPR? Would the answer be different if you used one of your own careful drawings of the same pot?

6. Is adding digital lava to a mountain really changing a place? Could archaeologists similarly manipulate images of sacred objects or places in a book or academic article as a compromise with Native peoples?

7. The illustration that accompanied this article in the original publication showed an ancient petroglyph and an almost exact copy of it on a modern ceramic plate. The authors posed the question, "Where is the line between fair use and the exploitation of someone's cultural past?" Discuss this and other examples of modern use of ancient designs and the degree to which those designs still belong to someone.

8. Dealers and collectors certainly consider themselves as stakeholders in ancient cultures. Can you think of an IPR they might claim in this context? Should archaeologists negotiate with them?

Further Readings

Brown, Michael F. 1998. Can Culture Be Copyrighted? *Current Anthropology* 39(2):193–222.

Cybulski, Jerome S. 2001. Current Challenges to Traditional Anthropological Applications of Human Osteology in Canada, In *Out of the Past. The History of Human Osteology at the University of Toronto*, edited by Larry Sawchuk and Susan Pfeiffer, CITD Press. Tspace.library.utoronto.ca/citd/Osteology/cybulski/html (accessed 4/22/05).

Nicholas, George P., and Kelly P. Bannister. 2004. Copyrighting the Past? Emerging Intellectual Property Rights Issues in Archaeology. *Current Anthropology* 45(3):327–350.

Riley, Mary (editor). 2004. *Indigenous Intellectual Property Rights*. Walnut Creek, CA: AltaMira Press.

Rowan, Yorke, and Uzi Baram (editors). 2004. *Marketing Heritage: Archaeology and the Consumption of the Past*. Walnut Creek, CA: AltaMira Press.

Lure of the Deep

24

JAMES P. DELGADO

This article reviews the history of shipwreck archaeology and salvage, particularly in North America, raising some important ethical questions along the way and drawing attention to some of the considerations and laws that distinguish archaeology under water from land-based work.

> *"It is probable that a greater number of monuments of the skill and industry of man will in the course of ages be collected together in the bed of the oceans, than will exist at any one time on the surface of the continents."*

—SIR CHARLES LYELL, Principles of Geology (1832)

FOR THOUSANDS OF YEARS the oceans have been great highways for communication and commerce. Many vessels have been lost and now rest on the ocean floor. Until recently, these shipwrecks, and the incredible record of the past that they contain, were beyond our reach. Now, thanks to new technologies, scholars as well as treasure hunters can safely descend to great depths to explore or plunder them.

At stake are a host of ancient wrecks—trading ships scattered about the Mediterranean seabed; gold-laden Spanish galleons off the coasts of North, Central, and South America; and Spanish and Portuguese ships off the Azores, their cargo of treasure from Asia, Africa, and the East Indies still intact. Many of these sites are incredibly well-preserved, with both ships and their contents in near pristine condition. Salvors have barely begun exploiting these cultural resources, but the potential for them to do so is increasing by the day, a cause for alarm among archaeologists.

Early technologies useful in the pursuit of sunken treasure were pioneered by the British adventurers John and Charles Deane, who in 1836 dove on Henry VIII's warship *Mary Rose*, which had sunk in 40 feet of water off England's southern coast in 1545. Wearing metal helmets and leather suits and breathing through tubes attached to an air pump on the surface, the brothers wrested huge cannon and well-preserved wood from the ship. Their quest was motivated in large part by financial gain from the salvage of the guns, but the age of the timbers and the history of the ship inspired them to preserve small pieces of wood as relics, which they used as covers for the souvenir books that accompanied a display of the cannon.

A century later, from 1918 to 1923, nearly $10 million in gold bullion was salvaged from the British ocean liner *Laurentic*, which sank in 120 feet of water after being torpedoed by the Germans in January 1917. This operation led to the development of the first decompression tables, which allow divers to calculate the time that can be spent at a given depth and the time needed between dives to avoid dangerous nitrogen buildup in the blood, a condition commonly known as "the bends."

After World War II the invention of scuba gear allowed forays as deep as 200 feet. Wartime technologies for locating enemy submarines, including sonar and magnetometers, were appropriated by treasure hunters searching for sunken ships. Recreational divers, souvenir hunters, and salvors quickly stripped wrecks in shallow waters. Alarmed by such pillaging, many countries adopted legislation to protect wrecks within their jurisdictions, generally three to 12 miles out to sea. These laws have slowed the plundering of shipwrecks within national boundaries. Wrecks in deep international waters were protected by their inaccessibility.

The first breakthrough in deep-sea salvage came in June 1963, when a U.S. Navy crew using the bathyscaphe *Trieste II* searched for and recovered the American nuclear submarine *Thresher*, which had sunk more than one and one-half miles in the Atlantic after experiencing mechanical problems. In 1965 the Navy was able to locate a hydrogen bomb that had dropped into the sea after a midair collision between a bomber and its refueling tanker off Palomares, Spain, by sending a remotely operated vehicle (ROV) down some 3,000 feet. The following year the Navy recovered the bomb using the manned submersible *Alvin*. Within a few years such military technology would be used by civilians to find historically significant wrecks in far deeper waters.

Clive Cussler's novel *Raise the Titanic!* published in 1976, described a futuristic salvage of the ocean liner *Titanic*, which sank with more than 1,500 passengers on her maiden voyage from Southampton to New York in 1912. Finding the legendary vessel in the deep waters of the North Atlantic was declared impossible after a series of well-publicized attempts to locate the ship by Texas oil millionaire Jack Grimm. He had searched for *Titanic* in the early 1980s using side-scan sonar, magnetometers, and a remotely operated camera towed 650 feet above the seabed, but missed the ship by more than a mile.

In 1985 Robert Ballard, then of the Woods Hole Oceanographic Institution, and Jean-Louis Michel, of the Institut Français de Recherche pour l'Exploration des Mers, succeeded in finding *Titanic* in more than 12,000 feet of water off the Grand Banks of Newfoundland. Like Grimm, they had towed an array of instruments behind their research ship, including high-resolution sonar and a camera, but they had "flown" them closer to the seabed. The following year they visited the wreck in *Alvin* and investigated its interior using a camera-toting ROV named *Jason, Jr.* that brought ghostly images of intact chandeliers and grand staircases into homes worldwide.

There has been much debate over what to do with *Titanic*. Some, including Ballard, believe it should be left untouched as a memorial to the dead. Others want artifacts and parts of the wreck salvaged and put on display. Still others have recovered items from the ship and are now selling them. In 1986 Congress passed the Titanic Memorial Act, urging that artifacts from the ship not be sold in the United States. The measure called for international discussions on preserving the wreck as a memorial, suggesting that plans be developed for "appropriate" recovery and salvage. Ignoring the act, Titanic Ventures, Inc., based in Connecticut, recovered some 1,800 artifacts from the ship in 1987, including dinnerware, bottles of champagne, and personal effects, using the French submarine *Nautile*. RMS Titanic, Inc., of New York, brought up still more artifacts in 1993, 1994, and 1995, including coal, the sale of which has been advertised in newspapers and magazines. While the Titanic Memorial Act expressed the wishes of Congress, the older Law of Salvage prevailed and RMS Titanic was awarded sole salvage rights to the wreck by the United States District Court for the Northern District of Virginia. The group has proposed exhibiting some of the artifacts in a floating museum that would visit ports around the world.

In 1987 the Columbus-America Discovery Group, a consortium based in Ohio, discovered the wreck of the American side-wheel steamer *Central America*, which sank in 1857 in 8,000 feet of water more than 260 miles off the coast of South Carolina. The salvors captured headlines with their recovery of gold bullion worth more than $2 million using an ROV named *Nemo*. One of *Nemo's* robot manipulator arms shot large quantities of epoxy onto the gold bars so they could be brought up en masse. In 1989 Seahawk, a company in Tampa, found and later recovered precious artifacts from a seventeenth-century Spanish galleon—possibly *Nuestra Señora de la Merced*, which was lost in 1622—in 1,500 feet of water in the Gulf of Mexico. Recently, salvors discovered the American liberty ship *John Barry*, loaded with $26 million in Saudi silver dollars, in deep waters off East Africa. The ship had been carrying money to support the Soviet Union's efforts against the Nazis when it was torpedoed by a U-boat in 1944. The *I-52*, a Japanese submarine that had been carrying gold bullion now worth

$25 million to Nazi Germany, was found last year by businessman Paul Tidwell and his Virginia-based company AU Holdings. Sunk by Allied forces on June 23, 1944, the submarine lies under more than 18,000 feet of water, making it the deepest wreck found to date.

Archaeologists have not been sitting idly by. In 1989 Ballard and archaeologist Anna Marguerite McCann, using *Jason, Jr.*, discovered and documented a fourth-century A.D. Roman wreck in 3,000 feet of water in the Mediterranean. Called *Isis*, the ship is the deepest known ancient wreck. Last summer Ballard, now president of the Institute of Exploration in Connecticut, began searching for more wrecks in the Mediterranean by retracing ancient trade routes—from Ostia to Carthage and along the coast of North Africa. At his disposal is the U.S. Navy's nuclear submarine *NR-1*. Launched in 1969, *NR-1* can dive to 3,000 feet and travel at a speed of more than ten knots. It can remain submerged for weeks, even months, its high-resolution side-scan sonar "seeing" more than 600 feet on either side of the vessel. Ballard and his team are mapping wrecks and pinpointing debris fields, all potential targets for archaeological research.

Such assistance from the Navy could give academic institutions and research professionals a competitive edge over commercial salvors, only a few of whom can afford such sophisticated technology. RMS Titanic estimates that it spent some $50,000 per artifact recovered, and to date the company is unsure how it will recoup its investment. Paul Tidwell estimates that it will cost $8 million to recover the bullion from *I-52*, gold to which he may not legally be entitled. If it is determined that the gold was payment for goods delivered to Japan, it might belong to Germany if that country should decide to assert a claim. If the gold is deemed a capturable asset the Allies may be entitled to it as war reparations.

Can or should archaeologists forge a working relationship with salvage groups? We should not participate in projects that profit from the sale of artifacts, and salvors who promise not to do so will also have to guarantee that they will properly excavate and record a site, and that there will be adequate financing to carry projects beyond the retrieval of artifacts to conservation, publication, and curation of the finds.

Despite a few well-publicized for-profit excursions into the deep, there are not that many treasure hunters working on the ocean floor. But the potential is there for a rapid expansion of salvage operations. Archaeologists must draw some battle lines. Are *Titanic* and World War II ships significant archaeological sites? We currently assess the importance of a site or an artifact by what it tells us about the past, and by its potential to yield new information. Not all wrecks of the past 100 years may be archaeologically significant, though all wrecks should be evaluated. We should focus our efforts on using the new technology to find and study archaeologically significant sites such as *Isis*, and offer the public "profit" through knowledge, not plunder.

Discussion Questions

1. The author asks, "Can or should archaeologists forge working relationships with salvage groups?" Why is this an issue? Defend your answer to his question.
2. Find out whether recreational scuba divers think that taking souvenirs from a shipwreck is different than, for example, picking up a "souvenir" arrowhead from an archaeological site on land. Do you think there is a difference? Defend your position.
3. What U.S. laws govern archaeological and salvage work on underwater sites and how do they differ from laws that protect archaeological sites on land? Should there be any difference in the way the two kinds of sites are treated, either by law or by the general public? How do other countries protect their underwater cultural resources?
4. What kinds of information might we expect to recover from the careful archaeological excavation of an ancient shipwreck that we could not learn from a (far less expensive!) land excavation?
5. Have you ever seen "pieces of eight" or other "treasure" from a shipwreck offered for sale? If so, did you think of them as looted archaeological objects? Do you think most people do? Are they?
6. How are the ethics for underwater archaeologists different from those of land-based archaeologists?

Further Readings

Arnold, Barto J. 1978. Underwater Cultural Resources and the Antiquities Market. *Journal of Field Archaeology* 5(2):232.

Bass, George F. 1985. Archaeologists, Sport Divers, and Treasure Hunters. *Journal of Field Archaeology* 12(2):256-258.

———. 2003. The Ethics of Shipwreck Archaeology. In *Ethical Issues in Archaeology*, edited by Larry J. Zimmerman, Karen D. Vitelli and Julie Hollowell-Zimmer, pp. 57–70. Walnut Creek, CA: AltaMira Press.

Delgado, James P. 2001. Diving on the Titanic. *Archaeology* 54(1):52–56.

Chronicler of Ice Age Life

25

BLAKE EDGAR

Although she is not a professional archaeologist, Jean Auel is one of the world's best-selling writers about archaeology. Beginning with her 1980 book, The Clan of the Cave Bear, *Auel's Earth's Children novels have sold close to 35 million copies and have been translated into 27 languages. This article summarizes Auel's career, her ability to connect with the public's imagination, and prompts us to consider why most professional archaeologists have not successfully written about their work for the general public.*

L ATE LAST APRIL, publishers and journalists from a dozen countries converged on the bucolic village of Les Eyzies, beside the Vézère River in the Dordogne region of southwestern France. They came to the self-styled "capital of prehistory" to celebrate 66-year-old Oregonian Jean M. Auel on the occasion of the publication of her fifth and latest novel, *The Shelters of Stone.* Les Eyzies contains the rock shelter of Cro-Magnon, a name synonymous with the first modern Europeans, and lies near many well-known sites occupied by these people and their Neandertal contemporaries. What better place to honor the woman who has introduced millions worldwide to the lives of our 30,000-year-old predecessors?

Between back-to-back interviews and press conferences with Auel, participants were treated to demonstrations of stone knapping and fire making with flint and iron pyrite. They saw spears hurled by an atlatl at a wooden pig. They visited the life-size sculpted horse frieze of Cap Blanc, Font de Gaume Cave's rampaging humpbacked bison and delicately drawn reindeer, and the rock shelter of Laugerie-Haute. In her new book, Auel has re-created the latter site as the Ninth Cave of the Zelandonii, the destination of her Paleolithic protagonists Ayla and Jondalar after a year-long journey.

Starting with *The Clan of the Cave Bear* in 1980, Auel's *Earth's Children* novels have made her an international publishing phenomenon with sales approaching 35 million copies in 27 languages. It has been 12 years since her last book, and *The Shelters of Stone* immediately soared to the top of bestseller lists across the world.

Auel has just returned from a book tour of the United States and Europe when we meet at Portland, Oregon's Multnomah County Central Library. She has resumed the usual nocturnal schedule that keeps her writing into the wee hours and awoke not long before our early afternoon interview. "I'm not even a trained novelist when it comes right down to it," says Auel with a chuckle. "I'm certainly not a trained scientist." Yet the bespectacled, grandmotherly author has earned archaeologists' admiration for her disciplined research, attention to detail, and considerable passion for prehistory that inspires her richly rendered accounts of the past.

"She knows what she's doing," says Jean Clottes, the former inspector general of decorated caves for France's Ministry of Culture. An authority on rock art and member of the team studying the world's oldest-known examples within Chauvet Cave in southeastern France, Clottes says, "There is nothing that's basically false in what she says. In fact, it's quite accurate." Clottes has been an Auel fan since he purchased a second-hand copy of *The Clan of the Cave Bear*. The author sent him a draft of *The Shelters of Stone*, and Clottes was pleased to find that she depicted a living rhinoceros with a dark band around its torso, just as they appear on the walls of Chauvet. He also noticed that Auel playfully pays homage to the discovery of Lascaux by four French boys in pursuit of a dog. In the book, Ayla follows her pet wolf into the as yet unpainted limestone cave.

Auel's novels have inspired students to explore anthropology while giving general readers their first glimpse of the early human past. "I think she has done us an enormous service," says Olga Soffer of the University of Illinois. "We [archaeologists] can't write for normal people, so I don't think we convey the excitement that drew us into the field." The release of a new Auel novel generates increased interest in Soffer's courses, "People of the Ice Age" and "Novel Archaeology," in which students read two of Auel's books.

For the uninitiated, Auel's saga follows the life of Ayla, a blond, blue-eyed orphan rescued from near death by a band of Neandertals. Auel's Neandertals lack full-blown verbal speech, but have an expressive language of gesture and posture. Unable to think abstractly or envision the future, their brains nonetheless store vast amounts of information and experiences spanning their species's history. Ayla comes under the tutelage of Creb, a partially blind, crippled holy man who soon notes her creative abilities. In the course of the books, Ayla becomes a skilled hunter and healer, raises a cave lion, tames a wild horse and a wolf, and discovers, then rediscovers, sexual pleasure with her Cro-Magnon companion Jondalar. From him, Ayla learns spoken language and modern human ways. Together, they embark on an epic journey across Ice Age Europe.

Auel was born in Chicago in 1936, one of five siblings. Her mother was a housewife and her father worked as a railroad switchman—Jean liked to tag along and watch him communicate by Morse Code—and later as a painter. Jean met her future husband, Ray, in grade school, and married him at age 18. After a few years on an air force base in Roswell, New Mexico, the couple relocated to Portland, Oregon. Auel gave birth to five children before age 25, and her clan now includes 15 grandchildren and two great-grandchildren.

Ray worked as a packaging designer for an electronics company, Tektronix, but their growing family prompted Jean to take a job in the company's billing department. A keen reader of Ray's college textbooks, Jean decided to take night courses in college-level algebra, trigonometry, calculus, and physics. "I wanted to learn how things work," she says, "and that's not what women learned in my day."

Eventually, Auel became one of the company's few women circuit board designers. After writing an in-house design manual for engineers, she became a technical writer of instruction manuals and was later promoted to credit manager. In November 1976, six months after earning an M.B.A, Auel quit Tektronix. She was 40 years old with three kids in college and expected to apply her hard-earned degree to a new business career. First, she caught up on sleep.

Then, late one January night, Auel decided to try writing a short story. She had written poetry sporadically for several years (one of her poems appears in *The Shelters of Stone*). Now she had an idea about a young woman living with people very different from herself—primitive people, though not necessarily prehistoric. They have suspicions about the woman, but allow her to stay because she cares for a crippled elder. "I didn't think I was suddenly going to be a writer. I just thought it was something fun to do," she recalls. Lacking a clear focus, Auel needed to do some research.

Her encyclopedia gave her some terms to ponder: Pleistocene, Mousterian, and so forth. Then Auel visited Portland's Multnomah County Library. After browsing the card catalog and the stacks, Auel pulled some books off the shelves and began reading and taking notes. Fortuitously, she selected archaeologist Ralph Solecki's Shanidar, *The First Flower People*, his 1971 account of excavating a Neandertal cave site in Iraq. The site became famous for the burial of an adult male Neandertal thought to have been interred with clusters of pollen from hollyhock, yarrow, and other herbal and medicinal flowers. Did this imply a religious sensibility, even a soul, for Neandertals? Another male buried in the cave had been blinded in one eye by a blow to the skull. His right arm and shoulder had withered, the hand and forearm possibly amputated. His right leg and foot revealed a healed fracture and degenerative disease that immobilized the limb. But the man had survived these traumas and presumably had been cared for by others.

Auel was stunned by what she read. "There's my old man with the crippled arm," she thought. "He really existed!" Pressing questions arose in her mind. How had he survived with such handicaps? Who loved him enough to care for him? Before long, reading between the lines of the research, she was developing characters. "That's how my mind worked when I read this material," she says. "I kept seeing the people in it."

Auel never completed that short story, but several months of furious writing produced a massive outline for the plots of six novels. That summer, she attended the Willamette Writers Conference in Portland. Auel was the conference's keynote speaker in August 2002, but 25 years earlier she had been one of many prospective authors. She met and received encouragement from a New York agent named Jean Naggar. Two years later, having finished the first novel, Auel sent Naggar a one-page letter describing the book and her idea for an entire series. "The passion for her characters and the period she was writing about really came through," says Naggar, who asked to see the novel.

The bulky manuscript sat on the overworked agent's living room table until her husband, Serge, perused it one evening. He read it through and told Naggar to make time for it right away. In 1979, Naggar held an auction for rights to *The Clan of the Cave Bear*—unheard of for an unknown author—and garnered Auel $130,000, the highest advance that had ever been paid for a first novel. Her debut novel spent 18 weeks on the *New York Times* bestseller list, and its successor, *The Valley of Horses*, became 1982's best-selling novel.

From the outset of her writing career, Auel has diligently learned as much as she can about her characters' environment and the archaeological evidence for Paleolithic behavior. What began as a bibliography on index cards in a recipe box has grown to a personal library of a few thousand books and articles. She subscribes to numerous professional journals, including *Current Anthropology*, *American Antiquity*, and the *Journal of Archaeological Science*. The Auels regularly attend the annual meeting of the Society for American Archaeology. In 1993, they hosted their own symposium near Portland, where an international gathering of scholars gave talks on Paleolithic symbolism and enjoyed Dom Pérignon and Château d'Yquem from the Auels' cellar.

Beyond her library research, Auel tries to directly experience prehistoric life. While writing *The Clan of the Cave Bear*, she helped build and slept in a snow cave on volcanic Mount Hood. In eastern Oregon, she learned volumes worth of traditional survival skills from primitive technology expert Jim Riggs, who Auel calls "the kind of person you could put into one end of a wilderness naked, and he'd come out the other end fed, clothed, and sheltered."

Riggs taught Auel how to tan buckskin by painstakingly scraping off the fur and inner hide and then soaking the leather in a bucket of pulverized deer brains. After being wrung, stretched, and hung to dry, the leather is smoked to make it waterproof. Auel crafted a hunk of buckskin into a pouch for carrying the obsidian tools and sinew she brought on her first book tour.

More recently, Auel audited pioneering experimental archaeologist Errett Callahan's workshop on producing intricate, pressure-flaked Neolithic daggers, watching how a master flint knapper passes on his proficiency to students. Auel has also foraged for edible weeds and other wild foods with nutritionist and botanist John Kallas. On a weekend workshop on the Oregon coast in 1999, she waded into chilly, chest-deep water in Netarts Bay to dig for cockles and harvested kelp and bladder wrack along the shore.

Auel's adventures don't stop at the Oregon border, however. She visits archaeological sites and museums to gather impressions that add texture to her stories. Her first research trip occurred after she completed *The Valley of Horses*. Archaeologist David Abrams of Sacramento State University approached her about touring Europe's Paleolithic sites. The two worked out an itinerary that would help Auel research her forthcoming books, *The Mammoth Hunters* and *The Plains of Passage*, and in the summer of 1982 the Auels spent several weeks traveling with Abrams and art historian Diane Kelly.

During a private tour of Lascaux (the first of three visits she's made), Auel vividly remembers walking down a gradual slope in the cave's dim light. As the light rose slightly, she lifted her head and gazed on the magnificent painted beasts. "By the time I started breathing," she says, "I was sobbing. It literally brought me to tears. It left me gasping." Not a conventionally religious person, Auel does feel enormous spiritual power in Lascaux, which she thinks from its ease of access was a cave used by women or families.

Later, in Czechoslovakia, archaeologist Jan Jelinek showed them the Paleolithic village site of Dolní Vestonice. Around 28,000 years ago, its occupants discovered how to fire in a kiln tiny clay figurines of humans and animals. In *The Plains of Passage*, a medicine woman—who serves as the sadistic leader of a group of horse-hunting women warriors—masters the technique for firing clay. Auel also incorporated Dolní Vestonice's intriguing triple burial into her novel. In 1986, archaeologists unearthed the skeleton of a young woman with a deformed spine flanked by the skeletons of two healthy, teenage males. One man's arms rested on the woman's pelvis, sprinkled with ocher; the other man's right arm rested atop the woman's left arm, but his skull had been turned to face away from her. Auel the novelist imagined the trio as victims of intentional poisoning.

Auel's use of artistic license has come in for its fair share of criticism. She admits to compressing time in her books, sometimes combining archaeological influences from different places at a single site, and speculating beyond the immediate evidence—she added structures, for instance, to the Dordogne's large limestone shelters. Maybe she pushes the advent of domestication and fermentation too far into the past. But some of her extrapolations have been prescient—placing Neandertals in the Caucasus long before a child's skeleton was found at Mezmaiskaya Cave, or creating a half-black character in *The Mammoth Hunters* before learning about a skeleton with African features from Kostenki, a site in Russia that she fictionalized as the Lion Camp.

Having immersed herself in archaeological evidence for so long, Auel has developed informed opinions about many of the field's debates. She discounts the idea that modern humans completely replaced Neandertal populations in Europe and believes that the two groups could have interbred. She is convinced that much of Lascaux's paintings predate the accepted age of 17,000 years, obtained from a few dates on pieces of charcoal. The temperate-climate animals depicted on the walls don't fit with the cold climate that existed at the time, so Auel concludes that these paintings were created at least 25,000 years ago.

Auel defends her conviction that Upper Paleolithic people possessed modern-day loves and hates, dreams and disappointments. She believes literary critics, not scientists, have trouble accepting this perspective. But in a *Baltimore Sun* review of *The Shelters of Stone*, archaeologist John Alden criticized what he considers Auel's misguided sentiment about people who were "profoundly different from us in ways we can demonstrate, ways we can guess, and presumably, in ways we can't even imagine."

Berkeley archaeologist Meg Conkey, whose research often involves feminist perspectives on prehistory, applauds Auel's efforts to show how women could make crucial contributions to prehistoric society. But she also finds that Ayla's ingenuity becomes less plausible with each new accomplishment. "Between the two of them [Ayla and Jondalar], they invent everything. That's a bit much," agrees Jean Clottes. Yet Clottes accepts that this is a fictional story, and that Ayla must play the heroine in Auel's accurate, if romanticized, prehistoric world.

Auel's Paleolithic world is also a place where storytellers play an esteemed social role. In her books, visits by traveling entertainers postpone the work of entire cave communities. Auel imagines our Ice Age forebears listening with rapt attention to everything from current gossip to ancient legend. "We've been telling each other stories for a long time," she says.

Discussion Questions

1. Auel had no training or background in archaeology when she conceived the idea for her series—a story entirely dependent on archaeology for its setting and much of its action. How did she pull it off? Are there constraints on archaeologists that prevent them from writing stories such as Auel's? Do you think archaeologists should leave popular writing and fictionalized accounts about moments in archaeology to non-archaeologists?

2. Do you find it problematical that Auel takes considerable liberties with the archaeological facts to fit everything she wants to into her story, whether it is plausible that it really happened as she suggests, or not? Explain your position.

3. Do you agree with the reviewer who criticized Auel's "misguided sentiment about people who were 'profoundly different from us'"? How might distortion or even inaccuracy in a fictionalized account of the past have serious repercussions?

4. Discuss the potential IPR issues (see Chapter 23) in Auel's work. Why do you imagine that archaeologists have generally been happy to share their information and interpretations with her?

5. What other recent novelists have used archaeological data and settings effectively? Do you think a course such as Soffer's "Novel Archaeology" is a good way to introduce beginners to archaeology?

6. *The Clan of the Cave Bear* was made into a film—that Auel apparently disliked. What other films have used archaeological settings? From an archaeological perspective, were they effective in their use of the discipline? What impression does each give of the discipline? Do you think courses like "Archaeology and Film" are a useful and effective way to introduce archaeology?

7. Auel's main character is Ayla, a woman. Why might it be important to show ancient human history through the eyes of a woman? Could a man write about Ayla from the same perspective?

Further Readings

Claasen, Cheryl (editor). 1994. *Women in Archaeology*. Philadelphia: University of Pennsylvania Press.

Holtorf, Cornelius. 2005. *From Stonehenge to Las Vegas: Archaeology as Popular Culture*. Walnut Creek, CA: AltaMira Press.

Jameson, John H., Jr. (editor). 1997. *Presenting Archaeology to the Public.* Walnut Creek, CA: AltaMira Press.

Linenthal, Edward T. 1994. Committing History in Public. *The Journal of American History* 81(3):986–991.

McManamon, Francis P. 1991. The Many Publics for Archaeology. *American Antiquity* 56(1):121–130.

Pokotylo, David, and Neil Guppy. 1999. Public Opinion and Archaeological Heritage: Views from Outside the Profession. *American Antiquity* 64(3):400–416.

Writing Unwritten History 26

JOE WATKINS

In this autobiographical account, Watkins discusses what it means today to be a professional archae-
ologist and a Native American, and reviews the rocky path he climbed to reach that point. He tried,
at first, to avoid the issue by working in France, to study the ancestors of (Euro-American) archae-
ologists. In graduate school, he found that professors assumed he could not be "objective" because he
was Indian. He persevered and, after receiving his doctorate, became increasingly involved in North
American archaeology, adding a native voice to archaeological practice. He now proudly refuses to be
"merely objective."

> *"Into each life, it is said, some rain must fall, some people have bad*
> *horoscopes, others take tips on the stock market. But Indians have been cursed*
> *above all other people in history. Indians have anthropologists."*
>
> —VINE DELORIA, JR.

I LAUGHED AS I READ THOSE WORDS EXCERPTED FROM *Custer Died for Your Sins*
in the August 1969 edition of *Playboy*, for I was gripped immediately by the
irony that here I was, an incoming freshman at the University of Oklahoma
majoring in anthropology, and also an American Indian. My interest in the unwritten history of Native Americans had drawn me to archaeology, and the University of Oklahoma was just 25 miles down Interstate 35 from my home in
Oklahoma City, the heart of "Indian Country."

According to Deloria, a Standing Rock Sioux activist with a master's from the
Lutheran School of Theology in Chicago, and a J.D. from the University of Colorado's School of Law, anthropology considered people "objects for experimen-
tation, for manipulation, and for eventual extinction." So why was I entering such
a profession? When I was a young boy, I found an Archaic projectile point on my

family homestead and showed it to my Choctaw grandmother. She told me (through my cousin, who translated) that it was part of the history of those who had lived there long before the Choctaw were forced to move to Oklahoma in the 1830s, and that it was important not to let that history get lost—that was why I wanted to be an archaeologist.

My undergraduate education occurred at a time of great social unrest. Minorities throughout the United States were demanding equal treatment, the conflict in Vietnam was polarizing students, and the "Great Society" of Lyndon B. Johnson was under attack. Archaeology was also under fire. American Indians were protesting the excavation of archaeological sites and the study of Indian remains. Anthropology professors laughed at and posted copies of cartoons and articles from American Indian newspapers that suggested Americans wouldn't be happy if Indians led excavations at Arlington National Cemetery. I don't believe anyone took those articles seriously, though they did illustrate the unequal treatment afforded American Indian burials by legions of scientists and policy makers. I understood the concerns American Indians had with the excavation of graves and the study of human remains and vowed I'd never excavate an American Indian burial. I decided, in spite of my early interest in the precontact history of the Americas, to pursue archaeology in the Old World and dig up the ancestors of archaeologists who were digging there!

In the summer of 1972, I worked in southwestern France at an excavation directed by François Bordes, famous for his system of classifying stone tools, which allowed archaeologists to make detailed comparisons of artifact assemblages from different sites. A rigid taskmaster and at times a tyrant, Bordes was, nonetheless, a personable man who kidded me that his ancestors ate buffalo before mine did, while I needled him that the French scalped more people than the Indians. He was one of the first archaeologists to learn the techniques of flaking flint to produce artifacts similar to the types he was finding in his excavations; the yard at his house was full of flint flakes on which neophyte flint knappers like me could develop skills.

France at that time seemed made for a 21-year-old—relaxed, friendly, and inexpensive, with local people willing to help an American with his halting French. I recall walking from our campsite to the town of Les Eyzies-de-Tayac-Sireuil and having my picture taken in front of the "Hotel Cro-magnon," a rock-shelter that, in 1868, had relinquished a human skull regarded as the prototype of modern Europeans. I spent my days immersed in the prehistory of the region, visiting sites I had read about and studied. By flashlight, I examined lifelike Palaeolithic animals painted and engraved on walls and ceilings of caves.

I came home with a renewed determination to work in the Old World, thinking that such a decision would keep me out of the growing conflict between archaeologists and American Indians. At the very moment that members of the American Indian Movement were occupying the town of Wounded Knee in an armed standoff with the South Dakota National Guard and the Federal Bureau of Investigation to draw attention to the plight of American Indians on the Pine Ridge Reservation, I was interviewing for a Ford Foundation Grant so that I could attend graduate school.

I enrolled at Southern Methodist University in Dallas because it was loaded with research opportunities in North Africa, the Near East, and Sub-Saharan Africa. I wanted to work in Sub-Saharan Africa with Garth Sampson, who was beginning to focus on the archaeology of recently abandoned Bushman (San) sites in South Africa and who was trying to weave experimental archaeology into his research. Shortly after my arrival in the department, I found out that Bruce Bradley, a noted flintknapper, was coming to work with Sampson. I had met Bruce on my first night at Bordes's house, where, after my long train trip with too much luggage and not enough food, a fellow American was a welcome sight. Once I reintroduced myself to him, we went looking for chert he could use in a flintknapping demonstration. Future trips in search of lithic sources cemented our friendship, and our discussions on these trips convinced me to focus on experimental archaeology as a means of understanding prehistoric technology. Here was a way I could sidestep the conflict between American Indians and archaeologists—take the people entirely out of the process and focus on their technology instead!

I soon discovered, however, that because I was a Native American, my professors didn't think I could be an objective scientist, while American Indians distrusted my motives in studying archaeology. I couldn't be an archaeologist because I was an Indian, and I couldn't be an Indian because I was an archaeologist. I was told by one instructor that the only reason I was accepted at SMU was because I was Indian and had my own funding, but that I still shouldn't have been allowed to enroll in the program. At a powwow in Dallas, I was introduced as an archaeologist to a Comanche Indian by the name of Leroy Mason. He asked me if I was one of those "bonediggers," and I answered that I had never excavated human remains, didn't want to, and never would. I am sure he didn't believe me.

In 1978, as part of an interview at UCLA, I was asked to give a public presentation. I chose to share my thoughts on archaeology and American Indians. Near the end of a question and answer session, a young American Indian woman stood up and asked, "Do you have to be an atheist to be an archaeologist?" I didn't ask her what she meant because I knew immediately what she was talking about. I probably should have tried to convince her of the amount of information available within a grave and the wealth of data that biologists can get out of human remains—something the objective scientist in me had come to believe—but I didn't. I responded with another question, asking her: "If graves must be dug, would you rather they be dug by someone who respects them, or someone who doesn't care?" She didn't respond, and I know that neither one of us got a real answer that day.

In December of that year, fresh out of graduate school and with no academic opportunities in sight, I set aside my Old World aspirations and returned to the New World dreams I'd nurtured as a boy. I entered the federal system as an archaeologist with the Interagency Archaeological Services (IAS)-Atlanta, an agency within the Department of the Interior that provided cultural resource management expertise to other government agencies.

The American Indian Religious Freedom Act of 1978 (AIRFA) required federal agencies to examine the ways their policies (such as the confiscation of eagle feathers by game rangers of the Fish and Wildlife Service) might affect American Indians' practice of religion. In 1979, as the IAS representative to the AIRFA Task Force, I reviewed IAS policies in search of any that might offer impediments to the free exercise of American Indian religion. The only relevant document I found at my agency was its "Policy for the Disposition of Human Remains," which provided a protocol for dealing with human skeletal remains encountered at archaeological sites. As part of the internal policy examination required by the act, I wrote a letter to the AIRFA Task Force defending the burial policy since it weighed scientific interests with the wishes of lineal descendants or those who could demonstrate an ethnic affinity to the remains. At an AIRFA Task Force consultation in Oregon later that year, I asked questions of the gathered Indians about the excavation of sites and the study of human remains. I listened to Indian speakers who wanted to reinter all human remains, equating archaeological sites with sacred sites. A National Park Service archaeologist subsequently chided me for asking those questions, commenting that archaeology would be better off if I would just leave well enough alone—that if we archaeologists didn't draw attention to ourselves, American Indians wouldn't notice us.

Instead, I tried to use the opportunity presented by the consultations to make the IAS burial policy even more amenable to American Indian concerns. T. J. Ferguson, tribal archaeologist of the Pueblo of Zuni, had pointed out that the policy had ignored the fact that many American Indian groups attributed great spiritual powers and values to human remains, and that it was biased toward the belief system of the dominant Euroamerican culture. He suggested that the policy should be restructured in such a way that American Indian values and beliefs concerning the disturbance of human remains received equal importance to those of archaeologists, especially in relation to the scientific study of those remains.

I suggested in a 1980 memorandum to the Department of the Interior's Consulting Archaeologist that policy makers should confront the issues that American Indians faced with regard to archaeology rather than turn a blind eye to them. I proposed revisions to the policy requiring consultation with affected groups prior to the initiation of excavations, time limits during which materials could be analyzed and curated, a system that allowed for reburial, and a set of procedures for situations where human remains were discovered in the course of an ongoing construction or archaeological project. I thought the revisions were a step in the right direction, but I never got a response to the memo. It would take another nine years before the government stepped in with serious repatriation and reburial legislation.

Meanwhile, my place within the federal system was unclear. A reorganization was looming that threatened possible transfer to Michigan or Philadelphia, too far away from my family. I went back to Oklahoma City, now determined to pursue New World archaeology, and started my own business consulting on cultural resources for private companies and public agencies before eventually taking a position with the Oklahoma Archaeological Survey at the University of Oklahoma doing assessments for highway realignments and bridge replacements.

In 1990, I became aware of test excavations at the East Wenatchee Clovis Cache along the Columbia River in southern Washington. While a cache of Clovis points of a size previously unrecorded and of an incredible variety of materials would be of interest to any archaeologist, a simmering conflict between archaeologists and American Indians piqued my interest. I watched it develop as American Indian groups in the area protested to gain control over the scientific excavation of cultural material more than 11,000 years old and grew interested in the ethical and legal ramifications of allowing tribal groups nearly 20,000 generations removed from the makers of the Clovis cache to control the disposition of the artifacts of a culture that might have been the precursors to the entire American Indian population.

While I had tended to view archaeology as a rather benign science and considered archaeologists to be generally well meaning, I was still unsure how other archaeologists felt about Native American issues. In 1991, as part of my dissertation research, I developed a questionnaire, based on the East Wenatchee Clovis Cache, that asked archaeologists to respond to sets of questions from which I could collect statistical information on their attitudes toward such issues. As a result of the research, I learned that archaeologists seemed more concerned about who owned the land on which cultural resources were located than the wishes of those whose ancestors produced the resources. In 1992, Randall McGuire, at the State University of New York at Binghamton, published a paper in *American Anthropologist* that suggested American archaeologists were more interested in studying dead Indians than working with live ones. It became apparent with this publication that other scholars were interested in examining the reasons behind the conflict between American Indians and archaeology.

At roughly the same time, the Society for American Archaeology (SAA) began examining its own code of ethics. This self examination—coupled with the passage of federal legislation in 1989 and 1990 requiring museums and federal agencies to return human remains, burial objects, and sacred objects to tribal groups—greatly influenced archaeologists' relationships with indigenous populations and forced the former to become more aware of American Indian perceptions of their discipline. These perceptions were often less than positive. American Indian testimony and presentations before Congress during the hearings on the Native American Graves Protection and Repatriation Act (NAGPRA) compared archaeologists to grave robbers. The decade that followed was one of questioning and posturing, with each side trying to convince the other of its views, culminating in the court case brought by six anthropologists against the Corps of Engineers, which had attempted to repatriate remains known alternately as "Kennewick Man" and "The Ancient One."

In 1993, I began my job as the agency archaeologist at the Bureau of Indian Affairs in southwestern Oklahoma. I remain intrigued by the relationships between archaeologists and American Indians and may now be in a better position to make a difference. I try to show American Indians the ways they can use archaeology to meet their goals, and believe that archaeology will function best not as an esoteric science that neatly sorts potsherds and arrowheads into even rows, but as a collection of methods and theories that offer us insights into the ways that people in the past coped with their daily lives and environments. Perhaps some archaeologists have forgotten that those were real people with hopes, fears, sorrows, and joys. I know that American Indians have not forgotten.

But I am still caught in the middle. The study of the past is often exciting and confusing, delightful and dangerous. American Indians are becoming involved in the practice of archaeology, but our numbers are so small (fewer than ten American Indians have a Ph.D. in archaeology, and perhaps no more than 20 have a master's degree) that we stand out at conferences. We sometimes feel, as Navajo anthropology student Davina Two Bears notes, "as though a Native American is not even a person or human, but a very complex, interesting thing." As archaeologists, we are asked to provide technical assistance to tribal groups about issues relating to federal compliance with specific legislation, but we are not trusted. Before we are given the opportunity to explain the ways federal regulations impact tribal groups, we must listen to recitations of the ills inflicted by past legions of anthropologists and federal officials. I recall being called a "Camp Indian" by a tribal representative because I tried to explain the utility of an archaeological inventory in opposition to his belief that non-tribal members must not know the locations of cultural sites. He felt I wanted to record the tribe's sites so that other archaeologists could come in and rob them of their artifacts.

While most archaeologists are interested in knowing about American Indian concerns with archaeology, I have heard some mumble about "that same old song" when I begin talking about the lack of American Indian voices in the discipline. Both American Indians and archaeologists are to blame for our small numbers. In the meantime, I am glad there are archaeologists like Larry Zimmerman of Indiana University-Purdue University Indianapolis and Randy McGuire, who keep nudging the discipline's conscience, but sometimes I get the urge to tell both sides to stop complaining and start working together.

Given the opportunity to start over, would I still become an archaeologist? I can answer "yes" with hardly a moment's hesitation. The past is more alive for me now than it has ever been, and the future looks more promising, with more American Indians getting involved in archaeology and finding their way into print.

But we remain at war over American Indian heritage. The reburial of Kennewick Man might destroy the information yielded by one of the New World's oldest skeletons. To be sure, I lament the loss to science, but perhaps this is one of those battles that archaeologists need to reexamine. What is at stake? Is it the freedom of Western science to continue to operate as it has in the past, as a self-appointed guardian of a self-defined truth, or is it the opportunity to develop a more meaningful blend of Western science and non-Western beliefs concerning the philosophy of the past? "There's a whole book of information [in Kennewick Man's bones]. To put him back in the ground is like burning a rare book so we'll learn nothing," Rob Bonnichsen of Oregon State University has said. On the other side of the fence is Armand Minthorn of the Confederated Tribes of the Umatilla Indian Reservation. "Some scientists say that if this individual is not studied further, we, as Indians, will be destroying evidence of our own history," he has stated. "We already know our history. It is passed on to us through our elders and through our religious practices."

Why don't more American Indians get involved in archaeology? I'm not sure there is an answer to that question—at least not an easy one, but perhaps a story will help. I was walking across Cambridge Common at Harvard, trying to find my way to the Peabody Museum. I must have looked a little lost, as I was, and perhaps broke an unwritten rule by walking across the grass. As I passed an elderly woman sitting on a park bench feeding popcorn to a flock of pigeons, I heard her say "Stupid foreigners," not quite under her breath.

I slowed and turned, curious as to whom she was speaking, and saw a look of distaste in her eyes that rocked me a bit. I realized she was talking about me. I stopped for a moment, and then smiled at the irony of it all. My ancestors on my father's side have been on this continent for perhaps 15,000 years, give or take a few hundred, while hers, giving her the full benefit of the doubt considering her dress and appearance, 380 years at the most. Maybe I didn't belong at Harvard, but who was the true foreigner? So has archaeology traditionally objectified Native Americans, making them feel like outsiders on their own soil, and making archaeology a very unlikely career choice.

Throughout my 30-plus years in archaeology, I have seen American Indians progress from protesting excavations, to gaining control of archaeological sites and cultural materials, to working within the system to get legislation such as NAGPRA passed. I have been committed to working within the system to publicize American Indian concerns about archaeology, and while I may not have been responsible for any profound changes, I like to think that my contributions may have helped in some small way.

What archaeology needs now more than ever is a spirit of humanity, a driving desire to give life to the people of the past rather than simply a penchant for describing and cataloging dusty objects. That is what I, as an American Indian archaeologist, can perhaps bring to the discipline, a viewpoint that refuses to be merely objective, but embraces the emotional, one that pursues not an ill-defined "truth," but an inkling of understanding, and one that includes all facets of what it is to be human.

As Thoreau said, "Wherever men have lived there is a story to be told, and it depends chiefly on the story-teller or historian whether that is interesting or not." I hope that, if I do nothing else, I can give the past its due.

Discussion Questions

1. The author remembers finding an arrowhead as his first encounter with archaeology. What was yours? Was an archaeologist involved, or just an artifact? Explore the possibilities of first archaeological encounters and their potential effects on one's feelings for archaeology over a lifetime.

2. If Watkins had stayed and developed his expertise in Old World archaeology, would he have avoided the controversies over NAGPRA and related ethical issues?

3. Watkins explicitly mentions thinking he could "sidestep the conflicts" by taking "people entirely out of the process and focus[ing] on their technology instead." Might this be a broader phenomenon in archaeology—and what effect does it have on the discipline?

4. Explore the impact on and meaning for the discipline of archaeology and for Joe Watkins, the person, of the comments he reports from his professors and from other Native Americans. How have things changed in this respect over the last quarter century?

5. How would you answer the young American Indian woman's question "Do you have to be an atheist to be an archaeologist?" and Watkins's response, so that both sides might have the "real answers" he felt were lacking?

6. In 1978, "with no academic opportunities in sight," Watkins turned to a government agency for employment. Indeed, it was about 25 years before a university department offered him a teaching position, in spite of the fact that during all those years he was (a) interested in a teaching position (b) very well known and active in professional organizations (c) published and (d) was (and is) one of very few Indians with a Ph.D. and lots of experience in a wide range of archaeology. Why did it take so long for the academy to hire him?

7. Watkins found, in 1991, that archaeologists were "more concerned about who owned the land on which cultural resources were located than the wishes of those whose ancestors produced the resources." Why do you think that was the case? What do you think his survey results would be if he re-ran the same questions today? Why?

8. Are more American Indians now pursuing careers in archaeology than were at the end of the century? How might these and other American Indians use archaeology to meet their goals? Try substituting any other minority group for "American Indian" in all of the above questions. Are the differences in your answers significant depending on whose unwritten history is concerned?

9. What are some of the "ills inflicted by past legions of anthropologists and federal officials" on American Indians? Consider Watkins's experience with Native Americans in relation to "Cloak and Trowel" (Chapter 12) and the St. Lawrence Island experience (Chapter 14).

10. How can archaeologists "embrace the emotional" in archaeology, while maintaining high scientific standards and not falling prey to the kinds of issues seen in earlier chapters such as "Faking Biblical History" and "Flashpoint Ayodhya"?

11. What does Watkins's experience say about the future of archaeology? What will archaeology and archaeological ethics look like in the years ahead?

Further Readings

Biolsi, Thomas, and Larry J. Zimmerman (editors). 1997. *Indians and Anthropologists: Vine Deloria Jr. and the Critique of Anthropology*. Tucson: University of Arizona Press.

McGuire, Randall H. 2004. Contested Pasts: Archaeology and Native Americans. In *A Companion to Social Archaeology*, edited by Lynn Meskell and Robert W. Preucel, pp. 374–395. Oxford: Blackwell.

Two Bears, Davina. 2000. A Navajo Student's Perception: Anthropology and the Navajo Nation Archaeology Department Student Training Program. In *Working Together: Native*

Americans and Archaeologists, edited by Kurt E. Dongoske, Mark Aldenderfer and Karen Doehner, pp. 15–22. Washington D.C: Society for American Archaeology.

Watkins, Joe. 2000. *Indigenous Archaeology: American Indian Values and Scientific Practice*. Walnut Creek, CA: AltaMira Press.

Watkins, Joe. 2003. Beyond the Margin: American Indians, First Nations, and Archaeology in North America. *American Antiquity* 68(2):273–285.

Sources and Permissions

The editors and publisher would like to acknowledge the following for rights to reprint articles in this volume.

1. Chase, Arlen F., Diane Z. Chase, and Harriot W. Topsey. 1988. Archaeology and the Ethics of Collecting. *Archaeology* 41(1):56–60, 87.
2. Braden, Maria. 1999. Trafficking in Treasures. *American Archaeology* 3(4):18–25.
3. Atwood, Roger. 2003. Guardians of the Dead. *Archaeology* 56(1):43–49.
4. Robbins, Elaine. 2004. The World Wide Web of Antiquities. *American Archaeology* 8(3):27–30.
5. Silberman, Neil Asher, and Yuval Goren. 2003. Faking Biblical History. *Archaeology* 56(5):20–29.
6. Curry, Andrew. 2004. Letter from Colorado: Anasazi in the Backyard. *Archaeology* 57(4):64–66, 68, 70.
7. Bryant, Kathleen. 2004. Celebrating 25 Years of Preservation. *American Archaeology* 8(4):27–32.
8. Romey, Kristin M. 2002. The Race to Save Afghan Culture. *Archaeology* 55(3):18–25.
9. Garen, Micah. 2004. The War within the War. *Archaeology* 57(4):28–31.
10. Raschka, Marilyn. 1996. Beirut Digs Out. *Archaeology* 49(4):44–50.
11. Romey, Kristin M. 2004. Flashpoint Ayodhya. *Archaeology* 57(4):48–55.
12. Price, David. 2003. Cloak and Trowel. *Archaeology* 56(5):30–35.
13. McIntosh, Roderick J., Susan Keech McIntosh, and Téréba Togola. 1989. People without History. *Archaeology* 42(1):1, 74–81.
14. Zimmer, Julie. 2003. When Archaeological Artifacts Are Commodities: Dilemmas Faced by Native Villages of Alaska's Bering Strait. Based on the paper in *Indigenous People and Archaeology: Proceedings of the 32nd Annual Chacmool Conference*, edited by Trevor Peck, Evelyn Siegfried and Gerald A. Oetelaar, pp. 298–312. Archaeological Association of the University of Calgary, Calgary.

15. Brent, Michel. 1994. The Rape of Mali. *Archaeology* 47(3):3, 26–35.
16. Bawaya, Michael. 2003. Archaeotourism. *American Archaeology* 7(4):12–19.
17. Meighan, Clement W. 1994. Burying American Archaeology. *Archaeology* 47(6):64, 66, 68. Zimmerman, Larry J. 1994. Sharing Control of the Past. *Archaeology* 47(6):65, 67–68.
18. Michel, Mark. 2004. Books Banned at National Parks' Bookstores. *American Archaeology* 8(4):7.
19. Preucel, Robert W., Lucy F. Williams, Stacey O. Espenlaub, and Janet Monge. 2003. Out of Heaviness, Enlightenment: NAGPRA and the University of Pennsylvania Museum of Archaeology and Anthropology. *Expedition* 45(3):21–27.
20. Golden, Juliet. 2003. Remembering Chełmno. *Archaeology* 56(1):50–54.
21. Lobell, Jarrett. 2004. Acropolis Museum Is Back on Track and Wants the Parthenon Marbles to Come Home. *Archaeology* 57(4):10–11.
22. Fagan, Brian. 1995. Archaeology's Dirty Secret. *Archaeology* 48(4):4, 14–17.
23. Nicholas, George P., and Julie Hollowell. 2004. Intellectual Property Issues in Archaeology? Based on the paper in *Anthropology News* 45(4):6, 8.
24. Delgado, James P. 1996. Lure of the Deep. *Archaeology* 49(3):41–43.
25. Edgar, Blake. 2002. Chronicler of Ice Age Life. *Archaeology* 55(6):36–41.
26. Watkins, Joe. 2000. Writing Unwritten History. *Archaeology* 53(6):36–41.

About the Contributors

Roger Atwood is a journalist who writes on the antiquities trade.

Michael Bawaya is the editor of *American Archaeology*.

Maria Braden was a journalism professor at the University of Kentucky. She passed away in 2004.

Michel Brent, trained in the law, is a career journalist who writes for *Le Vif-L'Express*, a Belgian news magazine.

Kathleen Bryant is a freelance writer whose work has appeared in *Arizona Highways*, *Plateau Journal*, and *Sunset*.

Arlen F. Chase and Diane Z. Chase teach anthropology at the University of Central Florida and do field work in Belize.

Chip Colwell-Chanthaphonh received his Ph.D. in anthropology from Indiana University in 2004. Since 1993, he has conducted field and laboratory work in Arizona, Wisconsin, Belize, and Belgium. His written work has appeared in *American Anthropologist*, *International Journal of Cultural Property*, *Museum Anthropology*, *American Indian Quarterly*, *Archaeologies*, *Anthropological Quarterly*, and the *Journal of Social Archaeology*. He is also the author (with T. J. Ferguson) of *History Is in the Land: Multivocal Tribal Traditions in Arizona's San Pedro Valley*. During the preparation of this volume, he was a fellow at the Center for Desert Archaeology, a private nonprofit organization in Tucson, Arizona. He is now a visiting scholar at the American Academy of Arts and Sciences in Cambridge, Massachusetts.

Andrew Curry is a general editor at *Smithsonian*.

James P. Delgado is executive director of the Vancouver Maritime Museum.

Blake Edgar is coauthor, with Richard G. Klein, of *The Dawn of Human Culture* (2002) and, with Donald Johanson, of *From Lucy to Language* (1996).

Stacey O. Espenlaub is NAGPRA coordinator at the University Museum, University of Pennsylvania.

Brian Fagan is professor emeritus at the University of California, Santa Barbara.

Micah Garen is a journalist, photographer, and documentary filmmaker in New York.

Juliet Golden is a freelance writer based in southwest Poland.

Yuval Goren is associate professor of archaeology and ancient Near Eastern cultures at Tel-Aviv University.

Julie Hollowell is a Killam Fellow (2006-2008) at the University of British Columbia and a research associate with Indiana University's Archaeology and Social Context Program.

Jarrett Lobell is assistant managing editor of *Archaeology*.

Roderick J. McIntosh and **Susan Keech McIntosh** teach anthropology and archaeology at Rice University and have done field work in Mali.

Clement W. Meighan, now deceased, was professor of anthropology for thirty-nine years at the University of California, Los Angeles.

Mark Michel is president of The Archaeological Conservancy.

Janet Monge is adjunct associate professor of anthropology at the University of Pennsylvania and keeper of the physical anthropology collections at the University Museum.

George Nicholas is associate professor of archaeology at Simon Fraser University.

Robert W. Preucel is associate professor of anthropology at the University of Pennsylvania and associate curator of North America at the University Museum.

David Price is associate professor of anthropology at Saint Martin's College in Lacey, Washington.

Marilyn Raschka is a journalist and writer who has lived in the Middle East for more than twenty-five years.

Elaine Robbins, a former executive editor of *Texas Parks & Wildlife* magazine, has written for *Sierra, Modern Maturity, Organic Style,* and other national magazines.

Kristin M. Romey is managing editor of *Archaeology.*

Neil Asher Silberman is a historian with the Ename Center for Public Archaeology in Belgium. His most recent book, with Israel Finkelstein, is *The Bible Unearthed* (2002).

Téréba Togola is a researcher at the Institut des Sciences Humaines in Mali.

Harriot W. Topsey was the Archaeological Commissioner for Belize until his untimely death in an automobile accident in 1995.

Karen D. Vitelli received her Ph.D. in classical archaeology from the University of Pennsylvania in 1974. She has done fieldwork, primarily on prehistoric sites, in Greece, Turkey, and the eastern United States. She has served as chair of the committee on ethics for the Society for American Archaeology and as Vice President for Professional Responsibilities for the Archaeological Institute of America. For many years she taught archaeological ethics at Indiana University, where she was a founding member of the Archaeology and Social Context Ph.D. program. She now lives in Maine, as professor emerita of anthropology, Indiana University.

Joe Watkins has been associate professor of anthropology at the University of New Mexico since 2003.

Lucy F. Williams is keeper of collections, American Section, at the University Museum, University of Pennsylvania.

Larry J. Zimmerman is professor of anthropology and museum studies at Indiana University–Purdue University at Indianapolis.